USING NATIONAL DATA BASES IN EDUCATIONAL RESEARCH

USING NATIONAL DATA BASES IN EDUCATIONAL RESEARCH

By

Thomas L. Hilton
Educational Testing Service

with
chapters by

Albert E. Beaton
Judith Pollack
Donald A. Rock
William B. Schrader
Spencer S. Swinton
William W. Turnbull
Educational Testing Service

Valerie E. Lee
University of Michigan

Susan Urahn
Minnesota House of Representatives

LEA
LAWRENCE ERLBAUM ASSOCIATES, PUBLISHERS
1992 **Hillsdale, New Jersey**   Hove and London

Lawrence Erlbaum Associates, Inc., Publishers
365 Broadway
Hillsdale, New Jersey 07642

Library of Congress Cataloging-in-Publication Data

Hilton, Thomas Leonard, 1924–
    Using national data bases in educational research / by Thomas L.
Hilton ; with chapters by Albert E. Beaton . . . [et al.].
        p.   cm.
    Includes bibliographical references (p.   ) and indexes.
    ISBN 0-8058-0840-X
    1. Information storage and retrieval systems—Education.
    2. Education—United States—Data processing.   3. Education—
Research—United States.   I. Beaton, Albert E.   II. Title.
    LB1028.26.H55   1992
    370'.7'8—dc20   91-27877
                                                     CIP

Printed in the United States of America
10 9 8 7 6 5 4 3 2 1

To
William W. Turnbull

Contents

Preface

With the advent of massive national surveys and high speed computers, the rate at which educational research data are accumulating is staggering. The amount of data available to educational researchers has grown exponentially in the last two or three decades. National longitudinal studies, such as Project TALENT, the National Longitudinal Study of the High School Class of 1972 (NLS), and High School and Beyond (HS&B), provide the researcher with an unprecedented amount of longitudinal data. In addition, annual or biennial testing programs and surveys such as the College Board Admissions Testing Program (SAT), the National Assessment of Educational Progress (NAEP), and the Graduate Record Examinations—all of which release tapes for public use—tremendously expand the amount of research data available. Furthermore, by combining data from two or more of the available longitudinal or cross-sectional files, the power of available data can be further expanded. In principle, it should be reasonably straightforward to merge data from large national data files. In practice, however, such merging is fraught with problems and pitfalls. One goal of this volume is to describe ways of overcoming some of these problems and avoiding the many pitfalls.

The purpose of this book is to enable future educational researchers to make better use of the huge longitudinal and cross-sectional data files that are now readily available. We make no assumptions about the professional training of the reader—the book is intended to be as readable and understandable by college undergraduates as it is by experienced researchers with advanced degrees. Where technical terms are used, we have tried to provide definitions and explanations. The book is not, however, a how-to book. The reader who wishes to take the next step and actually use the data bases described will need to possess data processing and data analysis skills or contract with someone who has them. Such readers also will need user's manuals for the data bases. We could not possibly include enough information in one volume to enable readers to use the data bases in question without the ponderous user's manuals that accompany the public release files which typically are purchased when a researcher wishes to use the data in question. Thus, the major purpose of the following pages is to facilitate research at the planning and design stage more than at the implementation stage. The studies described herein demonstrate what can be done with large national data bases and, perhaps equally important, what cannot be done or what cannot be done unless certain precautions are taken.

Most of the chapters grew out of a major study conducted at the Educational Testing Service (ETS) for the National Science Foundation (NSF). The study was referred to as the Data Base Project. Its purpose was to investigate the feasibility of assembling a comprehensive, unified data base for science indicators. By means of the data base, NSF would monitor the development of cohorts of students in order to derive science indicators and also to conduct studies of the future supply of scientists and engineers.

Our approach to the feasibility question was to conduct a number of studies that required the merging of data from more than one data source, our assumption being that if a particular study produced useable results then the data sources for that study would be candidates for inclusion in a comprehensive data base. One study used data from NAEP, the SAT Program, and HS&B. Another study used data from Project TALENT and HS&B. A third study used data from NLS and HS&B, and a fourth study made use of both SAT and HS&B.

To make a long study short, we concluded that it was not feasible at the time to merge all of these data bases into one unified base in view of the many difficulties that we encountered in trying to use merged data in the individual studies. In the process of conducting these studies, however, we accumulated a valuable core of experience. The distinguished Advisory Committee to the project was unanimous in its judgment that the individual studies that were conducted are informative in themselves and should be disseminated. Several members of the Committee, and also friends who are teaching in universities, mentioned how much they would like to have the manuscripts printed in book form for collateral reading in undergraduate and graduate seminars. Hence, this book.

To supplement the studies conducted as part of the Data Base Project, we added reports on seven closely related studies, none of which has been published except as project reports or ETS research reports.

Collectively, the chapters address the following questions:

1. What variables are present in each of the major national bases?
2. For which variables are the definitions and item formats in the various data bases sufficiently similar to permit accurate comparisons between data bases?
3. For which variables is this clearly not the case?
4. What are the problems and dangers in making comparisons across data bases?
5. What steps can be taken to reduce the risk in making such comparisons?
6. In what important ways did the administration of the data collection instruments in the various national surveys differ and what effect do these differences have on the validity of comparisons?
7. How do the cognitive tests administered in the various national surveys compare?
8. What steps, if any, can be taken to make the scores comparable?
9. What factors invalidate comparisons of test scores across data bases?
10. In what ways can data from certain data bases be physically merged with data from other data bases?
11. In what ways can data from certain data bases be weighted so as to make them comparable to data in other data bases?

ACKNOWLEDGMENTS

The interpretation of the data analyses conducted in the Data Base Project was greatly aided by the advisory committee previously mentioned. It met twice, first in the early stages of the project and later when preliminary results were available. These advisory committee members and their affiliations were as follows:

Dr. Sue Berryman—Columbia University

Dr. Kimiko O. Bowman—Oak Ridge National Laboratory

Dr. Willie Pearson, Jr.—Wake Forest University

Dr. Marshall S. Smith—Stanford University

Dr. Wayne W. Welch—University of Minnesota

Although the impetus for the study came from the ETS staff, it simply would not have come about had not Richard Berry of NSF recognized its potential value and strongly encouraged the first author to persist in planning the study and writing the proposal for it. Once the grant was awarded, Dick's guidance and judicious monitoring of progress was invaluable. The authors are deeply indebted to him.

The authors also are indebted to a large number of assistants and secretaries. Notable among these is Irene Smith, who managed the typing of the manuscript and Eleanore De Young who assisted Irene.

Lastly, we acknowledge our indebtedness to the late William Turnbull who attended most of the meetings of the Data Base Project staff, who was always available for advice, counsel, and support, and who performed with distinction as discussant at the American Educational Research Association symposium in which the preliminary results of the project were reported. Dr. Turnbull's remarks precede the summary chapter of this book.

CHAPTER ONE

Introduction

Thomas L. Hilton
Educational Testing Service

In examining the condition of science education in the United States, the National Research Council's Committee on Indicators of Precollege Science and Mathematics Education stated that "The renewed interest and investment in precollege mathematics and science education make it especially important to understand the current condition of these fields and to be able to track future changes" (Raizen & Jones, 1985, p. 1). The Educational Testing Service (ETS) project that generated a major part of the research described in this volume was undertaken in response to the Committee's conclusion that there is need to assemble a comprehensive data base as a source of indicators of student attainment in science fields. Recognizing the magnitude of the total task, the author proposed first to conduct a study of the feasibility of developing a statistical system and data base that would provide current indicators of the number and the educational achievement of science and engineering students.

Background

Quite independently, the author of this volume had concluded that a standing base of student data would be of great value to the National Science Foundation (NSF). For a number of years, ETS has been supplying NSF with trend data for its biennial editions of *Science Indicators*. These data are retrieved from the test score files and the published and unpublished periodicals of several ETS testing programs, including the

Scholastic Aptitude Test (SAT), the Graduate Record Examinations (GRE), the Advanced Placement Program (APP), the National Teacher Examinations (NTE), and the National Assessment of Educational Progress (NAEP). The results of this periodic data retrieval have been valuable. Test scores, designed—with the exception of NAEP scores—to serve students and the schools to which they apply, have been used to show trends in the developed verbal and quantitative ability of students who report they intend to major in math or science or engineering. (We prefer the term *developed ability* over *aptitude* for the kind of skill measured by the SAT and the GRE.) There are, however, undesirable aspects in this spasmodic data retrieval.

Shortcomings of Ad Hoc Data Files

The first shortcoming is *wasteful start-up costs*: Every 2 years we reinvent the wheel. Computer programs written for a particular retrieval tend not to be saved. If they are saved, they tend not to be suitable, given changes in hardware and software, changes in personnel, and—most serious of all—changes in the measuring instruments. A prime example is the Student Descriptive Questionnaire, completed by most students who take the SAT. Two years ago, in an effort to improve the items in the questionnaire, a well-meaning committee managed to change many of the items just enough to preclude comparisons of 1985–1986 data with data of previous years. For example, "Counseling about educational plans and opportunities" was shortened to "Developing educational plans." These clearly are different behaviors. On another item, the choice between "Yes" and "No" was changed to "Yes," "No," and "I don't know." For some purposes this change is an improvement, but it obviously created a headache for researchers interested in trends.

The second undesirable aspect is that piecemeal consideration of each file of test scores or questionnaire responses makes it difficult and *costly to study relationships* among the data in separate files. Each time a new set of relationships is examined, a new file of merged data has to be assembled.

Third, some files are huge and thereby *costly to access*. The SAT file, for example, includes over a million cases for a single year. Simply to read the file can cost several hundred dollars.

Fourth is the *problem of self-selection*. Instead of being a national probability sample, as in the longitudinal studies sponsored by the National Center for Education Statistics, the available data may be for a self-selected sample, as in the case of the SAT takers. Such self-selection creates two problems: (a) the students who have scores are not likely to be representative of all members of a national age cohort, and (b) some fraction of a sample drawn from a particular age cohort will have no scores. These two problems point to the desirability of some method of estimating the scores that might have been obtained had all members or some well-defined subgroup of the cohort completed a particular measuring instrument. If such a method could be developed, we might—in the case of the SAT—estimate what the annual national mean would have been had all members of the college-going population taken the SAT; we might thereby also be able to judge to what extent an observed change may have resulted from a change in the composition of the SAT population in contrast to a pervasive change in the developed ability of SAT takers. Chapter 7 in this volume is addressed to estimating such mean SAT scores.

Alternative Approaches

What, then, can be done about the four shortcomings of what might be referred to as the ad hoc approach to data assembly? One alternative would be to create a standing data base incorporating data from a range of sources. The data would be merged in such a way that relationships between components of the file could be investigated at minimum cost and inconvenience and could be updated whenever more recent data for a particular component became available. For example, one component might be annually updated American College Testing (ACT) scores for a broad range of subpopulations.

In accord with the Committee on Indicators, we recognized that achievement is only one of the desired outcomes of science instruction. Favorable attitudes toward science and mathematics are probably of equal importance. But, as a first step, we decided to give priority to measures of achievement. We also gave priority to student variables, setting aside the important schooling and process variables that the Committee on Indicators also discussed.

Although our immediate concern was precollege education, the scope of the proposed work was not limited to that level, primarily because we believed that understanding the role of precollege indicators and demonstrating their validity required a more comprehensive system, encompassing postsecondary outcome variables to which earlier indicators should be importantly related.

An important feature of the unified data base would be, insofar as possible, uniform definitions and item response alternatives. This presumably would be achieved by collapsing categories like regions of the country or ethnicity or educational levels in such a way that comparisons could be made across data bases. "Hispanic," for example, would mean the same in each data base.

Economy could be achieved in at least two ways. First, randomly drawn samples of a population would be included in the unified base. One might, for example, include 1,000 cases drawn from each annual SAT population. Second, summary scores would be included for any subgroups. What the unit of aggregation would be is a critical and complex question. A possibility would be the cell obtained by crossing sex, race/ethnicity, socioeconomic status (SES), and intended or actual college major. Thus, a unit might be the cell for high-SES Black females who have intentions to major or are now majoring in math or science or engineering. A statistic for this unit might be the mean SAT Math score for the individuals in the cell. It would be updated annually.

Pursuing this example a bit further, we can compute the number of data cases that would result from the assumed level of data aggregation. If there are two sex categories, seven racial/ethnic categories (White, non-Hispanic Black, Mexican American or Chicano, Puerto Rican, other Latino, American Indian or Alaskan native, and Asian or Asian American), three levels of SES, and four field-of-study categories (math, science, or engineering [MSE]; humanities and fine arts; other; and not enrolled or no college plans), then there would be 168 data cases ($2 \times 7 \times 3 \times 4$). Our working assumption would be that, for many research purposes, dealing with aggregated data would be preferable to dealing with a large number of individual cases, and it would be technically adequate.

Although we anticipated many unsolved problems, the advantages of a unified data base such as the one just described were sufficiently appealing for us to request support from NSF for the development of such a data base. But knowing there were, indeed, many unsolved problems, we proposed first to conduct a study of the feasibility of constructing a unified data base. The Foundation provided funds for the work in July 1985, and the project was undertaken immediately.

Requirements of Unified Data Base

Our first task was to specify what features a unified data base should have. Some of these are as follows:

1. The data file should include a means of accurately identifying the sex, ethnicity, and race of each individual, and it must be sensitive to the history and educational access of the subgroups studied. With rare exceptions, research on access to higher education has not given sufficient attention to subgroup population demographics and especially to the society and culture of ethnic/racial minorities. Actuarial studies of data

on minority group members relevant to access to higher education reveal important relationships between the educational opportunities and background characteristics of minorities. Well-established findings tend to be generalizable across subgroups; for example, the well-documented finding that aptitude test scores, high school grades, and undergraduate college grades are related to students' socioeconomic background. However, there are unique characteristics of ethnic/racial groups that must be considered in understanding their educational attainment and presence in the pool of students in higher education. Each major ethnic/racial group has a unique historical presence in the United States and a unique pattern of access to higher education and graduate school. How detailed the ethnic/racial breakdowns should be is difficult to specify. Should, for example, separate categories be provided for Asian/Pacific Island Americans? We recommended that the design of any data base err on the side of too many categories, because related categories can be combined in any subsequent data analysis. The rapid increase in the enrollment of women in undergraduate and graduate education generally, and in science programs particularly, makes it especially important to examine the data for women, separately and in detail, to document trends and to project future circumstances.

2. The file should contain data on a comprehensive set of individual variables, including the individual's social, economic, educational, and psychological environment. Some reasons for this requirement were discussed previously.

3. Ideally, the data should cover a span of at least 21 years. Several studies indicate that certain curriculum decisions early in senior high school, such as whether to take algebra (Hilton, 1967), are highly related to which educational pathway the student subsequently follows. The student may be as young as 13 at this point. At the other end, one would want data on the placement of advanced-degree recipients in permanent full-time positions (as opposed to positions regarded by the individual as filling the gap until graduate work is completed or a long-term position is obtained). Given the extended period for completion of undergraduate and graduate school (8 years each for an appreciable number of students) and allowing 5 years for high school completion, we suggest a span of 21 years.

4. The data file should include enough subjects to permit separate examination of important subpopulations of the total group. If, for example, one wishes to subdivide the Hispanic student population into students with Mexican, Puerto Rican, Cuban, and other Latin American backgrounds—a minimal subdivision for most purposes—then a total cohort size of 50,000 students is desirable. (High School and Beyond, sponsored by the National Center for Education Statistics, which started

with 36,000 high school seniors, has 308 students who classified themselves as being of Puerto Rican descent—even though Hispanic students were oversampled. By the time of graduate school, this number will probably shrink to fewer than 25.) If, as is likely, further subdivisions of the sample will be needed—by gender and by high school curriculum, for example—then an even larger sample would be desirable.

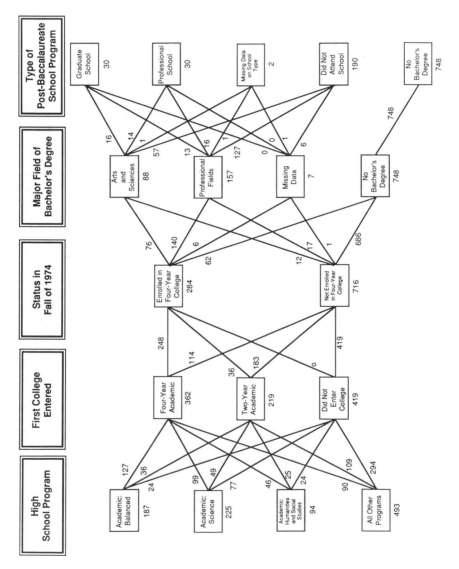

FIG. 1.1.   Pathways for high school seniors: estimated number per 1,000 sample members (actual N = 16,740).

5. The data base should provide for the fact that students follow different pathways to graduate school and switch from one pathway to another. There is no single pipeline to higher education, as shown in Fig. 1.1, taken from the study of pathways to graduate school by Hilton and Schrader (1987). The proportions of one subgroup that follows a certain pathway may be very different from that of another subgroup. Also students drop out of the system at various points. A growing fraction later return to the system and provision must be made for this reality. In addition, individuals return to the system after long absences and large numbers of foreign students enter the system at various points. A large majority of these foreign students take the Test of English as a Foreign Language (TOEFL) for which reason these test files were considered as a possible data source.

6. The data base should allow for the fact that students differ in the number of years they require to complete each phase of their education.

7. There should be detailed documentation of how the data in the file were collected and processed. In the absence of such information, it is difficult to evaluate the validity of the data and to merge one segment of the file with data from another source. We would ask: What was the sampling frame, and how was it sampled? Was the response rate adequate? How were missing data treated? How were write-in responses coded? In the instrument used, how, for example, were the race/ethnicity questions worded?

The preceding were the requirements that motivated our search for suitable data bases and for methods of making use of the data in them. In the following chapters, a number of efforts to draw conclusions from multiple data bases are described. Some were pursued as part of the Data Base Project. Others were conducted independently but are included in this volume because of their exceptional relevance to its goal. Most of the chapters are shortened versions of long reports submitted to the federal government and never published in the usual sense. For some, the full text may now exist only in the archives of ETS.

CHAPTER TWO

General Problems in Using Results from Two or More Data Bases

Thomas L. Hilton
Educational Testing Service

In this chapter, we first describe twenty-odd data bases that the Data Base Project identified as candidates for inclusion in a unified data base. Then the temporal relationships among the data bases are examined. Schaie's work on cross-sectional and longitudinal models provided a conceptual framework for relating the various data collections. Five levels of data bases are discussed, and examples are given. Finally, a possible way of merging data from different cohorts of subjects is briefly described. The balance of the book is devoted to detailed descriptions of a number of efforts to draw conclusions from multiple data bases.
—*Thomas L. Hilton*

In our search for existing national data bases that might be included in a unified data base, our first task was to search the literature to identify any data bases that we did not already know about. We limited the search to large national data bases but did not require that the data bases be national probability samples. We excluded several well-known smaller data bases, such as Terman's base for gifted students and Bachman's annual surveys, even though they are valuable for other purposes. We also excluded several excellent overseas data bases, such as those from the Scottish and Swedish longitudinal studies, and also data bases limited to single states, such as those for Illinois and California, even though for some purposes these also are valuable sources of data. The data bases identified are listed in Table 2.1. The Appendix provides a brief description of each base, along with information about how to obtain copies of the data bases.

Having identified a large number of possible sources of national data,

TABLE 2.1
Selected National Data Bases
(in order of modal or initial age of subjects)

Data Base	Modal Age
Research Triangle Institute National Science Survey	6–12
National Assessment of Education Progress (NAEP)	9–17
Longitudinal Study of American Youth (LSAY)	13–19
National Longitudinal Surveys of Labor Market Experience	14–?
International Math Survey (U.S. Component)	14–18
National Education Longitudinal Study (NELS)	14–?
Project TALENT	15–30
Metropolitan Achievement Tests	16
Iowa Tests of Education	16
1980 High School and Beyond (HS&B)	16–?
Armed Services Vocational Aptitude Battery (ASVAB)	17
American College Testing Service	18
National Longitudinal Study of the High School Class of 1972	18–?
College Entrance Examination Board Admissions Testing Program (Scholastic Aptitude Test, Achievement tests, Advanced Placement Examinations)	18
High School Equivalency Test	19
Cooperative Institutional Research Program (CIRP)	19
Integrated Postsecondary Education Data System (IPEDS)	19–25
Current Population Surveys	All
Graduate Record Examinations	22
National Teacher Examinations	22
Recent College Graduate Survey	22
Graduate Enrollment Survey	26
Survey of Graduate Science Students and Postdoctorates	26
Survey of Earned Doctorates	26

our next step was to ask how one might go about merging the various data bases. The first and most obvious method is appropriate when two data bases have common members. An example of this is the SAT and the *National Longitudinal Study of the High School Graduating Classes of 1972* (NLS) (Hilton & Rhett, 1973; Riccobono, Henderson, Burkheimer, Place, & Levinsohn, 1981), sponsored by the National Center for Education Statistics (NCES) and also NCES's High School and Beyond (Sebring, P., Campbell, B., Glusberg, M., Spencer, B., & Singleton, M., 1987), the name given to the longitudinal study begun in 1980 that parallels the 1972 NLS, which is described in detail in chapter 3. In NLS, survey administrators in each of the participating high schools retrieved SAT and ACT[1] scores

---

[1]The Scholastic Aptitude Test (SAT) is the college admissions test taken annually by over one million secondary school seniors in the United States. It is developed and administered by ETS under contract with the College Entrance Examination Board. Additional details about the test are given in several chapters of this book.

ACT is the acronym by which the college admissions test developed and administered by the American College Testing Program is known. It is administered annually to approximately one million high school seniors who tend to reside in the Middle West of the United States.

from the files of the high schools for any students who had taken either or both of the admissions tests. In HS&B, as described in chapter 4, SAT scores were retrieved from the history files of the SAT program at ETS for all members of the 1980 seniors whose scores could be located. For the 1980 HS&B, sophomore cohort scores were taken from high school transcripts as part of the Transcripts Survey. Also retrieved at the same time were PSAT scores (mathematics and verbal); ACT scores (English, mathematics, natural science, social science, composite); and Advanced Placement test scores whenever any of these scores were present on the transcript. It seems that a substantial number of SAT scores—if not other scores—were not posted on the transcripts, because the mean of the SAT scores is substantially higher than the published mean (College-Bound Seniors). Thus, for several thousand students there now exists a method for relating the SAT and ACT to the test scores, biographical data, and school data in the NLS and HS&B public release files, as well as a method for relating the SAT and the ACT to each other.

Figure 2.1 is an effort to depict these relationships and others. The vertical axis shows the year in which the data were collected or, in the longitudinal studies, the year in which the base-year data collection was conducted. The horizontal axis shows the age of the subjects at the time the data were collected. The intersection of the vertical and horizontal lines indicates that the data for a national survey or admissions programs were collected at the same time but not necessarily for the same subjects. For example, in one phase of the Department of Labor's National Longitudinal Survey (Parnes, Milius & Spitz, 1969), referred to as the Youth Survey, data were gathered for a national sample of 17-year-olds in 1979. At the same time, a national sample of 17-year-olds participated in the Armed Services Vocational Aptitude Battery (ASVAB). The probability of any student being in both samples is a very small number.

Another intersection exists for the 1980 HS&B senior cohort for whom SAT and ASVAB scores were retrieved in a 1983 study conducted at ETS for the Army Recruiting Command (Hilton, Schrader, & Beaton, 1983; also see chapter 5). Although the computerized search routine did not produce scores for all of the students who said they had taken the SAT, the retrieved scores are representative of all SAT takers, in that the mean of the scores retrieved agrees to one decimal point with the national mean published by the College Board.

A POSSIBLE MODEL

The next step in the feasibility study was to select a schema for representing the unified data base. In thinking about possible schema, we were strongly influenced by Schaie's (1965) general model for the study of

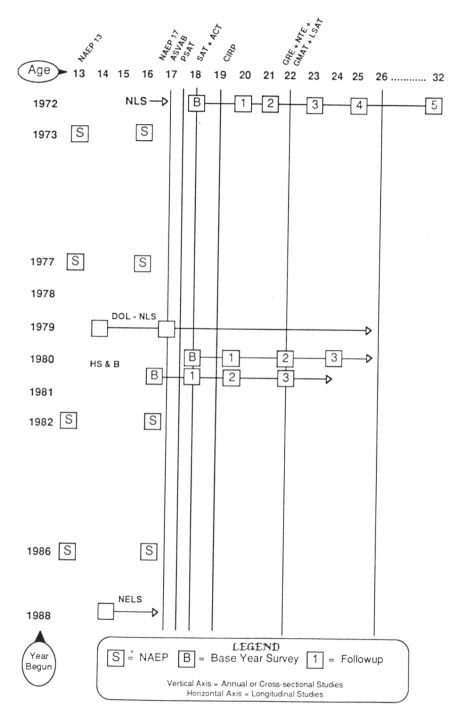

FIG. 2.1. Selected annual and longitudinal data bases.

development. Figure 2.2 depicts this model for a hypothetical example of two cohorts of students who were surveyed repeatedly. The first cohort was surveyed at ages 12, 14, 16, 18, and 20. Four years later, the surveying of a second cohort started and followed the same schedule. Following Schaie's model, we define three sources of change: (a) any systematic difference between the two cohorts (Cd), (b) any difference attributable to the second cohort's being surveyed 4 years later than the first (Td), and (c) any changes within each cohort attributable to the increasing age of the members (Ad). The cross-sectional difference then becomes the sum of the age difference (Ad) and the cohort difference (Cd). The longitudinal difference in the sum of age differences (Ad) and time differences (Td), and what Schaie calls the "time lag difference" is the sum of time differences (Td) and cohort differences (Cd). We have found

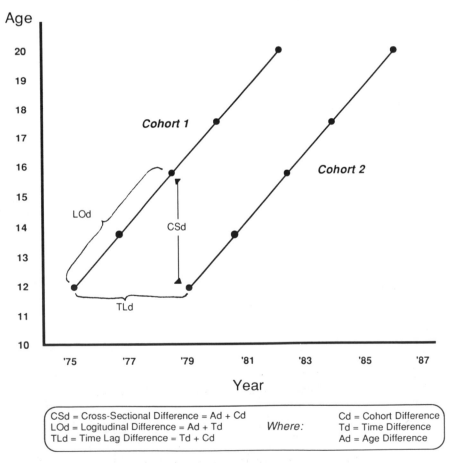

FIG. 2.2.   Schaie model.

this way of decomposing differences useful even though the nonrandom nature of the data we have had available has precluded our fully implementing Schaie's model.

The first decision in designing a unified base was easy, namely, to use the national longitudinal studies sponsored by NCES as a framework for the unified data base. A way of depicting these longitudinal studies is shown in Fig. 2.3. What has become known as the 1972 NLS—not to be confused with the Department of Labor National Longitudinal Survey (Parnes et al., 1969)—is shown at left. Beginning in 1972, a national probability sample of approximately 23,000 high school seniors was surveyed in the fall of their senior year and then, at roughly 2-year intervals, was resurveyed four times. Seven years later, in 1986, a fifth follow-up was conducted. The dashed boxes indicate that questionnaire items in later surveys permit one to pin down the status of the students at these times. Eight years after the base-year survey of NLS, HS&B was undertaken. Samples of 36 seniors were surveyed in a national sample of 1,000 high schools and, at the same time, a sample of 36 sophomores was surveyed in each participating high school. These subjects have now been followed up three times. The reader should note from Fig. 2.3 that questionnaire items were designed to enable researchers to ascertain the status of the students at intervals matching that of the 1972 cohort. This design feature provided us with a unique opportunity to investigate trends (time lag differences) from 1972 to 1982 but, as is shown shortly, the comparisons are not without pitfalls and uncertainties.

FIVE LEVELS OF DATA BASES

The next step was to consider actual ways of creating a unified data base. To this end, we suggest some language with which to describe five levels of unified data. The first level is what might be referred to as *pooled data*. Simply for logistical convenience, two or more data bases are included in one file, whether it be an actual file drawer, a magnetic tape, a Bernoulli box, or some other storage device.

The second level concerns what might be called *matched multicohort data*, whereby data from different cohorts that span the same age range or grade levels are pooled in one data base. Pooling data from the base year and the first two follow-ups of the 1972 NLS with the base year and the first two follow-ups of the 1980 HS&B senior cohort would be an example of matched multicohort data. But we know—as shown in Fig. 2.3—that the segments do not line up precisely, because the interval between follow-up surveys was not the same for both NLS and HS&B. We also know, however, that the intervals can be equated by focusing on certain items in each longitudinal data base.

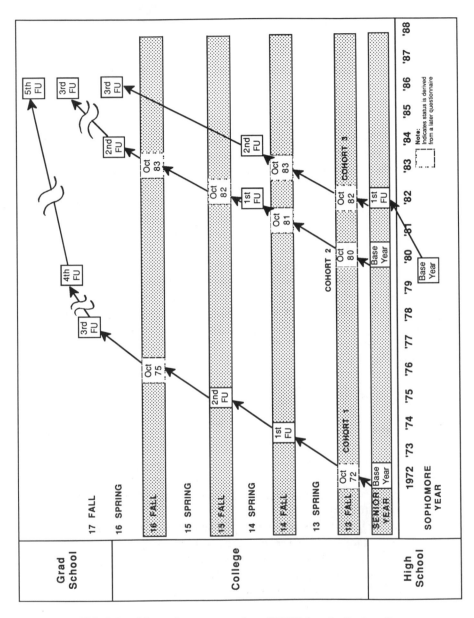

FIG. 2.3.   Schematic representation of NCES longitudinal studies.

14

If only the data for these items are included in the unified data base, we might refer to the base as *matched longitudinal segments*. In terms of Schaie's model, there are both a cohort difference and a time difference between the two longitudinal segments.

The third level is what might be called *linked cohort-data*. At this level, segments of data for the same age cohort are linked together in the same data file. Several possible examples of such linking are shown in Fig. 2.4. The first example is the linking of data from NAEP and data from the College Board Admissions Testing Program (including SAT scores). In 1971, a national sample of 13-year-olds completed a reading test as part of the NAEP testing for that year. Four years later, the same age cohort, now 17 years old, was tested again for reading. The 1975 students were not the same students as in 1971, except for the small subsample who were drawn by chance in both samples. But the students in both samples were born in the same year. Thus, in Schaie's language, there was no cohort difference between these particular NAEP samples.

One year after the second NAEP administration, a subset of the age cohort took the SAT. Because approximately one third of each age cohort now takes the SAT, and 30,000 members of each age cohort participates in NAEP, we would expect 10,000 students to be common to the NAEP 17 and SAT samples.

Four years after the 1971 NAEP administration, a new sample of 13-year-olds was tested in reading, and then, 5 years later, a third sample of students was similarly tested. This schedule of testing raised an intriguing question: Did changes in NAEP scores from 1971 to 1975 and from 1975 to 1980 forecast changes in SAT scores 5 years later? If the answer is yes, then National Assessment may be more than a thermometer that measures the momentary health of American education; it may be a barometer that forecasts changes in the health of education. Chapter 8 describes a preliminary study of this question.

The fourth level of data base is what might be called *simulated longitudinal data*. In this case, the data from one age cohort are linked to the data from a different age cohort as if the two cohorts comprised the same individuals. At the time of the data analysis of the present study, data were available for two follow-ups of the HS&B sophomores covering—for students continuing their education without interruption—high school graduation through 2 years of college. For the 1972 NLS cohort, however, data from four follow-ups were available, including the last 2 years of undergraduate school and, for some, enrollment in graduate school. These data introduced the possibility of somehow linking the two files together, and a possible way of doing this is described in chapter 12. Assume for a moment that we are interested in estimating, for a particular cohort of students, how many make the transition in the third

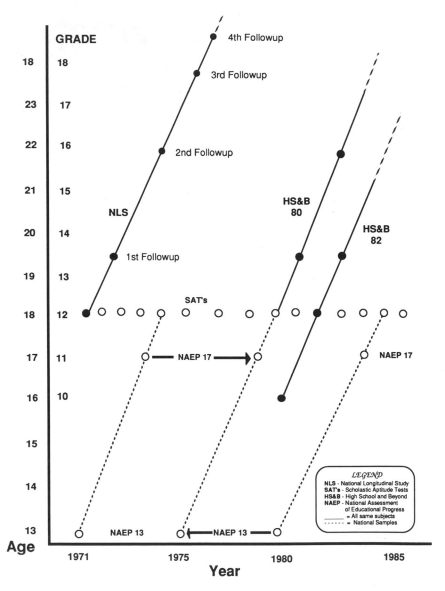

FIG. 2.4.   Illustrative data links.

year of higher education from 2- and 4-year colleges to 4-year colleges. The needed number is the product of the number of students in 4-year colleges in the second year and the proportion making the transition plus the product of the number in 2-year colleges and the proportion making the transition. We know that the number in various pipelines—or, as I prefer, pathways—changes from one cohort to another, but our observation is that the transitional probabilities change less. An example of this is shown in chapter 12. If we accept the proposition that transitional probabilities are relatively stable from one cohort to another, then we have a possible way of merging two overlapping or contiguous longitudinal data sets, such as those from the 1972 NLS and the 1980 or 1982 HS&B, not at the individual level but at the subgroup level. Chapter 12 of this book further explains this possibility.

The last level is *merged individual data*. An example is the merging of SAT scores with the data in the public release file for the 1980 HS&B seniors. This is the ideal way of creating a unified data file but one that we seldom have the opportunity to implement. Our hope is that the following chapters suggest some second-best steps that will provide reasonable estimates of the statistics we need in education research.

CHAPTER THREE

Pooling Questionnaire and Test Data from Three National Surveys: An Example Involving Project TALENT, the Coleman Study, and NLS

William B. Schrader
Thomas L. Hilton
Educational Testing Service

Project TALENT (Flanagan et al., 1962), the Equality of Educational Opportunity Survey (Coleman et al., 1966), and the Base-Year Survey of the National Longitudinal Study (Hilton & Rhett, 1973; Riccobono et al., 1981) questioned and tested national probability samples of American High School seniors in 1960, 1965, and 1972. This study, reported in this chapter, was concerned with the feasibility of using these data for studying trends in educational attainment.

Three separate aspects of the problem were considered. First, a detailed review of sample selection, weighting, and school participation showed that the data would provide a sound basis for comparing performance, and identified certain implications of the existing data for making and interpreting comparisons. Second, comparisons were made of students' high school experiences, their educational and occupational aspirations and plans, and their parents' education and occupation. The pattern of results for the three survey samples, although obscured by differences in questions and by population trends, indicated that comparisons of test performances of the groups would be warranted. Third, a detailed design was prepared for studying the equivalence of selected tests used in the three surveys and for equating test scores on pairs of equivalent tests. Part of this proposed study was actually implemented, as described in chapter 4. The present chapter describes in detail the many factors that must be considered in deciding whether two or more educational data bases contain comparable data.

—Thomas L. Hilton

Project TALENT, the Equality of Educational Opportunity Survey (EEOS), and the Base Year Survey of the NLS provide data on the test performance of a national probability sample of American high school seniors. A systematic review of the design and execution of this aspect of the three surveys should be distinctly useful in evaluating the feasibility of using these data for comparing twelfth grade students in 1960, 1965, and 1972. This chapter is intended to provide such a review.

PURPOSE AND SCOPE OF THE SURVEYS

Consideration of the purpose and scope of the three surveys is essential to an understanding of both the sampling design and the operational procedures that were used. As summarized in Table 3.1, all three surveys had very ambitious purposes. It seems fair to say that TALENT emphasized measurement, guidance, and manpower considerations; EEOS gave prominence to minority group questions and to the role of the schools in developing abilities; and NLS was particularly concerned with describing students and schools and with the use of data in long-range planning and research. Despite these differences in emphasis, the measurement of student abilities served as a major focus in each research effort. Table 3.2 provides a summary of relevant aspects of the scope of each survey. Each of the surveys was a massive enterprise calling for widespread involvement of schools in the collection of large quantities of data about students and schools. Table 3.2 also provides evidence of significant differences in the allocation of resources for data collection among the three surveys. As is shown later in this chapter, the smaller number of students in the NLS survey is offset by the precision with which the student sample was defined.

CHARACTERISTICS USED IN STRATIFICATION

A comparison of the basic student and school characteristics used in stratification for selecting the public school sample in each survey yields certain insights on similarity and differences in sampling design. Table 3.3 shows a summary of the basic stratification characteristics. Although all of these surveys used the geographical location of the school in stratification, as would be expected in a national survey, the classifications used were different. It is clear that the stratification scheme in TALENT is relatively simple, that EEOS placed heavy stress on the number and percent of non-White students in sample selection, and that NLS used a greater variety of characteristics in sample selection. In all three surveys, the selection of a sample of schools was of critical importance in the design for sampling. Table 3.3 suggests that the data available for sampling are, on the whole, less tightly linked to the significant characteristics of pupils in particular schools than would be optimal for stratification purposes.

TABLE 3.1
Major Purposes

TALENT	EEOS	NLS
To provide relevant information on seven areas of national concern:	As mandated by Congress, the general purpose was to investigate inequality of educational opportunity in public educational institutions. Specific objectives included:	The base-year study of the NLS was envisaged both as providing basic data for a continuing follow-up of students participating in it and as a prototype for surveys of later cohorts of high school seniors.
1. Available talent 2. Relationships among aptitudes, interests, and other factors 3. Limiting effects resulting from lack of interest and motivation 4. Factors affecting vocational choice 5. Predictors of creativity and productivity 6. Effectiveness of various types of educational experience 7. Procedures for realizing individual potential	1. Developing comprehensive statistical information on items considered relevant to school equality, 2. Comparing schools mainly attended by minority students with schools attended mainly by majority students on these indexes, and 3. Studying the relation between characteristics affecting quality of education and student performance on aptitude and achievement tests.	The specific objectives of the base-year survey included the following: 1. Describing high school seniors with respect to a wide range of personal characteristics—attitudes, abilities, interests, plans, knowledge of educational and occupational opportunities, and membership in ethnic and other significant subgroups, 2. Describing the high schools attended by participating students and the characteristics of counselors in those schools, and 3. Developing appropriate data files and access procedures to facilitate the use of the base-year data both for follow-up studies and for other research.

TABLE 3.2
General Scope of Survey

TALENT	EEOS	NLS
Main Sample: Five percent of high school seniors (between 400,000 and 500,000 students)	*School Sample:* Approximately 700,000 public school students in selected grades, with approximately half of the sample to be White and the other half to be non-White.	*Desired Sample:* 21,600 12th-grade students in 1,200 high schools.
Grade Levels: 9–12	*Grade Levels:* 1, 3, 6, 9, 12	*Grade Level:* 12
Amount of Student Time Needed: Two school days	*Amount of Student Time Needed:* One school day.	*Amount of Student Time Needed:* Approximately 3 hours.
Data Collection Instruments: Completed by student:	*Data Collection Instruments:* 1. Completed by 12th-grade students:	*Data Collection Instruments* 1. Completed by students:
23 aptitude and achievement tests	7 aptitude and achievement tests	6 aptitude and achievement tests
Preference test	Questionnaire	Student questionnaire
Themes	2. Completed by others:	2. Completed for each student by survey administrator:
Student activities inventory	Principal questionnaire	Student School Record
Interest inventory	Teacher questionnaire	Information Form
	Superintendent questionnaire	3. Completed by others:
		School questionnaire
		Counselor questionnaire

Note: Only those phases of each survey which included the national 12th-grade sample are considered in this summary.

21

TABLE 3.3

Variables and Characteristics Used in Selection of Public School Sample

TALENT	EEOS	NLS
1. *Geographical Location:* Used 56 strata as follows: 5 largest cities, District of Columbia, and 50 states (with 5 largest cities removed).	1. *Geographical Location:* Used seven groups of states and distinguished between counties included in a Standard Metropolitan Statistical Area (SMSA) and counties not included in an SMSA.	1. *Geographical Location:* Used four groups of states.
2. Size of senior class	2. *Percent non-White in SMSA or county*	2. *Size of senior class*
3. Retention ratio (holding-power) of school	3. *Estimated number of non-White students in secondary school and in its feeder schools.*	3. *Percent minority in school or in county in which school is located*
	4. *Percent non-White in school*	4. *Proximity to higher education of SMSA or county in which school is located*
		5. *Income class of ZIP Code area or county in which school is located*
		6. *Degree of urbanization of city, SMSA, or county.*

22

SAMPLING AND WEIGHTING

SAMPLING AND WEIGHTING IN TALENT[1]

Sampling of Schools

Definition of Sampling Frame. The sample design for the high school sample in Project TALENT called for the selection of approximately 5% of all senior high schools, and, for schools that did not include a ninth grade, appropriately selected feeder schools. Thus, the desired sampling frame would include all public, private, and parochial schools that included Grades 9 through 12. In all, about 26,000 high schools were located. The main list of public schools was obtained from the United States Office of Education, which also provided three supplementary lists and a list of parochial schools. In addition, a list of schools supplied by the Bureau of Internal Revenue included names, but not enrollment data, for some additional schools.

Selection of Stratified Public School Sample. The characteristics used in stratifying the public school sample are shown in Table 3.4. The size of senior class was the only basis used for assigning different sampling ratios to different strata. The following sampling ratios were used:

	Sampling Ratio
Public schools with fewer than 25 seniors	1:50
Public schools with 25–99 seniors	1:20
Public schools with 100–399 seniors	1:20
Public schools with 400 or more seniors	1:13

Because it was planned from the outset to test all students in the designated grades, simple random sampling of schools within size strata would have yielded a sample in which each student would have had an equal chance of inclusion. This approach, however, would have selected a large number of small schools and relatively few large schools. Consequently, sampling ratios different from 1 to 20 were used for the largest and smallest schools, and corresponding weights were used in the analysis to compensate for this difference. In selecting schools within the strata

---

[1]This discussion of sampling and weighting is based on a number of Project TALENT publications as follows: Flanagan, Dailey, Shaycoft, Gorham, Orr, and Goldberg (1960); Flanagan et al. (1962); Flanagan et al. (1964); Shaycoft, Dailey, Orr, Neymen, and Sherman (1963); and Project TALENT (1972). Citations of specific reports are made only when detailed information is cited from a particular report.

TABLE 3.4
Definition and Sources of Variables and Characteristics Used
in Selecting Public School Sample in Project TALENT

Variable	Definition	Source
Geographical Location	5 largest cities District of Columbia 50 states (excluding 5 largest cities)	U. S. Bureau of the Census
Size of senior class	Groupings: (a) Less than 25 seniors (b) 25–99 seniors (c) 100–399 seniors (d) 400 or more seniors	U. S. Office of Education
Retention ratio (holding power) of school	Ratio of number of graduates in 1958–1959 school year to number of 10th graders in 1957–1958 school year	U. S. Office of Education

thus defined, schools were ordered with respect to the retention ratio, and systematic sampling was used for the final selection.

Selection of Parochial and Private School Sample.   Private and parochial schools were stratified only on the basis of the 56 geographical locations. The sampling ratio was 1:20 for these schools. In all, 125 parochial and 59 private senior high schools were selected for the sample, as compared with 879 public senior high schools.

Sampling of Student Data for Analysis

The enormous number of students (nearly 400,000) included in the TALENT survey made sampling of the data for analysis virtually indispensable. Although a number of different samples were created, it is necessary in this discussion to consider only the sample used for the analysis of the test performance of the twelfth-grade sample. This sample (designated A-10.0-3 by the authors) included all students who had a 6-digit testing number ending in 3 and whose records were incorporated in the 1963 edition of the master tape file.

Weighting

Several weighting plans were utilized in different phases of Project TALENT. The weighting that is relevant to this report, however, was designed to reproduce the national population represented by the national high school sample. The weight for each student in a particular school is equal to the reciprocal of the sampling ratio applied in selecting the school divided by the proportion of invited schools in a given stratum that participated in the testing. The first element in the product compensates for the differential selection ratios for different schools. The second element in the product is based on the implicit assumption that the best available estimate of characteristics for students in nonparticipating schools are the characteristics of students enrolled in participating schools in the same stratum. Because a very large proportion of the schools that were invited decided to participate, the effect of this estimation for nonparticipants on the results is small. The simplicity and clarity of the sampling design and the high degree of participation of the invited schools indicate that the weighting system, although necessary, played a relatively minor role in determining the descriptive statistics on twelfth-grade students.

SAMPLING AND WEIGHTING IN EEOS[2]

First-Stage Sampling

Definition of Sampling Frame.   For the first-stage sampling in EEOS, it was decided to use counties rather than school districts as primary sampling units both because census and other statistics were more readily available for counties and because it was judged that counties had greater internal heterogeneity than school districts. The desirability of internal heterogeneity arises because cluster sampling has greater adverse effects on the precision of results for a given sample size when variation between clusters is relatively large and variation within clusters is relatively small. Once the decision to use counties (or the equivalent) was made, the sampling frame for the first-stage sampling was fully defined by current census documents.

Selection of Stratified Sample of SMSAs and Counties.   At any given time, every county or county equivalent in the United States can be classified unambiguously as belonging to a Standard Metropolitan Statistical Area (SMSA) or as not belonging to an SMSA. The classification of a county on this basis, however, may change, because new SMSAs are created when new combinations of counties meet the standard for inclusion. In the first-stage sampling for EEOS, SMSA was treated as the primary sampling unit for all counties that belonged to an SMSA. At the time the sample was selected, there were 209 SMSAs and 2,674 counties not belonging to an SMSA.

---

[2]Sampling and weighting for EEOS are discussed in Coleman et al. (1966, pp. 550–554, 558–560, 571–572).

A decisive consideration in the sample selection process was the desire that about half of the pupils in the sample be non-White. Because it was also judged necessary that all pupils in the designated grades be included in the sample for any school selected for the sample, it was necessary to stratify the SMSAs and nonmetropolitan counties on the basis of their non-White populations and to give greater representation in the first-stage sample to primary sampling units having a large proportion of non-Whites while maintaining broad geographical distribution in both the metropolitan and nonmetropolitan units selected.

The description of the sample selection procedures does not state explicitly all the considerations that determined the sampling ratios for the various strata. The sampling ratios for each stratum, which are shown in the report, make it clear that the estimated size of the non-White population in a stratum was a major factor in determining the allocation of the first-stage sample. For purposes of this discussion, the totals for all seven geographical regions should provide a sufficient basis for describing the first-stage sample selection.

	Primary Sampling Units	
Stratum	Number in Universe	Number Selected
SMSAs		
Included in sample with certainty	21	21
Proportion non-White:		
30–under 70	13	4
10–under 30	46	17
Under 10	129	28
Nonmetropolitan counties		
Proportion non-White		
70 and over	19	10
30–under 70	381	105
10–under 30	368	110
Under 10:		
100 or more non-White students	498	55
Less than 100 non-White students	1,408	52

The 21 SMSAs that were included in the sample with certainty were those whose estimated total non-White enrollment in the designated grades was equal to or greater than the corresponding non-White enrollment for the stratum divided by the number of SMSAs to be selected from the stratum.

The actual selection of the sample within each stratum was performed by ordering all elements in the stratum on the basis of estimated number of non-White students in the designated grades and then using systematic sampling with a random start to select the first-stage sample. This is the crucial point that insures that the sample is, in fact, a probability sample. There was one stratum containing four SMSAs, none of which was selected for the first-stage sample. This would seem to constitute a minor discrepancy in the sampling procedure.

Second-Stage Sampling

The second-stage sampling was based on a substantial amount of information about each secondary school and its feeder schools. These data were obtained mainly from State Departments of Education.

As in the first-stage sampling particular emphasis was placed on the number and percentage of non-White students in determining the number of schools to be selected in a given stratum. Schools in each of the 209 SMSAs and 2,674 nonmetropolitan counties were further stratified according to the percentage of non-White students, yielding the following categories: (a) 75.1–100.0, (b) 50.1–75.0, (c) 25.1–50.0, (d) 10.1–25.0, and (e) 0–10.0. The 209 SMSAs included 2,741 high schools, of which 349 were selected for the final sample. The 2,674 nonmetropolitan counties included 1,781 high schools, of which 821 were selected for the final sample. The operation of the second-stage sampling in the nonmetropolitan counties resulted in the inclusion of 467 of the 540 high schools which had 10% or more non-White students, and 354 of the 1,241 high schools which had 10% or less non-White students.

The geographical distribution of the schools selected for the final sample is as follows:

Geographical Location	Number of Schools
Nonmetropolitan	
Southeast	512
Southwest	125
All other regions	184
Metropolitan	
Southeast	89
Southwest	42
New England and Middle Atlantic	97
Great Lakes and Plains	85
Rocky Mountain and Far West	36
Total schools	1,170

Thus, 768 of the 1,170 schools included in the survey samples were from the Southeast or Southwest. For comparison, 310 schools from these two regions were included in the 879 schools selected in the public school sample for Project TALENT.

SAMPLING AND WEIGHTING IN NLS[3]

Sampling of Schools for Data Collection

Definition of Sampling Frame. The basic sampling frame for public schools included all schools listed on the United States Office of Education school universe tape that indicated that they had a twelfth grade plus those schools that indicated that eleventh grade was their highest grade. For seven states, it was necessary to use listings from the 1969–1970 school universe tape for all or part of the listings. Private schools were obtained from a tape supplied by the National Catholic Education Association and from an Office of Education listing of private schools. As with public schools, all schools that reported eleventh or twelfth grade as their highest grade were included. Finally, a listing of area vocational schools was obtained from a current directory of such schools. It was recognized that the sampling frame was incomplete and provision was made in the study design to locate additional schools and incorporate them in the sample (WESTAT, 1972, pp. 4–5).

Formulation of Stratification Plan for Public Schools. As shown in Table 3.5, an extensive array of stratification variables was utilized in defining the NLS sample. The first grouping of schools was based on the size of twelfth-grade enrollment, geographical region, and proximity code. Schools in the "less than 300 seniors" group were classified into the four geographical regions and three groups based on proximity codes (shown in Table 3.5) yielding 12 groups. For the remaining schools, proximity code was divided into only two categories: schools in SMSA's or counties containing the 100 largest central-city school districts versus all others. For these schools, there were two categories by enrollment size, four categories by geographical region, and two categories by proximity code, yielding 16 further groups. At this point, then, 28 groups of schools had been identified. For each of these 28 groups of schools, a two-way table was constructed, using percent minority (8 levels) and income class (11 categories).

The 28 tables created in the preceding step provided the basis for

---

[3]Sampling design is discussed in WESTAT (1972, pp. 1–32, 42–45) and in Hilton and Rhett (1973, sect. 2–14 to 2–16).

TABLE 3.5
Definition and Sources of Variables and Characteristics Used in Selecting Public School Sample for NLS

Variable	Definition	Source
Size of Senior class in school	Groupings: (a) Less than 300 seniors (b) 300–599 seniors (c) 600 or more seniors Note: For schools listing grade 11 as their highest grade, 11th grade enrollment was used.	U. S. Office of Education school universe tapes.
Percent minority in school or in county in which school is located.	Groupings: (a) Under 5% (b) 5–9% (c) 10–19% (d) 20–39% (e) 40–59% (f) 60–79% (g) 80% or over (h) Unknown	Records of the office of Civil Rights (OCR) 1970 census data by counties (used if OCR data not available)
Proximity to higher education of SMSA or county in which school is located	Groupings: (a) SMSAs or counties containing the 100 largest central-city school districts (b) Schools in all other SMSAs or counties which contain a public 2-year or 4-year college (c) All other schools	U. S. Office of Education higher education universe tape
Income class of ZIP code area or county in which school is located	For SMSAs, and counties having 50,000 or larger population, adjusted gross income in 5-digit ZIP code area in which school is located was used. For counties having a 1960 population of less than 50,000, however, ZIP code data were not used. Instead, median county income based on the 1960 census was used, because ZIP code area had been found not to be a satisfactory indicator of income level for schools in such counties. 1960 data were adjusted to make them comparable to the 1966 IRS data. The following 11 categories were used: (a) less than $2,000; (b) $2,000–$2,999; (c) $3,000–$3,999; (d) $4,000–$4,999; (e) $5,000–$5,999; (f) $6,000–$6,999; (g) $7,000–$7,999; (h) $8,000–$8,999; (i) $9,000–$9,999; (j) $10,000 and over; (k) Unknown.	For ZIP code areas, Internal Revenue Service tape based on 1966 individual tax returns. For counties, 1960 census reports

(Continued)

TABLE 3.5
(*Continued*)

Variable	Definition	Source
Degree of urbanization of city, SMSA, or county in which school is located	Schools contained in: (a) Ten largest central city school districts (b) Next 90 largest central city school districts (c) Other schools in same SMSA or county as Group (a) (d) Other schools in same SMSA or county as Group (b) (e) All other schools included in SMSAs (f) Nonmetropolitan counties having urban population of 75% or more (g) Nonmetropolitan counties having urban population between 50%–74% (h) Nonmetropolitan counties having urban population between 25%–49% (i) Nonmetropolitan counties having urban population less than 25% (j) Undetermined	Percent urban for nonmetropolitan counties based on 1970 census data.

dividing all schools into Type A and Type B schools. The classification of schools into those two types was based on a decision to sample schools in communities having family incomes less than $5,000 or having more than 20% minority students (Type A Schools) at double the rate assigned to other (Type B) schools. This procedure would yield a final sample of which approximately half the schools would belong to Type A.

The 28 tables included a total of 2,464 (28 × 8 × 11) possible subgroups. These were consolidated into 263 relatively homogeneous major strata. Care was taken that each major stratum contain only Type A or Type B schools. The 263 major strata for public schools were then subdivided into 559 final strata on the basis of the degree of urbanization. Categories for this characteristic are shown in Table 3.5. Final strata were used both in the selection of the sample and to yield a covariance term for the estimation of sampling error.

Allocation of the Sample to Strata. In determining the number of schools to be selected from each stratum, the initial allocation was based on the type of school (A or B) and on the size of senior class. For Type A schools and Type B schools separately, allocation was proportional to the total senior enrollment, so rounded that an even number of schools would be assigned to each group. Results were as follows (WESTAT, 1972, p. 21):

Enrollment Size	Number of Schools	
	Type A	Type B
Less than 300	304	286
300–599	188	214
600 or more	108	100
Total	600	600

In the subdivision of major strata into final strata, an effort was made to make the size of the group included in each final stratum as uniform as possible, within each of the six groups shown in the preceding table. Once the 600 final strata were created, the initial sample was formed by drawing two schools from each final stratum. For strata composed of schools having senior classes less than 300, selection was proportional to size. For strata composed of larger schools, simple random selection of schools was used. This procedure is equivalent to selecting schools in the larger school sizes in proportion to the average size of the schools in the two size groups rather than in proportion to the actual size of the school. This procedure resulted in an advantageous simplification in the work of sampling with no appreciable loss of precision.

The detailed stratification plan developed for the initial sample facilitated the selection of a sample of replacement schools to be invited to participate if any school initially invited found it impossible to participate. Two replacement schools were selected from each final stratum that included at least four schools. Substantially all final strata met this requirement. To the extent that schools within strata are more homogeneous than schools generally, this procedure reduces the effect on the results of replacing nonparticipating schools.

Sampling of Students Within Schools in NLS

From a methodological viewpoint, the provision for sampling of individual students in the NLS study has important advantages over the procedure of testing all students in the designated grade within a school. In particular, it yields greater precision for a given number of students who are tested or who complete questionnaires. Moreover, it seems likely to require the school to define more sharply which students are in twelfth grade, and to permit fuller coverage of the defined group than when all students present on the testing day are tested. On the other hand, the effort involved in identifying and assembling a small group of students tends to offset the efficiency gained by testing only a small proportion of students in a particular cluster, and administration of the tests and questionnaires to a fraction of the students may provide less realistic conditions than would be obtained by administration in regular classrooms and homerooms.

In the procedure used by NLS, schools were asked to supply a list of their twelfth-grade students, excluding adult education students, students who were early graduates no longer in attendance, and any foreign exchange students. If there were more than 18 students in the senior class, the NLS project staff selected a sample of 18 students by simple random sampling, and 5 replacement students were selected at random (provided that enrollment was 23 or greater). Each step involved in preparing the student samples was carefully checked. For practical reasons, in about one fifth of the schools, sampling was done by telephone rather than by the more formal procedure originally planned. The NLS procedures included a check of the student listing in 59 schools, in connection with a site visit. The error rate in the listing of students was about 1 in 1,000. The experience with the selection of students is discussed at some length in the NLS report (Hilton & Rhett, 1973, pp. 2-16–2-22). On the whole, the procedure was judged to be feasible and quite accurate.

Determining Weights for NLS

Because NLS sampled students within schools, the probability that a student will be selected is the product of the probability that a student's school will be selected and the probability that the student will be selected. Account must be taken of the fact that the sampling design permitted replacement of a school in the primary sample by another and of the fact that nonresponse may occur either for a school or for students within the school.

PARTICIPATION IN THE SURVEYS

The critical importance of securing a high degree of participation both by schools and by students was fully recognized in the planning of all three surveys. TALENT invited participation by a mid-November mailing to superintendents for testing in March. TALENT also provided 90 regional coordinators, who were outstanding educators and psychologists in all parts of the United States selected in part on the basis of their ability to work with school people. The role of these coordinators in securing a high degree of participation is acknowledged in the report (Flanagan et al., 1960, p. III-29). EEOS contacts with the schools began with a letter sent early in June to each chief State School Officer from the U. S. Commissioner of Education, asking that a staff member be appointed to coordinate the program within the state. Each state department of education was asked to supply certain data needed for selecting the sample. As soon as possible after authorization was received, a carefully prepared invitation was sent to the superintendent of each selected school. Some 434 consultants in all parts of the United States were appointed by Educational Testing Service to assist schools in any aspect of the survey. There was great pressure of time in these activities, because the main testing was scheduled for the end of September (Coleman et al., 1966, pp. 549–550, 554, 556). In NLS, the National Center for Education Statistics asked the Chief State School Officer in each state and the District of Columbia to appoint a state coordinator, and contacts with the superintendents were made through the state coordinator. When principals were invited to participate, they were informed of the prior approval by the state coordinator and the superintendent. Each principal was asked to appoint a survey administrator to manage the survey activities within the school. An honorarium of $50 was provided for each school or for the school's survey administrator at the discretion of the state department of education and the school administration. A similar sequence of approvals was followed for parochial schools. The telephone was used extensively in securing decisions by schools and in resolving problems arising in participation. As in EEOS, there was great pressure of time. The study began early in February, and school terms ended for nearly all schools by the middle of June (Hilton & Rhett, 1973, pp. 2-6–2-12).

Participation in TALENT was quite high, amounting to 92.9% of the schools that were invited to participate. The following table shows the number invited and the percentage participating for public, parochial, and private high schools (Flanagan et al., 1962, p. 55).

	Number in Sample	Percent of Schools Participating
Public	879	93.5
Parochial	125	91.2
Private	59	86.4
Total	1,063	92.9

Although the percentage of students tested within schools was not determined, there were indications that in many communities, school attendance for the special testing was higher than usual (Flanagan et al., 1962, p. 167).

The participation rate for schools was noticeably smaller in EEOS than in TALENT. Participation figures showing the percentage of schools that administered both tests and questionnaires to twelfth-grade students, classified jointly by geographical location and by non-White percent, are given in the report (Coleman et al., 1966, p. 567). The overall participation was 67%.

Information on participation in NLS differs from that of the other two surveys in several important ways. First, the study design provided for replacing a school that did not participate with another school from the same final stratum, and for replacing a student who did not participate with another student chosen at random within the same school. Second, because the NLS sample was defined in terms of specific students, percent participation of students was reported. Third, in analyzing nonresponse, it was recognized that nonresponse was different for different components of the survey. For example, nonresponse was noticeably smaller for the School Record Information Form than for the questionnaires and tests. One consequence of these refinements is that it is difficult to formulate the response rates in a form comparable to the other two surveys, although a substantial amount of detailed information is available (Hilton & Rhett, 1973, pp. 4-53–4-67, 5-1–5-4, Appendix A, A-12–A-41). The following table provides one basis for considering nonresponse. In this table, a distinction is made between schools in the primary sample and schools in the supplementary sample. The following table, adapted from Table 5-1 of the NLS report, shows the number of students from the primary sample of schools and the total number of students who had data on the tests, on the student questionnaire, and on the School Record Information Form (SRIF) separately, and it shows the number who had data on at least one of the three. The percentages were obtained by dividing these numbers by 21,600, which was the number of students called for by the sampling design.

Kind of Data	Number of Students from Primary Sample	Percent of Desired Number	Number of Students in Total Sample	Percent of Desired Number
Questionnaire	15,563	72	16,409	76
Test	14,962	69	15,625	72
SRIF	16,093	75	17,693	82
Questionnaire, Test, or SRIF	16,126	75	17,726	82

Note that the introduction of replacement schools did not have much effect on the response rate as defined. The table also makes it clear that, among students in the total sample who had data for at least one of the three kinds, 88% had test data and 93% had questionnaire data (Hilton & Rhett, 1973, p. 5-3).

In summary, the participation rate of schools and of students makes it unlikely that the participants in TALENT differed appreciably from the sample as designed. In EEOS and NLS, on the other hand, it cannot safely be assumed that the characteristics of the participants correspond closely to the characteristics of the sample called for by the study design. The extent of nonparticipation in NLS and EEOS does not, of course, imply that the results of these studies are biased. What it does is reduce substantially the precision that can be attributed to the results as descriptions of twelfth-grade students in the United States.

SUMMARY AND CONCLUSIONS

The three surveys differed markedly in the procedures and characteristics used in defining the samples but all three samples of twelfth-grade students were well-designed, national probability samples. Moreover, the large number of schools involved in the sample selected for each of the three studies provide adequately for the statistical inefficiency inherent in the use of the school as a key sampling unit in all three studies. One important difference in the sampling frames, however, must be taken into account in any comparison of test performance of the three groups. EEOS was limited to public school students, but TALENT and NLS sampled both public and private school students. Strictly speaking, this would entail developing appropriate descriptive statistics for TALENT and NLS for public school students only.

Weighting presents somewhat more difficult questions. Although the weights used in the three surveys are reasonable, it is conceivable that weights devised specifically for the purpose of estimating test performance in the target population would yield a sufficient gain in precision to justify their use. In particular, the special weights devised for summarizing test data should be used for developing estimates for NLS data. The development of special-purpose weights for use with the EEOS regression subgroups, although not essential, deserves consideration as a way of sharpening the year-to-year comparisons.

Two points arising from program operations have definite implications for year-to-year comparisons. In TALENT, the necessary statistics should be based on the TALENT Data Bank sample rather than the sample analyzed for the 1964 report. Second, allowance needs to be made for growth in ability from early fall, when EEOS tests were administered, to spring, when TALENT and NLS tests were administered. Although the order of magnitude of this growth is probably small (perhaps 5% of a standard deviation), it is relevant to the interpretation of year-to-year comparisons.

Finally, the effect of nonparticipation by schools in the EEOS and NLS surveys must be considered. It must be acknowledged that nonparticipation is too great to justify any claim that the year-to-year comparisons would be definitive. On the other hand, it may reasonably be stated that they offer a better basis for comparisons across the years 1960 to 1972 than any alternative data sources.

CHARACTERISTICS OF HIGH SCHOOL SENIORS IN 1960, 1965, AND 1972 SAMPLES

DEVELOPMENT OF THE QUESTIONNAIRES

Student questionnaires constituted an important data source in all three surveys. Both TALENT and EEOS used discrete, multiple-choice items only. All twelfth-grade students were asked to respond to 374 items, and college-bound students were asked to reply to 20 additional items in the TALENT survey. EEOS included a 116-item questionnaire. NLS utilized a more flexible format that permitted grouping of items concerned with the same topic and that permitted the use of the same options. In the NLS survey, all twelfth-grade students were asked to respond to 46 items that called for 198 separate choices and to 9 free-response items. They were also asked to reply to an appropriate subset of the remaining 59 items, depending on what they were planning to do during the year following high school graduation.

This section is concerned with identifying questions that are sufficiently similar in the three surveys to permit comparison of the students in the three samples with respect to important characteristics. In discussing these topics, attention is given first to the student's current activities as a high school student, second to the student's educational and occupational aspirations and plans, and third to the important but difficult topic of parents' education and occupation.

Each of the questionnaires was prepared with care. In TALENT, an extensive list of questions was assembled. These questions were screened, rewritten, and checked for clarity in pilot interviews with students. Judgments by distinguished advisory panels and project staff took into account previous research in which the questions had been used (Flanagan et al., 1962, p. 155). The EEOS report does not describe the specific steps involved in the formulation, writing, review, and revision of the questions used in that survey. Instead, emphasis is placed on the pretesting of the items, in which special effort was made to include both White and Black students and lower ability and lower middle class students in the sample. The Grade 12 questionnaire was pretested on 67 students (Coleman et al., 1966, pp. 576–577). The NLS questionnaire was developed initially by the Research Triangle Institute. Both the TALENT and EEOS questionnaires were used, along with other sources, in developing items, and new items were written to cover additional topics. A draft version was administered to nine high school seniors and revised by USOE before pretesting. A pretest was administered to 727 seniors in 10 states, and the responses were evaluated in detail. The version developed by Research Triangle Institute embodied the flexible design and the branching that characterized the final questionnaire (Horvitz et al., 1972, Vol. 1, pp. 23–52, Vol. 2, Appendix H). A revised version 'of the pretested questionnaire was embodied in the Request For Proposal (RFP) for the base year study. The NLS project staff introduced further revisions designed to reduce ambiguities, to make the language appropriate to high school seniors and inoffensive to minority students, and to embody questions that had been used successfully in other ETS programs. Further revisions were made in response to requests from the National Center for Education Statistics based on requests from the Department of Defense and other user groups within the Department of Health, Education, and Welfare (HEW). Finally, the questionnaire was pretested again with high school students (Hilton & Rhett, 1973, pp. 2-33, 2-34).

CONSIDERATIONS IN INTERPRETING RESULTS

In interpreting TALENT questionnaire results, information provided by the authors (Flanagan et al., 1964, p. 5-5) on the percentage of students who completed items 1, 100, 150, 200, 250, 300, 350, and 374 is relevant. Data are given for males and females separately and for students of each sex classified into 10 groups on the basis of aptitude level. Students were urged repeatedly in the instructions for the first six sections (items 1–374) to "answer each question sincerely and thoughtfully." Dropout was less than 5% for all of the 20 groups on items 1, 100, 150, and 200. Even at item 300, only students in the lowest tenth in ability had a dropout rate greater than 10%. At item 350, however, dropout exceeded 10% for all male groups except the top tenth and for the five female groups in the lower half in ability. There was a noticeable trend for a smaller percentage of students in the lower-scoring groups to respond. On item 374, the highest percent response was 85.3, for females in the second tenth in ability, and the lowest percent response was 47.1, for females in the lowest tenth in ability.

In preparing the summary tables on student characteristics in this report, separate percentages for men and women, reported to one decimal place by TALENT (Flanagan et al., 1964, pp. 5-5–5-35), were combined using the weighted N based on all students answering each item. The tabulations were based on all students having complete records in the master tape at the time the analyses were done. Because an appreciable number of students who participated in the survey were not included in the analysis, the results differ to an unknown, but probably small, extent from the results that would have been obtained for all participating students. Although the actual N is not cited specifically for these results, it is clear that over 62,700 students were included in the response tabulations. The percentages were based on weighted Ns, and nonresponses were allocated on a *pro rata* basis among the options. For this summary, percent omits have been calculated, using a total weighted N of 1,304,200 as shown in Table 2-1 on page 2-6 of the 1964 TALENT report.

The results for EEOS are based on unpublished analyses conducted by Albert E. Beaton as part of the basic analysis for that survey. As described in chapter 1 of this book, the sample for these analyses included 20 subsamples of approximately 1,000 students each, so selected that each sample would be self-weighting. In combining the 20 subsamples to arrive at a national figure, weights based on national population data were employed. It may be useful to compare the proportion of students in various ethnic groups as determined by the EEOS weights and as determined by the weighted student responses in the NLS study. Results are as follows:

	EEOS	NLS
Black	13.9	9.4
Mexican American	2.8	2.7
Puerto Rican	1.0	0.4
Other Latin American	—	0.7
Oriental	0.9	1.0
American Indian	1.3	1.1
Other	1.1	2.9
Unknown	0.9	—
White	78.1	81.8
	100.0	100.0

Except for the somewhat greater proportion of Black students in the EEOS sample, the two samples seem to be in agreement with respect to ethnic compositions particularly in view of the technical difficulties in obtaining data on this topic.

Directions to students for the EEOS questionnaire differed somewhat from those used in TALENT. They were as follows: "Mark the space on the answer sheet corresponding to the answer that is correct for you for each question. Mark only one answer for each question. You may leave out any question you prefer not to answer, but we hope you will answer all of them" (Coleman et al., 1966, p. 644). In the EEOS data discussed in this summary, as in the basic EEOS analysis, "omit" is treated as a separate option. Fewer than 5% of students omitted most items under consideration. In a few instances, omits have been prorated among the options to facilitate comparison.

Two respects in which EEOS differed from the other two surveys should also be noted. First, the EEOS sample was limited to public school students. Second, EEOS was administered in the fall and the other two surveys were administered in the spring.

For NLS, an important factor in interpreting the results arises from the fact that in this survey students were permitted or encouraged to regard the completion of any instrument as optional and to feel free to omit any items they might regard as an invasion of privacy. The leaflet inviting students to participate included the statement that "Participation in this study is *strictly voluntary.*" Each section of the questionnaire included the following heading: "Please answer every question unless you are asked to skip to another one. You may omit any question that you or your parents would consider objectionable" (Hilton & Rhett, 1973, Appendix A). The emphasis on the student's freedom to omit items was considered essential by the research staff to forestall adverse reactions by students to the survey.

It is difficult to assess the effect of these permissive instructions on the extent to which students omitted items. In the NLS data analysis, provision was made for prorating nonresponses among the options. However, the percentage of students omitting an item is shown in each table. The percentage of "omits," like the percentages for the various options, is based on weighted Ns in order to describe the population from which the sample was drawn. The actual number of students who completed questionnaires and who were included in the analysis is 16,409. Results summarized in this report were taken from Appendix B of Hilton & Rhett, 1973.

STUDENT'S HIGH SCHOOL EXPERIENCES

Results describing the *curriculum* or *program* in which a student is enrolled are shown in Table 3.6. One striking feature of these results is the similarity in the percentage of students who report being enrolled in an academic or college preparatory program, ranging only from 41.4 in EEOS to 42.9 in NLS. Results for most other high school programs are similar for TALENT and EEOS, although the percentage of students in a commercial or business program is smaller for EEOS (18.6) than for TALENT (22.5). In NLS, the percentage for the general program is 32.9, as compared to 21.8 and 22.3 in the other two programs. Interpretation of this shift is difficult because NLS used a somewhat different format

TABLE 3.6

High School Curriculum or Program

TALENT	EEOS	NLS
Which one of the following high school programs or curriculums is *most like* the one that you are taking? *If you have not yet been assigned to a program, which do you expect you will take?* (Question 91)	Which one of the following best describes the program or curriculum you are enrolled in? (Question 43)	Which of the following best describes your present high school program? (Question 2)
Response	*Response*	*Response*
%[a]	%	%[a]
21.8 General—*a program that does not necessarily prepare you either for college or for work, but in which you take subjects required for graduation and many subjects that you like.*	22.3 General	32.9 General
	41.4 College preparatory	42.9 Academic or college preparatory
42.8 College Preparatory—*a program that gives you the training and credits needed to work toward a regular Bachelor's degree in college.*	18.6 Commercial or business	Vocational or Technical:
	6.6 Vocational	1.6 Agricultural occupations
22.5 Commercial or Business—*a program that prepares you to work in an office; for example, as a secretary or bookkeeper.*	1.6 Agriculture	12.0 Business or office occupations
	3.0 Industrial arts	2.5 Distributive education
7.7 Vocational—*a program that prepares you to work in a shop or factory, or to enter a trade school, or become an apprentice after high school.*	4.5 Other	0.9 Health occupations
	2.0 Omit	1.1 Home economics occupations
2.1 Agriculture		6.0 Trade or industrial occupations
2.9 A program very different from the above.		

[a]Omits: TALENT, 1.3%; NLS, 1.4%.

for the question, grouping all programs except general and academic under "vocational or technical." In addition, NLS did not offer a category for other programs than those listed. The NLS analysis plan made it possible to compare the student's self-reported program with his program classification determined by the survey coordinator at the high school from the student's school record. For nearly all students, this classification rather than the student's own report was used in classifying students by program in the main questionnaire analysis. (This analysis was based only on students for whom data on sex, program, race, and father's education were available.) The following table was adapted from data in Hilton & Rhett, 1973, Appendix B-1:

| | Percent in Each Program | |
	Self-Report	Coordinator
General	32.1	30.0
Academic	44.1	46.0
Vocational-Technical	23.7	23.9

Of students classified by the coordinator as enrolled in the general program, 60.8% reported enrollment in that program. Of students classified by the coordinator as enrolled in the academic program, 78.8% reported enrollment in that program. Of students classified in a vocational-technical program, 67.1% reported enrollment in a vocational-technical program. These results suggest that conceptions of what constitutes a general, academic, or vocational-technical curriculum are not as sharply defined or as uniformly understood as would be desirable from a statistical viewpoint.

Results for student's self-reported *grades* are shown in Table 3.7. Here, the creativity of the questionnaire authors has gone far to forestall any meaningful comparisons. This particular topic would seem to permit almost limitless variations and improvements. Attempts to resolve the difficulties presented by those variations have not provided a basis for drawing any conclusions from the data. This outcome is particularly regrettable because the data do suggest that fewer EEOS students report A and B grades than is true for the other two surveys. There is no way, however, of judging the effect of asking for an average grade rather than for the student's subjective impression of what his or her report cards looked like.

Data concerning study hours might be expected to throw some light on similarity of samples, although such comparisons would be confounded with possible trends in student motivation. As it happened, TALENT asked for study hours in school and out of school per week, EEOS asked about studying outside of school on school days, and NLS asked only

TABLE 3.7
High School Grades

TALENT

Items 106–113. The following questions ask you to report your grades in courses you have taken in the ninth grade or later. *Please consider only semester grades. If you have not taken any courses in the topic, skip the item.* In these questions choose the one answer that best describes your grades.

[If your school does not use letter grades, please use the following equivalents:

For a grade of A:	Excellent;	90–100
For a grade of B:	Good;	80–89
For a grade of C:	Average;	70–79
For a grade of D:	Fair;	60–69
For a grade below D:	Failing;	59 or lower]

My grades in *all courses starting with the ninth grade* have been: (Question 113)

$\%^a$	Response
3.8	All A's or equivalent
11.0	Mostly A's or equivalent
30.4	Mostly A's and B's or equivalent
40.7	Mostly B's and C's or equivalent
13.1	Mostly C's and D's or equivalent
1.0	Mostly D's or below or equivalent

EEOS

What is your grade average for all your high school work? (Question 88)

%	Response
7.0	A(either A –, A, or A +)
37.1	B(either B –, B, or B +)
42.7	C(either C –, C, or C +)
3.5	D(either D –, D, or D +)
6.7	Don't know
3.0	Omit

NLS

Which of the following best describes your grades so far in high school? (Question 5)

$\%^a$	Response
9.2	Mostly A (a numerical average of 90–100)
19.4	About half A and half B (85–89)
20.7	Mostly B (80–84)
28.1	About half B and half C (75–79)
14.6	Mostly C (70–74)
6.8	About half C and half D (65–69)
1.0	Mostly D (60–64)
0.2	Mostly below D (below 60)

^{a}Omits: TALENT, 3.8%; NLS, 0.7%.

TABLE 3.8
Study Hours

TALENT		EEOS	
On the average, how many hours do you study each week? *Include study periods in school as well as studying done at home.* (Question 97)		On an average school day, how much time do you spend studying outside of school? (Question 61)	
%[a]	Response	%[a]	Response
		8.0	None or almost none
2.0	None	9.3	About ½ hour a day
19.9	About 1–4 hours per week	18.4	About 1 hour a day
31.4	About 5–9 hours per week	16.6	About 1½ hours a day
24.9	About 10–14 hours per week	23.7	About 2 hours a day
14.3	About 15–19 hours per week	16.7	About 3 hours a day
7.5	About 20 or more hours per week	7.3	4 or more hours a day
9.0	Median	1.7	Median

[a]Omits: TALENT, 1.3%; EEOS, 1.7%. Omits for EEOS were prorated.

about homework. Table 3.8 shows that TALENT students reported a median of 9.0 hours per week, and EEOS students reported a median of 1.7 hours per school day. Although no conclusions can be drawn about differences in the samples from these data, the results seem to be reasonably consistent for the two groups.

The questions about work for pay were virtually identical in TALENT and EEOS. It is true that TALENT asked about work "during the school year" and EEOS limited its concern to work "during the last year." The NLS questionnaire, which asked about all work whether paid or not, was judged not to be comparable to the other two. Table 3.9 shows results

TABLE 3.9
Work for Pay

TALENT		EEOS	
During the school year, about how many hours a week do you work for pay? *Do not include chores done around your own home.* (Question 37)		During the last school year about how many hours a week did you work for pay? Do not include chores done around your own home. (Question 89)	
%[a]	Response	%[a]	Response
42.3	None	47.2	None
15.8	About 1–5 hours	14.5	About 1 to 5 hours
11.1	About 6–10 hours	9.6	About 6 to 10 hours
8.5	About 11–15 hours	6.2	About 11 to 15 hours
8.8	About 16–20 hours	6.7	About 16 to 20 hours
13.5	About 21 hours or more	15.7	About 21 hours or more
2.9	Median	0.7	Median

[a]Omits: TALENT, 0.9%; EEOS, 3.3%. Omits for EEOS were prorated.

for TALENT and EEOS. In general, it appears that TALENT students were performing more work for pay during the school year than EEOS students. The median number of hours for the TALENT sample was 2.9; for EEOS, it was 0.7. As it happened, however, the percentage of students working 21 hours or more was 15.7 for EEOS and 13.5 for NLS, reversing the pattern.

Table 3.10, which is concerned with participation in debating, drama, and music, illustrates the approach of the three surveys toward extra-curricular activities. TALENT asked students who participated in an activity to rate their degree of participation on a five-step scale. EEOS used only two degrees of participation (active vs. not very active). NLS asked participants to distinguish between active participation and participation as leaders. The following table combines certain responses to aid in comparing the results:

TALENT % Responses		EEOS % Responses		NLS % Responses	
23.1	Extremely active or very active	---	---	---	---
---	---	28.7	Active	33.0	Participated actively or leader
14.8	Fairly active	---	---	---	---
8.3	Not very active or rarely active	9.1	Not very active	---	---
53.7	Not a member	63.6	Not a member	67.1	Have not participated
---	---	1.8	Omit	---	---

If there is a difference in the level of participation, the manner in which the questions are formulated seems to have obscured it rather effectively. The trend, if any, appears to be toward reduced participation in the later surveys.

Although a number of questions in each survey dealt with extracurricular activities, differences in groupings of activities were judged to be too great to warrant detailed comparisons. Questions concerning hobby clubs might be comparable, but a detailed comparison of the surveys on this point seemed unlikely to yield useful information.

The surveys paid a good deal of attention to student attitudes. As a result of the different interests and emphasis of the authors, however, virtually no meaningful comparisons could be made between the samples.

TABLE 3.10
Student's Participation in Debating, Drama, or Music

TALENT	EEOS	NLS
Organizations	Did you participate in any debating, dramatics, or musical clubs last year? (Question 72)	Have you participated in any of the following types of activities, either in or out of school this year? (Question 10C)
Items 1–10. How active have you been in any one or more of the following organizations?		
Debating, dramatics, or musical clubs or organizations (Question 3)	*Response*	Debating, drama, band, chorus
%^{a} *Response*	% *Response*	%^{a} *Response*
10.9 Extremely active	60.3 No	67.1 Have not participated
12.2 Very active	28.7 Yes, I was an active member	26.6 Have participated actively
14.8 Fairly active	5.8 Yes, but I wasn't very active	6.4 Have participated as a leader or officer
4.7 A member, but not very active	3.3 Our school does not have such clubs	
3.6 A member, but rarely active	1.8 Omit	
53.7 Not a member of any of these organizations		

[a]Omits: TALENT, 0.5%; NLS, 2.6%.

45

STUDENT'S EDUCATIONAL
AND OCCUPATIONAL PLANS

Both EEOS and NLS asked students how much education they "wanted to" (EEOS) or "would like to" (NLS) achieve. As shown in Table 3.11, the specific options differed in the two surveys. Moreover, the high percentage (31.5) of NLS students who omitted this item raises some question about whether it is reasonable to prorate nonresponses among the options. It seems likely that a higher proportion of students with low aspirations than students with high aspirations would omit the item. Of the EEOS students, about 60% reported that they wanted to achieve at least some college training. In NLS, over 75% wanted to attend college. In part, this difference presumably reflects an increasing interest in college attendance between 1965 and 1972. The fact that NLS specifically listed junior college as an option, whereas EEOS did not, would contribute to the difference, as would the fact that parochial and private school students are included in the NLS but not in the EEOS sample.

Educational expectations (TALENT) and plans (NLS) are compared in Table 3.12. For this question, as for the preceding one, the percentage of NLS students who omitted the item is relatively high (24.7). Although the percentage of nonresponse is fairly high (7.8) for TALENT also, this high degree of nonresponse is probably attributable in part to the fact that the question occurs late in the questionnaire (item 304). Direct comparison of expectations of some college attendance is prevented by the fact that the TALENT question groups junior college with vocational

TABLE 3.11
Student's Educational Aspirations

EEOS		NLS	
How far do you want to go in school? (Question 49)		To answer this question, circle one number for the highest level of education you would like to attain. (Question 29A)	
%	Response	%[a]	Response
1.9	I do not want to finish high school	0.7	Less than high school graduation
13.2	I want to finish high school only	5.7	Graduate from high school but not go beyond that
25.8	I want to go to technical, nursing, or business school after high school	19.2	Graduate from high school and then go to a vocational, technical, business, or trade school
11.0	Some college training, but less than 4 years		
29.6	I want to graduate from a 4-year college	8.4	Go to a junior college
		29.2	Go to a 4-year college or university
17.2	I want to do professional or graduate work after I finish college	36.8	Go to a graduate or professional school *after college*
1.5	Omit		

[a]Omits: 31.5%.

TABLE 3.12
Student's Educational Expectations

TALENT	NLS
What is the greatest amount of education you expect to have during your life? (Question 304)	To answer this (question, circle one number for the highest level of education you plan to attain. (Question 29B)

%[a]	Response		
1.0	I don't expect to finish high school.	%[a]	Response
25.8	I expect to graduate from high school.	2.2	Less than high school graduation
21.0	I expect to obtain vocational, business school, or junior college training.	17.0	Graduate from high school but not go beyond that
		18.5	Graduate from high school and then go to a vocational, technical, business, or trade school
9.9	I expect to obtain some (less than 4 years) regular college training	12.6	Go to a junior college
27.1	I expect to graduate from a regular 4-year college.	36.9	Go to a 4-year college or university
15.1	I expect to study for advanced college degrees.	12.8	Go to a graduate or professional school *after college*

[a]Omits: TALENT, 7.8%; NLS, 24.7%.

and business school training in the same option. However, the data do permit obtaining the total percentage of students who expect to attend a four-year college or to go beyond college. It turns out that the percentage is higher for TALENT (52.1) than for NLS (49.7).

Parent's attitudes toward educational goals are described in Table 3.13. These results show a modest downward trend for the percentage of parents who want only a high school education for children who have reached the senior year of high school, and a modest upward trend in the percentage who want their children to attend professional or graduate school. Fifty percent of parents in the TALENT sample and 48.1% of fathers and 52.7% of mothers in EEOS wanted a college degree or advanced training beyond college for the students. Fifty-five percent of fathers and 60.7% of mothers in the EEOS sample and 57.7% of fathers and 61.1% of mothers in the NLS sample wanted at least some college for the students. These findings are, if anything, too consistent. Taken at face value, they suggest that parents' attitudes toward having their children obtain a college education showed little change between 1960 and 1972. For the present, no satisfactory hypothesis for accounting for this pattern is apparent.

Results on students' occupational preference for TALENT and NLS are presented in Table 3.14. Substantial differences in the options offered by the questionnaires complicates the interpretation, as does the relatively

TABLE 3.13
Parents' Attitudes toward Educational Goals

TALENT

How much education do your parents or guardians want you to have? (Question 337)

%[a]	Response
1.1	They don't care whether I stay in high school
11.5	High school only
22.2	Vocational school, business school, or junior college
41.8	A college degree
8.2	Professional or graduate school
15.3	I don't know

EEOS

How much education does your father (mother) want you to have? (Questions 27 and 28)

Father %	Mother %	Response
1.4	1.0	Doesn't care if I finish high school or not
9.9	9.5	Finish high school only
18.3	20.7	Technical, nursing, or business school after high school
6.9	8.0	Some college but less than 4 years
38.4	42.0	Graduate from a 4-year college
9.7	10.7	Professional or graduate school
3.8	0.7	Father is not at home
9.3	5.8	Don't know
2.2	1.6	Omit

NLS

As far as you know, how much schooling do your father and mother (or guardian) want you to get? (Questions 91A and 91B)

Father %[b]	Mother %[b]	Response
0.2	0.2	Wants me to quit high school without graduating
7.0	6.4	Wants me to graduate from high school and stop there
20.5	21.6	Wants me to graduate from high school and then go to a vocational, technical, trade, or business school
9.7	11.0	Wants me to go to a 2-year or junior college
36.2	37.5	Wants me to go to a 4-year college or university
11.8	12.6	Wants me to go to a graduate or professional school after graduating from 4-year college or university
14.5	10.8	I don't know

[a]Omits: 15.5%.
[b]Omits: Father, 11.5%; Mother, 10.1%.

TABLE 3.14
Student's Occupational Preference

TALENT	NLS

TALENT

Which *one* of the following occupations would you most *like* to enter? *If your choice is not on the list, mark the one that is closest to it. Mark one of these even if you have not definitely made up your mind.*

(Question 212)

%[a]	Response[b]
3.7	Accountant
3.5	Artist or entertainer
1.3	Biological scientist (biologist, botanist, physiologist, zoologist, etc.)
1.0	Clergyman (minister, priest, rabbi, etc.)
0.6	College professor
1.1	Dentist
8.9	Engineer (aeronautical, civil, chemical, mechanical, etc.)
4.9	Elementary school teacher
1.6	Forester
5.2	High School teacher
2.5	Lawyer
1.1	Mathematician
5.9	Nurse
0.9	Pharmacist
2.2	Physical scientist (chemist, geologist, physicist, astronomer, etc.)
2.1	Physician
2.5	Pilot, Airplane
0.3	Political scientist or economist
2.2	Social worker
1.6	Sociologist or psychologist
1.3	Writer
0.5	Engineering or scientific aide
1.5	Medical or dental technician
2.6	Armed forces officer
0.7	Enlisted man in the armed forces
2.9	Businessman
0.6	Salesman or saleswoman
0.5	Craftsman
3.0	Skilled worker (electrician, machinist, plumber, printer)
0.7	Structural worker (bricklayer, carpenter, painter, paperhanger, etc.)
12.0	Secretary, office clerk, or typist
2.7	Barber, beautician
0.6	Policeman or fireman
2.0	Farmer
5.5	Housewife
9.5	Some other occupation different from any above

NLS

In the column under YOU, circle the one number that goes with the best description of the kind of work you would like to do. The exact job may not be listed but circle the one that comes closest. (Question 25A)

%[a]	Response[b]
44.7	PROFESSIONAL such as accountant, artist, clergyman, dentist, physician, registered nurse, engineer, lawyer, librarian, teacher, writer, scientist, social worker, actor, actress
6.7	TECHNICAL such as draftsman, medical or dental technician, computer programmer
2.4	MILITARY such as career officer, enlisted man or woman in the armed forces
3.1	MANAGER, ADMINISTRATOR such as sales manager, office manager, school administrator, buyer, restaurant manager, government official
1.8	PROPRIETOR OR OWNER such as owner of a small business, contractor, restaurant owner
3.0	SALES such as salesman, sales clerk, advertising or insurance agent, real estate broker
7.7	CRAFTSMAN such as baker, automobile mechanic, machinist, painter, plumber, telephone installer, carpenter
2.3	OPERATIVE such as meat cutter; assembler; machine operator; welder; taxicab, bus, or truck driver; gas station attendant
14.7	CLERICAL such as bank teller, bookkeeper, secretary, typist, mail carrier, ticket agent
4.2	SERVICE such as barber, beautician, practical nurse, private household worker, janitor, waiter
2.2	PROTECTIVE SERVICE such as detective, policeman or guard, sheriff, fireman
1.6	FARMER, FARM MANAGER
2.5	LABORER such as construction worker, car washer, sanitary worker, farm laborer
3.0	HOMEMAKER OR HOUSEWIFE

[a]Omits: TALENT, 3.5%; NLS, 22.9%.
[b]Order of responses has been changed.

high nonresponse percentage (22.9) for NLS. The order of responses has been changed to facilitate comparisons. For strict comparability, the fact that TALENT asked students what occupation they would "like to enter," whereas EEOS asked students what they would "like to do," is troublesome because the term *enter* may suggest an early career stage to some students. In any case, if the first 21 occupations listed for Project TALENT in Table 3.14 are regarded as professions, 54.4% of TALENT students would like to enter a profession as compared to 44.7% of NLS students who chose "Professional" to describe their career preference. For technical careers, only 2.0% of TALENT students chose the two options presented, whereas 6.7% of NLS students chose the technical category. In TALENT, 12.0% chose "Secretary, office clerk, or typist," as compared with 14.7% in NLS who chose "CLERICAL such as bank teller, bookkeeper, secretary, typist, mail carrier, ticket agent." On the whole, the results for occupational preference suggest that differences in patterns between the two samples are not large enough to be clearly discernible in the available data.

PARENT AND FAMILY CHARACTERISTICS

Before discussing the characteristics of the parents of students in the three twelfth-grade samples, it seems desirable to consider briefly some of the factors at work in determining these data. First of all, it should be recognized that a dramatic increase in retention rate of high schools occurred between 1960 and 1966. The number of high school graduates per 1,000 students entering fifth grade 8 years earlier rose from 621 to 732 (U.S. Bureau of the Census, 1973, p. 131). Preliminary figures for 1972 graduates showed an increment to 750. If there had been no shift in parents' educational and occupational status during the period, this factor would be expected to result in a downward trend, particularly between TALENT and EEOS.

It is clearly important, but very difficult, to estimate the effect of trends in the educational level of parents during the period covered. Some data on parents' ages are provided by TALENT (Flanagan et al., 1964, p. 5-22). The median father was 47 years old, and the median mother was 43 years old, according to the students. One fourth of the fathers were 53 or older, and one fourth of the mothers were 48 or older. At the other end of the distribution, one fourth of the fathers were 42 or under, and one fourth of the mothers were 40 or under. Assuming that the same distribution of ages is roughly appropriate for the other two studies, it is possible to calculate the year in which the middle half (25th percentile to 75th percentile) of parents reached age 18 for the three studies, as follows:

	Father	*Mother*
TALENT	1925 to 1936	1930 to 1938
EEOS	1931 to 1942	1936 to 1944
NLS	1937 to 1948	1942 to 1950

It is clear that many parents in these groups reached high school graduation age during the depression or during World War II years. On the other hand, it is difficult to evaluate the impact of these events on the educational and occupational careers of the parents.

Results for parents' education in the three samples are shown in Table 3.15. The following table shows the percentage of fathers and mothers who were reported to have finished college or who had taken graduate or professional training beyond college:

	Father	*Mother*
TALENT	12.3	9.0
EEOS	11.0	7.0
NLS	19.2	11.5

Results are also available for parents who attended but did not complete college, as follows:

	Father	*Mother*
TALENT	6.7	6.1
EEOS	8.9	7.5
NLS	11.3	10.4

Finally, results can be summarized for parents who graduated from high school but who did not attend college:

	Father	*Mother*
TALENT	27.8	39.8
EEOS	38.4	41.8
NLS	37.4	51.1

The trends for EEOS and NLS seem to be reasonable, assuming a generally increasing level of education in the United States.

Data on father's occupation are shown in Table 3.16. Responses have been rearranged to facilitate comparison. On the whole, these results

TABLE 3.15
Parents' Education

TALENT

Mark the *one* answer indicating the *highest* level of education your father (mother) reached. *Mark the one best answer even if you are not sure.* (Questions 218 and 219)

Father %[a]	Mother %[b]	Response
7.3	4.1	None, or some grade school
16.2	12.8	Completed grade school
21.6	22.7	Some high school, but did not graduate
22.3	32.4	Graduated from high school
5.5	7.4	Vocational or business school after high school
6.7	6.1	Some junior or regular college, but did not graduate
6.4	6.1	Graduated from a regular 4-year college
1.5	1.0	Master's degree
1.1	0.7	Some work toward doctorate or professional degree
3.3	1.2	Completed doctorate or professional degree
8.3	5.6	I don't know

EEOS

How far in school did your father (mother) go? (Questions 19 and 20)

Father %	Mother %	Response
6.9	4.0	None, or some grade school
11.7	9.4	Completed grade school
21.8	23.3	Some high school, but did not graduate
23.7	34.9	Graduated from high school
4.7	6.9	Technical or business school after high school
8.9	7.5	Some college but less than 4 years
6.9	5.2	Graduated from a 4-year college
4.1	1.8	Attended graduate or professional school
9.4	5.6	Don't know
1.9	1.6	Omit

NLS

What was the highest educational level each of the following persons completed? If you are not sure, please give your best guess. (Questions 90A and 90B)

Father %[a]	Mother %[b]	Response
3.0	2.0	Doesn't apply
29.2	25.0	Did not complete high (secondary) school
30.6	42.9	Finished high school or equivalent
1.3	2.0	Adult education program
5.5	6.2	Business or trade school
11.3	10.4	Some college
10.4	7.4	Finished college (four years)
2.7	1.8	Attended graduate or professional school (for example, law or medical school, but did not attain a graduate or professional degree
6.1	2.3	Obtained a graduate or professional degree (for example, M.A., Ph.D., or M.D.)

[a]Omits: TALENT, 4.2%; NLS, 11.3%.
[b]Omits: TALENT, 5.3%; NLS, 10.5%.

TABLE 3.16
Father's Occupation

TALENT	EEOS	NLS
Which one of the following comes *closest* to describing the work of your father (or the male head of your household)? *Mark only one answer. If the works on more than one job, mark the one on which be spends most of his time. If be is now out of work, or if he's retired, mark the one that he did last.* (Question 206)	What work does your father do? You probably will not find his exact job listed, but check the one that comes closest. If he is now out of work or if he's retired, mark the one that he usually did. Mark only his main job if he works on more than one. (Question 18)	Under FATHER, circle the one number that best describes the work done by your father (or male guardian). The exact job may not be listed but circle the one that comes closest. If either of your parents is out of work, disabled, retired, or deceased, mark the kind of work that he or she used to do. (Question 25B)

$\%^a$	Response^b	$\%$	Response^b	$\%^a$	Response^b
6.1	Professional—such as actor, accountant, artist, clergyman, dentist, engineer, lawyer, librarian, scientist, etc.	7.7	Professional—such as accountant, artist, clergyman, dentist, doctor, engineer, lawyer, librarian, scientist, college professor, social worker, etc.	14.4	PROFESSIONAL such as accountant, artist, clergyman, dentist, physician, registered nurse, engineer, lawyer, librarian, teacher, writer, scientist, social worker, actor, actress
2.9	Technical—such as draftsman, surveyor, medical or dental technician, etc.	2.3	Technical—Such as draftsman, surveyor, medical or dental technician, etc.	3.0	TECHNICAL such as draftsman, medical or dental technician, computer programmer
2.4	Official—such as manufacturer, officer in a large company, banker, government official or inspector, etc.	4.0	Official—such as manufacturer, officer in a large company, banker, government official or inspector, etc.		
7.3	Manager—such as sales manager, store manager, office manager, business manager, factory supervisor, etc.	14.7	Manager—such as sales manager, store manager, office manager, factory supervisor, etc.	13.8	MANAGER, ADMINISTRATOR such as sales manager, office manager, school administrator, buyer, restaurant manager, government official
8.6	Proprietor or owner—such as owner of a small business, wholesaler, retailer, contractor, restaurant owner, etc.		Proprietor or owner—such as owner of a small business, wholesaler, retailer, contractor, restaurant owner, etc.	7.0	PROPRIETOR OR OWNER such as owner of a small business, contractor, restaurant owner
4.4	Salesman—such as real estate or insurance salesman, factory representative, etc.	4.3	Salesman—such as real estate or insurance salesman, factory representative, etc.	6.0	SALES such as salesman, sales clerk, advertising or insurance agent, real estate broker

(Continued)

TABLE 3.16
(Continued)

TALENT		EEOS		NLS	
$\%^a$	Response[b]	%	Response[b]	$\%^a$	Response[b]
20.0	Skilled worker or foreman—such as a baker, carpenter, electrician, enlisted man in the armed forces, mechanic, plumber, plasterer, tailor, foreman in a factory or mine (but not on a farm), etc.	22.0	Skilled worker or foreman—such as baker, carpenter, electrician, enlisted man in the armed forces, mechanic, plumber, plasterer, tailor, foreman in a factory or mine, etc.	17.8	CRAFTSMAN such as baker, automobile mechanic, machinist, painter, plumber, telephone installer, carpenter
7.5	Semi-skilled worker—such as factory machine operator, bus or cab driver, meat cutter, etc.	17.5	Semiskilled worker—such as factory machine operator, bus or cab driver, meat cutter, etc.	11.6	OPERATIVE such as meat cutter; assembler; machine operator; welder; taxicab, bus, or truck driver; gas station attendant
2.8	Clerical worker—such as bank teller, bookkeeper, sales clerk, office clerk, mail carrier, messenger, etc.	2.8	Clerical worker—such as bankteller, bookkeeper, sales clerk, office clerk, mail carrier, messenger, etc.	2.8	CLERICAL such as bank teller, bookkeeper, secretary, typist, mail carrier, ticket agent
1.1	Service worker—such as barber, beautician, waiter, etc.	1.1	Service worker—such as barber, waiter, etc.	2.2	SERVICE such as barber, beautician, practical nurse, private household worker, janitor, waiter
1.6	Protective worker—such as a policeman, detective, sheriff, fireman	1.6	Protective worker—such as policeman, detective, sheriff, fireman, etc.	2.5	PROTECTIVE SERVICE such as detective, policeman or guard, sheriff, fireman
8.8	Farm or ranch owner and/or manager	4.7	Farm or ranch manager or owner	5.1	FARMER, FARM MANAGER
0.6	Farm or ranch foreman	2.0	Farm worker on one or more than one farm	11.0	LABORER such as construction worker, car washer, sanitary worker, farm laborer
1.8	Farm or ranch worker	11.4	Workman or laborer—such as factory or mine worker, fisherman, filling station attendant, longshoreman, etc.	2.7	MILITARY such as career officer, enlisted man or woman in the armed forces
16.5	Workman or laborer—such as factory or mine worker, fisherman, filling station attendant, longshoreman, etc.	5.3	Don't know	0.2	HOMEMAKER OR HOUSEWIFE
0.2	Private household worker—such as a servant, butler, etc.	4.2	Omit		
7.0	I don't know.				

[a] Omits: TALENT, 4.6%; NLS, 21.2%.
[b] Order of responses has been changed.

suggest that the samples are reasonably similar. A large number of relatively minor differences in the questions and analysis can be identified, and exact comparisons cannot be made. However, the following summary of percentages gives a rough idea of the outcomes:

Occupational Group	TALENT	EEOS	NLS
Professional	6.1	7.7	14.4
Technical	2.9	2.3	3.0
Official, Manager, Proprietor, Owner	18.3	18.7	20.8
Sales	4.4	4.3	6.0
Skilled worker or Foreman	20.0	22.0	17.8
Semi-skilled worker, Clerical worker, Service worker, Protective worker	13.0	17.5	19.1
Farm or ranch manager, owner, foreman, or worker	11.2	6.7	5.1
Workman or laborer	16.5	11.4	11.0
Others and Don't know	7.2	9.5	2.9
Omit	---	4.2	---

The larger percentage in the professional group and the decrease in farm workers over time is reasonable in light of population shifts, especially if allowance is made for detailed differences in the wording of the questions in the three surveys. The increase in the percentage in the group of occupations including semiskilled, clerical, service, and protective workers is probably attributable also to a general shift in the occupational structure. The smaller percentage of fathers in the skilled worker or foreman group in NLS may have arisen because "foreman" was omitted from the description of that group in NLS. The larger percentage in sales in the NLS results is probably the result of the fact that sales clerk was included in "sales" in NLS but was classified as "clerical" in the other two surveys. The percentage for "workman or laborer" in the TALENT sample is higher than would be expected for a group of 1960 high school seniors.

Results for mother's occupation are shown in Table 3.17. If it can be assumed that a mother who does not have a job outside the home is a housewife, the percentage of housewives is 53.4 for the TALENT sample, 50.1 for the EEOS sample, and 55.5 for the NLS sample. The higher figure for NLS may reflect the fact that in TALENT, a student was told not to check housewife if his or her mother had worked for pay in the last 3

TABLE 3.17
Mother's Occupation

TALENT	EEOS	NLS
Which *one* of the following comes *closest* to describing the work of your mother (or the female head of your household)? *Mark only one answer. If she does housework in addition to outside work, count only the outside work. If she works on more than one job, mark the most important one. If she usually works, but is now out of work, mark the one that she did last.* (Question 208)	Does your mother have a job outside your home? (Question 23)	Under MOTHER, circle the one number that best describes the work done by your mother (or female guardian). The exact job may not be listed but circle the one that comes closest. If either of your parents is out of work, disabled, retired, or deceased, mark the kind of work that he or she used to do. (Question 25C)
	% *Response*	
	33.1 Yes, full-time	
	15.5 Yes, part-time	
	50.1 No	
	1.3 Omit	
%[a] *Response*[b]		%[a] *Response*[b]
53.4 Housewife only; she has not worked for pay in the last 3 years.		55.5 HOMEMAKER OR HOUSEWIFE
5.5 Professional—such as actress, accountant, artist, dentist, physician, engineer, lawyer, librarian, scientist, etc.		9.1 PROFESSIONAL—such as accountant, artist, clergyman, dentist, physician, registered nurse, engineer, lawyer, librarian, teacher, writer, scientist, social worker, actor, actress
0.4 Technical—such as draftsman, medical or dental technician, etc.		0.7 TECHNICAL—such as draftsman, medical or dental technician, computer programmer
1.6 Manager—such as sales manager, store manager, office manager, business manager, factory supervisor, etc.		1.7 MANAGER, ADMINISTRATOR—such as sales manager, office manager, school administrator, buyer, restaurant manager, government official
0.5 Official—such as manufacturer, officer in a large company, banker, government official or inspector, etc.		1.2 PROPRIETOR OR OWNER—such as owner of a small business, contractor, restaurant owner
1.6 Proprietor or owner—such as owner of a small business, wholesaler, retailer, restaurant owner, etc.		

3.5 SALES—such as salesman, sales clerk, advertising or insurance agent, real estate broker

0.7 CRAFTSMAN—such as baker, automobile mechanic, machinist, painter, plumber, telephone installer, carpenter

3.2 OPERATIVE—such as meat cutter; assembler; machine operator; welder; taxicab, bus, or truck driver; gas station attendant

15.9 CLERICAL—such as bank teller, bookkeeper, secretary, typist, mail carrier, ticket agent

5.7 SERVICE—such as barber, beautician, practical nurse, private household worker, janitor, waiter

0.2 PROTECTIVE SERVICE—such as detective, policeman or guard, sheriff, fireman

1.1 FARMER, FARM MANAGER

1.3 LABORER—such as construction worker, car washer, sanitary worker, farm laborer

0.2 MILITARY—such as career officer, enlisted man or woman in the armed forces

1.3 Sales—such as real estate, life insurance salesman, etc.

1.6 Skilled worker or forewoman—such as a baker, inspector, etc.

5.9 Semi-skilled worker—such as factory machine operator, cab driver, etc.

11.5 Clerical worker—such as bookkeeper, secretary, typist, sales clerk, store clerk, etc.

4.5 Service worker—such as beautician, waitress, etc.

0.2 Protective worker—such as policewoman, etc.

0.3 Farm or ranch owner and/or manager

0.3 Farm or ranch worker

3.5 Worker or laborer—such as charwoman, laundry worker, etc.

3.1 Private household worker—such as housekeeper, maid, laundress, etc.

4.8 I don't know.

[a]Omits: TALENT, 3.5%; NLS, 18.0%.
[b]Order of responses has been changed.

years, and the figure of 50.1 cited for EEOS does not include any of the 15.5% of mothers who had a job outside the home at the time of the survey. In NLS, on the other hand, the student could judge whether housewife or job constituted his or her mother's main occupation. Comparisons of TALENT with NLS results for jobs outside the home show an increase in percentage in professional employment from 5.5 to 9.1 and for clerical employment from 11.5 to 15.9. In view of shifts in occupational patterns in the American population, and because of various detailed differences in the questions, the data for mother's occupation do not provide a basis for evaluating the representativeness of the samples in the three surveys.

SUMMARY AND CONCLUSIONS

The most salient finding of this review of questions used in the three surveys is the pervasiveness of change in the way questions on essentially the same topic are formulated. No doubt, this outcome is a side effect of highly desirable features of sound questionnaire development activities—pretesting, multiple reviews, committee discussions of questions, sensitivity to current concerns, responsiveness to the purposes of the study, need for comparing results with other surveys, and the efforts of the questionnaire authors to be both imaginative and realistic in seeking the perfect formulation of each question. This review suggests the desirability of specific attention to the identification of "marker" items on key topics that would be reproduced verbatim. For these items, the burden of proof would fall on the proponents of improvements. Where possible, supplementary items could be used to obtain needed information not adequately defined in the original formulation. It may be added that the questions discussed in this chapter are those most nearly comparable across surveys. The approaches to certain other topics of interest, including subjects studied in high school, foreign language spoken in the home, and the role of various advisors in students' planning, were judged to be too different to warrant detailed discussion in this report.

EQUATING THE TESTS
IN THE THREE NATIONAL SURVEYS

As the final step in this investigation of the feasibility of using data from Project TALENT, the Coleman Study, and NLS to study national trends in educational attainment, the tests administered in the three surveys were examined. Tests of reading comprehension and of mathematical ability were given in each survey. Because different tests were employed in each survey, however, the existing results provide no useful information on possible trends in student performance. In order to evaluate the usefulness of these results as a basis for describing trends in the verbal and mathematical abilities of high school seniors, a carefully-designed study is needed. The purpose of this study would be to determine whether the reading comprehension and mathematical ability tests of the National Longitudinal Study (NLS) can properly be equated to corresponding tests in Project TALENT and the Equality of Educational Opportunity Survey (EEOS), and if so, to determine equivalent scores for these tests.

CHOICE OF TESTS

In determining the tests to be included in the equating-equivalence study, the goal is to include those tests that have greatest usefulness as indicators of general educational development and that are likely to prove to be parallel and therefore to justify equating. It is considered desirable to limit the study to the essential test pairs in order to minimize demands on school and student time and to permit a thorough study of the tests included.

Six tests were judged to be particularly suitable for inclusion.

1. NLS Reading.

This 15-minute test included 20 items based on reading passages. The passages were relatively short (100–200 words) and emphasized straight-forward comprehension. Items considered particularly relevant for minority group students were drawn from the Project Access Reading Tests. Analysis of the test data for a sample of 1,955 students who were slightly more able than the total group tested yielded a reliability coefficient of .797, determined using Kuder-Richardson Formula No. 20. The test was judged to be suitable in difficulty for the group. With respect to speededness, it was found that 82% of the students completed the test but that about 4% did not complete 75% of the items, suggesting a slight degree of speededness. The mean biserial correlation of items with total score was .58. On the whole, the statistical characteristics of the test may be considered satisfactory (Hilton & Rhett, 1973, pp. 2-26, 2-27; Appendix D, pp. 3, 4, 6).

Evidence on sex differences and differences between racial groups are available for the twelfth-grade sample (Hilton & Rhett, 1973, Appendix D, p. D-578).

For sex, statistics are as follows:

	Mean	Standard Deviation	Percent Based on Weighted N	Actual N
Male	9.84	4.98	49.9	6,766
Female	10.05	4.91	50.1	6,926
Total	9.94	4.94	100.0	13,692

In order to facilitate comparisons with group differences observed on other tests, the observed difference in mean raw scores was divided by the standard deviation for the total group. The result is algebraically equivalent to expressing each mean as a standard score for the total group and subtracting. When this procedure was followed, the advantage of the female students expressed in standard score units was .04.

For race, statistics are as follows:

	Mean	Standard Deviation	Percent Based on Weighted N	Actual N
White	10.41	4.77	90.1	11,816
Black	5.67	4.45	9.9	1,876
Total	9.94	4.94	100.0	13,692

The advantage of White students divided by the standard deviation for the total group is 0.96.

2. TALENT Reading Comprehension.

This 30-minute test included 48 items based on reading passages. Topics included social studies, natural science, and literary materials, including poetry (Flanagan et al., 1962, pp. 105–106). Reliability coefficients for this test were obtained by several methods (Flanagan et al., 1964, pp. 2-14, 2-15, 2-51). Because it was judged that the test was slightly speeded, reliability coefficients based on separately timed halves were preferred, even though they were based on experimental rather than final forms of the test. The observed correlation between halves was adjusted in two ways: First, the Spearman-Brown formula was used to adjust for test length, and, second, the coefficient was adjusted for range of talent using data for a 10% sample of the high school senior group. The reliability coefficient for boys was .855; for girls, it was .825.

Evidence on sex differences is available for a 10% sample of twelfth-grade students, as follows (Flanagan et al., 1964, pp. 3-4, 3-5):

	Mean	Standard Deviation	Percent Based on Weighted N	Actual N
Male	33.023	10.483	47.7	2,946
Female	33.555	9.806	52.3	3,302
Total	33.301	10.138	100.0	6,248

The advantage of female students divided by the standard deviation for the total group is 0.05, which corresponds closely to the value of 0.04 for the NLS test.

3. EEOS Reading.

This is a 35-minute test that includes 35 items. It was taken from the reading test of the Cooperative Sequential Tests of Educational Progress series. As in the other two tests, items were based on reading passages varied as to topics and skills measured. Although data on the reliability of this test are not available, it is possible to obtain an approximate figure. Using data for 100 eleventh-grade students tested as part of the norming program of the Sequential Tests of Educational Progress, and using the Spearman-Brown formula to adjust for test length, the estimated reliability of the EEOS reading test would be .85. Although no formal analysis of speededness was made, a review of item responses showed little evidence of speededness (Cooperative Test Division, 1957, p. 10).

Data on scores for Black and White students on the EEOS Reading test are presented in the Supplemental Appendix of the EEOS report (Coleman et al., 1966, pp. 59, 73). The actual sample for each group included 1,000 students from each of 8 strata. Results are as follows:

	Mean	Standard Deviation	Percent Based on Weighted N
Black	58.22	17.12	15.1
White	75.64	16.62	84.9
Total	73.00	17.82	100.0

The advantage of White students divided by the standard deviation for the total group is 0.98, which is slightly higher than the corresponding figure of 0.96 based on the NLS Reading test.

4. NLS Mathematics.

Mathematical ability was measured by a test designed to measure basic competence in mathematics while minimizing computation and excluding algebraic, geometric, or trigonometric skills. The item-type used in this test is called quantitative comparison. The student is given two quantities and asked to decide which of the two is larger, to state that they are equal, or to state that insufficient data are provided to justify a decision (Hilton & Rhett, 1973, pp. 2-27, 2-30).

On the whole, the mathematics test seemed to be appropriate for the group (Hilton & Rhett, 1973, Appendix D, pp. 3, 4, 6). Test reliability estimated by Kuder-Richardson Formula No. 20 was .866. With respect to speededness, 85% of the students completed the test, but about 4% of the students did not complete 75% of the items, suggesting a slight degree of speededness. The difficulty level was well suited to the group.

Data on the comparative performance of male and female and of Black and White students are available (Hilton & Rhett, 1973, Appendix D, p. D-582).

For sex, statistics are as follows:

	Mean	Standard Deviation	Percent Based on Weighted N	Actual N
Male	14.05	7.26	49.9	6,766
Female	12.21	7.09	50.1	6,926
Total	13.13	7.23	100.0	13,692

The advantage of male students divided by the standard deviation for the total group is 0.25.

For race, statistics are as follows:

	Mean	Standard Deviation	Percent Based on Weighted N	Actual N
Black	6.38	6.03	9.9	1,876
White	13.87	6.96	90.1	11,816
Total	13.13	7.23	100.0	13,692

The advantage of White students divided by the standard deviation for the total group is 1.04.

5. TALENT Mathematics.

This test, which was administered with a single 50-minute time limit, included three parts (Flanagan et al., 1964, pp. 122–124). Part I (16 items) deals with arithmetic reasoning. Part II (24 items) emphasizes concepts and methods studied in ninth-grade algebra, but about 40% of the items are devoted to mathematical topics usually taught before ninth grade (e.g., fractions and decimals). Part III (14 items) samples a variety of topics from courses taught in Grades 10 through 12 in college preparatory courses, including plane and solid geometry, more advanced topics in algebra, trigonometry, and analytic geometry and calculus. In addition to scores on each part, subtotals of adjacent parts and total score on all three parts were analyzed in the TALENT research.

Reliability coefficients were determined by Kuder-Richardson Formula No. 21 for both part and total scores and by the formula for the reliability of a sum for the subtotals and total. Results, for twelfth-grade male and female students separately are as follows (Flanagan et al., 1964, pp. 2-14, 2-15):

	Reliability for:	
Part	Male Students	Female Students
I	.766	.729
II	.846	.783
I + II	.890	.853
III	.727	.590
II + III	.891	.831
I + II + III	.915	.874

Data on the comparative performance of male and female students on the various scores are as follows (Flanagan et al., 1964, pp. 3-6, 3-7):

	Male		Female		Total	
Score	Mean	Standard Deviation	Mean	Standard Deviation	Mean	Standard Deviation
I	9.81	3.67	8.77	3.54	9.27	3.64
II	12.38	5.63	10.25	4.85	11.27	5.34
I + II	22.18	8.64	19.03	7.59	20.53	8.26
III	4.41	3.05	3.10	2.31	3.73	2.77
II + III	16.79	8.22	13.35	6.60	14.99	7.61
I + II + III	26.58	11.14	22.10	9.23	24.24	10.43
Percent Based on Weighted N	47.7		52.3		100.0	
Actual N	2,946		3,302		6,248	

The advantage of male students divided by the standard deviation of the total group is as follows:

Score	Ratio
I	0.29
II	0.40
I + II	0.38
III	0.47
II + III	0.45
I + II + III	0.43

Of the various scores, only Part I yields a ratio that is reasonably similar to the value of 0.25 obtained for the NLS Mathematics test.

6. EEOS Mathematics Achievement.

Like the Reading Comprehension test used in the survey, this was taken from the Mathematics test of the Cooperative Sequential Tests of Educational Progress (Coleman et al., 1966, p. 583). It included 25 items to be answered in 35 minutes. The problems in this test emphasize concepts of measurement and geometry and of function and relation. The form that was used for twelfth-grade students was designed for use in tenth, eleventh, and twelfth grades.

Using data for eleventh-grade students tested as part of the norming program of the Sequential Tests of Educational Progress, and using the Spearman-Brown formula to adjust for test length, the estimated reliability of the EEOS mathematics test would be .72 (Cooperative Test Division, 1957, p. 10).

Data on scores for Black and White students on the EEOS Mathematics Achievement test are presented in the Supplemental Appendix of the EEOS report (Coleman et al., 1966, pp. 59, 73). The actual sample for each group included 1,000 students from each of eight strata. Results are as follows:

	Mean	Standard Deviation	Percent Based on Weighted N
Black	37.50	18.40	15.1
White	56.82	17.03	84.9
Total	53.90	18.61	100.0

The advantage of White students divided by the standard deviation for the total group is 1.04, which is the same as the corresponding value of 1.04 obtained for the NLS Mathematics test.

The three surveys included a wide variety of tests in addition to the six proposed for inclusion in this study. In particular, the NLS vocabulary test might be related to the sentence completion and synonyms tests of EEOS, and to a vocabulary test included in the TALENT survey. However, the NLS test is very short (5 minutes), and the TALENT test was not separately timed. It appears that the added information provided by these tests would be insufficient to warrant their inclusion in the study.

EVALUATION OF EQUIVALENCE

Although available information about the tests selected for inclusion in this study indicates that they are measuring reasonably similar abilities and have reasonably similar statistical characteristics, a more systematic evaluation of the question of equivalence is an essential part of this proposed study. Angoff (1966) showed that attempts to equate tests that are not parallel are likely to yield results that may be seriously misleading when used in interpreting scores. The dangers are particularly great when the equating results are used in comparing individual students who took different tests. However, the question of parallelism must be given serious consideration in any application of equated scores.

Two approaches to the evaluation of parallelism are included in this study. The first depends essentially on the correlation between the two tests and their reliability coefficients. Analysis of the data using this approach is done before the equating analysis is initiated, because certain possible outcomes may affect the equating procedures in specific instances. The second approach calls for score equating of the two tests based on different student groups. Although the usefulness of this approach depends on the insight with which the student subgroups are chosen, it has the advantage of showing the extent to which the equating lines for different tests differ when different student subgroups (e.g., boys and girls) are used for determining the equating line. Data analysis using this approach is described as part of the equating design. All basic data needed for the first approach are also required for score equating. Use of the second approach, however, requires the administration of a student questionnaire to provide a basis for differentiating the subgroups.

The initial analysis of equivalence involves a comparison of the correlation between each pair of tests with reliability coefficients for each test using Kuder-Richardson Formula No. 20. Data on the speededness of each test will be obtained in view of the fact that the Kuder-Richardson formula was designed for unspeeded tests.

It is expected that several of the scores yielded by the TALENT mathematics test will be found not to be sufficiently equivalent to NLS mathematics scores to warrant equating. If particular pairs of tests are found to be measuring the same ability, but differ substantially in reliability, true scores rather than observed scores will be used in the equating.

EQUATING DESIGN

Four equatings are called for in the proposed study: (a), NLS Reading (15 minutes) and TALENT Reading Comprehension (30 minutes); (b) NLS Reading (15 minutes) and EEOS Reading (35 minutes); (c) NLS Mathematics (15 minutes) and TALENT Mathematics (50 minutes); and (d) NLS Mathematics (15 minutes) and EEOS Mathematics Achievement. The plan does not provide for the direct equating of EEOS tests to the corresponding TALENT tests, a decision based on the desire to equate the NLS tests to each earlier test as precisely as possible for a given expenditure.

The following are considered to be important characteristics to be embodied in the equating design:

1. The equating procedures should permit the line of relation between scores to be curvilinear. (This provision is necessary because test specifications, particularly for the distribution of item difficulties, cannot be assumed to be the same for corresponding tests in different surveys.)

2. Data collected as part of the equating study should permit an evaluation of the equivalence of each pair of tests to be equated and should also permit the calculation of standard errors of equating at various score levels.

3. The study should be designed so that the standard error of equating is not likely to exceed 4% of the standard deviation in the vicinity of the mean score.

4. Although it should not be necessary that the equating sample yield precise twelfth-grade norms, all reasonable steps should be taken to make the equating sample resemble a norms sample, so that the line of relation will be well defined for the national norms group.

5. Tests should be administered for equating with the same time limits and the same directions used when they were administered in the national surveys.

6. The total testing time for any participating student should be modest (less than 2 hours) and the administrative task to be undertaken by any participating school should also be modest.

It is proposed that the equating procedure be an adaptation of Angoff's Design II (Angoff, 1971, pp. 573–576). In this design, the two tests to be equated are administered so that one random half of the equating sample takes the two tests to be equated in one order and the other random half takes the two tests in the reverse order.

This approach has several significant advantages. First, it can be shown that if scores on the two tests are fairly highly correlated, as is likely to be true for the tests in this study, a substantial gain in precision of equating arises from the fact that the identical group of students takes both tests. Second, this design permits the calculation of the correlation between the tests and of the Kuder-Richardson Formula No. 20 reliability of each test. This information will be useful in evaluating the equivalence of the tests to be equated (Angoff, 1971; Lord, 1950).

The possibility that taking the first test may affect performance on the second test presents some theoretical difficulties. Balancing the order of presentation of the two tests does not completely eliminate this problem, because the effects may not be symmetrical between the two orders.

Although this problem is minimal when alternate forms of the same test designed to the same specifications are to be equated, it is a matter of greater concern when, as in the proposed study, the tests to be equated differ in length and in item type. In order to minimize carry-over effects between testings, the study design should provide that the two tests to be equated be administered in different school weeks rather than at a single sitting. This provision is likely to be particularly important for the equating of TALENT Mathematics and NLS Mathematics because the TALENT test includes advanced material that may be frustrating to some of the students. The analysis of the equating data should be performed separately for the two orders of administration and the results should be examined for possible evidence of differential effects of the two orders.

In conducting the testing for the equating study, separate samples of schools should be drawn for each of the four equatings and each order of administration. Each school would be asked to test only one student group. This feature of the study design would make the administrative procedure for each school as simple as possible.

In performing the equating operations it is proposed that for reading and mathematics tests separately, the TALENT or EEOS test be equated directly to the corresponding NLS test. The procedures to be used for equating are drawn from those used in the Anchor Test Study (Bianchini & Loret, 1972, Vol. 1, pp. 138–140, 144–146). The following steps will be performed separately for reading and mathematics tests:

1.   Equate each pair of tests using the equipercentile method. As in the Anchor Test study, distributions will be determined using a raw score class interval of 1 and will be smoothed using the Tukey–Cureton method before percentiles are determined. If necessary, further smoothing based on judgment will be done. Linear interpolation will be used in determining selected percentiles, and in determining, for each raw score on the NLS test, the corresponding raw score (to one decimal place) on the test being equated to it.

2.   Using the two equating lines arising from the two orders of administration for a given pair of tests, calculate for each raw score on the NLS test the mean of the two estimated values on the test being equated to it.

A design calling for equating NLS directly to TALENT and to EEOS and for equating TALENT to EEOS through NLS was preferred to a somewhat more complex design in which each test would be equated directly to the other two. This preference is based in part on the conception of NLS as a pivotal test both for comparisons with past surveys and with future surveys.

In order to obtain some information about possible effects of the first testing on the second, the scores on each non-NLS test will be transformed to the NLS scale, using the average line based on both orders of administration. Means and standard deviations for NLS scores and the scores obtained by transforming scores on other tests to the NLS raw-score scale will then be compared. Although this procedure will not provide a rigorous evaluation of the effects of the first testing on the second, the results should throw some light on the order of magnitude of the effects.

In addition to the equating based on all students, separate equatings will be performed on designated subgroups of students. If equating results differ substantially from one subgroup to another, after taking account of sampling error, the tests cannot be regarded as parallel.

The particular comparisons to be made will call for dichotomization of the total group on the following five variables: (a) sex, (b) parents' education, (c) type of program in which enrolled (academic *vs.* all others), (d) self-reported high school grades, and (e) amount of mathematics study in Grades 9 through 12 (mathematics equating only). In the three variables calling for a choice of cutting point for dividing the total group into the two subgroups, the cutting point will be chosen so that the two subgroups are as nearly equal in size as the data permit.

Data for forming the designated groups will be obtained from a brief (five-item) questionnaire to be administered along with the NLS test in each pair. Except for the question on mathematics preparation, the appropriate questions from the NLS questionnaire can be used.

EVALUATION OF EQUATING ERROR

Because information on the sampling error of the equating will be of critical importance in applications of the equating results, it is essential to have detailed information on this point. For this purpose, the method of balanced repeated replication described by McCarthy (1969) and by Kish and Frankel (1970, 1974) is proposed. Essentially, this method depends on defining a limited number of principal strata and making two independent selections from each stratum. It is then possible to create pairs of non-overlapping half-samples by assigning one of the two selections from each stratum to one half-sample and assigning the other selection from the stratum to the other half-sample. For greatest efficiency in using the available data, a systematic balanced design for the definition of half-samples is desirable. The necessary design principles are provided by Plackett and Burman (1943–1946).

An important feature of the balanced half-sample design is that the number of balanced half-samples must be a multiple of 4. This restriction does not apply, however, to the number of principal strata. If the number of principal strata is not a multiple of 4, then the square matrix for the next larger multiple of 4 is used. In the design matrix, rows correspond to half-samples and columns to strata. If the number of strata is not a multiple of 4, only as many columns of the matrix are used in designing the analysis as there are strata. Thus, if there were nine principal strata, nine columns and 12 rows of a 12 × 12 design matrix would be used (McCarthy, 1969).

Although the balanced half-sample design should provide useful information on the extent of equating error, McCarthy (1969) pointed out that: "the exact characteristics of estimates of variance are for the most part, unknown" (p. 245). Kish and Frankel (1970, 1974), on the basis of extensive empirical studies, concluded that balanced repeated replication designs provide the best available method for estimating sampling error for complex statistics.

SAMPLE DESIGN

Certain decisions about the plan for test administration clearly narrow the options available for efficient sample design. First, the decision to test in the classroom situation is likely to accentuate the effect of cluster sampling, especially if classes are differentiated for students in different programs and if tracking is used by a school. Second, the decision to administer only one sequence of a particular pair of tests in any one school prevents matching of samples on the basis of class or school, which would be desirable from a sampling viewpoint.

Because this study is concerned with equating rather than with norming, and especially because the equating method to be used takes advantage of the presumably high correlation between the tests to be equated, the foregoing difficulties should not prevent the development of an adequate sample design. Moreover, to the extent that the tests to be equated approximate strict parallelism, the characteristics of the sample should have no systematic effect on the line of relation between scores. The precision of equating at different score levels would be affected, however.

For the present study, stratification on the basis of school characteristics related to test performance is important for the following reasons: (a) to increase the efficiency of the sample, (b) to permit the substitution of a similar school for a school that declines to participate, and (c) to make the schools administering a given pair of tests in one order as similar as possible to the schools administering that pair of tests in the reverse order. Stratification may also be used to insure diversity in the sample even if the characteristic is not known to have a high correlation with test performance. A further consideration is that the analysis could be adapted to study the standard error of the samples considered as norms samples and thus provide concrete evidence on the extent to which the method is less efficient than simple random sampling of the same number of students. Although this analysis would be incidental to the main study, it would make a useful contribution to empirical evidence on sampling design.

DATA ANALYSIS

Because the study design and data analysis are so closely connected in a study of this kind, the following statement of analysis steps is essentially a recapitulation.

Editing.   Only students who took both tests under defined conditions will be included in the analysis sample. Data will also be edited on the basis of teacher's irregularity reports, and answer sheets that have two or fewer items answered will be excluded.

Weighting.   A weight for each student will be determined based on the following two factors: (a) one eleventh divided by the proportion of all twelfth-grade students who belong to his or her principal stratum; and (b) 25 divided by the number of usable cases in his or her class. The same weight will be used in all phases of the analysis for a given student. Under this weighting plan, all members of a particular class will have the same weight.

Equating.   Equating results for the four pairs of tests will be obtained by averaging the equipercentile equating results for the two orders of administration for the following groups of students for each test pair:

1. All students.
2. Boys and girls separately.
3. Students dichotomized on the basis of parents' education.
4. Students dichotomized on the basis of type of school program (Academic vs. all others).
5. Students dichotomized on the basis of self-reported high school grades.
6. For mathematics tests only, students dichotomized on the basis of amount of high school study of mathematics.
7. Each of the 11 half-samples of the group taking each test pair, for use in determining equating error.

In the event that results for one or more of the subgroup equatings done to aid in evaluating equivalence are ambiguous, equating errors for each of the two subgroups will be developed using balanced half-sample replication.

Error of Norms.   Although this study is not a norms study, the balanced half-sample replication design will permit the evaluation of the sampling error of the mean score on the NLS Reading test and the NLS Mathematics test, when taken as the first test in a pair. This sampling error will be useful in evaluating the results obtained when the corresponding EEOS or TALENT test scores obtained in the samples that took them as the first test of the pair are expressed in NLS units. The line of relation obtained in the study would be used for this conversion. In addition, the results will provide useful information on the size of the error arising when classes rather than individual students or schools are sampled at the high school level.

Practice Effect.   By converting scores for tests other than NLS to the appropriate NLS scale, it will be possible to obtain means and standard deviations for all initial and final tests on the NLS scale. This analysis should throw some light on whether or not practice effects operate symmetrically for the two members of a test pair.

Parallelism.   The correlation between the two tests in each pair can be evaluated in relation to the reliability of scores for each test in the pair. For this analysis, Kuder-Richardson Formula No. 20 reliabilities will be determined for each test, using the sample that took that test first.

Application of Conversions to Survey Data.   Assuming that the outcome of the equivalency comparisons warrants the conversion of scores of tests in one survey to those in another, NLS data files will be utilized to convert scores for NLS tests to the appropriate scores in each of the other two surveys and to provide the same statistics for corresponding groups as have been provided in the earlier surveys.

For maximum precision of the comparisons, certain additional tabulations of TALENT, EEOS, and NLS data should be performed. Obtaining NLS distributions, means, and standard deviations based on weighted Ns, using the weights devised for the test participants rather than those for all participants would be useful. These statistics should be obtained for the total group having test scores, for male and female students separately, and for Black and White students separately. Moreover, to permit comparison with EEOS statistics, tabulations based on public school students only should be obtained. For EEOS, separate tabulations for male and female students should be obtained, provided that this can be done without excessive cost. Finally, the Project TALENT Data Bank should be utilized to obtain distributions, means, and standard deviations for public school students only and for the total group. For both of these groups, data should be analyzed separately by sex and for the two sexes combined. The TALENT results for reading comprehension should be compared with the results of a 1960 to 1970 comparison based on administration of the TALENT test in 1970 (Flanagan & Jung, 1971). The stratifications by sex and race do not, of course, exhaust the possible subgroups that might be examined to provide trend data for significant student groups.

ACKNOWLEDGMENT

This chapter is a revision of the final report of National Institute of Education Project No. NIE-G-74-0050 (Schrader & Hilton, 1975) which was completed in April 1975. Copies of the full final report may be obtained by requesting Project Report 75-13 from Educational Testing Service, Princeton, NJ, 08541.

CHAPTER FOUR

Equating Test Results from Two National Surveys: A Study of the SAT Score Decline

Albert E. Beaton
Thomas L. Hilton
William B. Schrader
Educational Testing Service

This chapter describes a major effort to pool data from two national surveys (Project TALENT and the National Longitudinal Study of 1972 (NLS)) and a large-scale test administration in order to investigate the possible causes of the infamous SAT Score Decline. Each national survey included a reading comprehension test which—when equated—permitted the authors to estimate how much of the decline was attributable to a change in the national level of verbal ability and how much was attributable to a change in the composition of the population of students taking the SAT. But equating the two reading tests was a complex problem as was the matter of achieving comparable biographical data from the two national surveys. The most formidable task, however, was developing a method of partitioning the mean change in SAT scores into meaningful components. The method is described in detail. Also included is a description of steps taken to achieve comparable data from questionnaire items with quite different formats and also steps taken to equate two tests of unequal reliability and with inaccurate scores.

—*Thomas L. Hilton*

That the average scores of students who took the SAT declined steadily and noticeably from 1964 is a fact. Because the SAT candidate group is self-selected, however, there is no certainty that a parallel decline in ability occurred for all college entrants or for all high school seniors. This study was initiated in order to obtain directly comparable data on changes between 1960 and 1972 in reading ability and other characteristics for high school seniors, college entrants, and SAT takers. Similarities and differences in the changes for these groups should be useful in evaluating various explanations for the SAT score decline.

METHOD

Sources of Data

The American Institutes of Research graciously cooperated in working out an arrangement by which SAT score files could be searched for a sample of 20,359 participants in the TALENT survey while the confidentiality of both data files was maintained. The data bases for the TALENT and the NLS surveys are well known and well documented. A detailed comparison of the two surveys has been made by Schrader and Hilton (1975) (see chapter 3); therefore, details of the samples and variables are not repeated here.

A critical variable in the present study was whether the student took the College Board examinations, a variable not included in the TALENT data but available on microfilm in the ETS files. Because looking up SAT scores for the entire 81,175 sample members would have been time-consuming and expensive, and because such a large sample is statistically unnecessary, we asked the American Institutes for Research for a subsample of about 25% of the cases (N = 20,359), a subsample comparable in size to the entire NLS sample. The final edited data base, therefore, contained a large number of test scores, questionnaire items, and SAT scores. The data file had no individual identification information. The Project TALENT sample used in this study was selected in such a way as to be self-weighting for high school seniors. Special weights, supplied by the Project TALENT staff, were used for persons included in the sample of nonrespondents selected for special follow-up.

For the 1972 data point, the present study used the records of 16,683 students who participated in the National Longitudinal Study. SAT scores were recorded by the schools. A follow-up survey was administered 2 years later to learn, among other things, about the career choices of these high school graduates. About 95% of the sample was located. The data file, including the results of the follow-up, was obtained from the National Center for Education Statistics.

Variables Used

Reading Comprehension. Both Project TALENT and the NLS administered reading comprehension tests to nearly all members of the samples. Project TALENT used a test with 48 items that was scored on a number-right basis. The NLS administered a 20-item test that was scored using formula scores (number right minus one fourth wrong). Because a comparable general test of intellectual ability was critical to the analyses discussed later, a substudy set about equating these two reading comprehension tests. For this study, special test administrations were conducted in 88 high schools, yielding usable data for 1,657 high school seniors. A detailed description and a discussion of the equating study were presented in the original report.

In this study, reading scores were used not only to describe various subgroups but also for stratifying the three main groups on the basis of reading ability. Six strata were defined, using the distribution of reading scores for the 1972 cohort, so as to include the top tenth, the second tenth, and the second, third, fourth, and bottom fifth of the 1972 high school senior group. (In determining the strata, the 90th, 80th, 60th, 40th and 20th percentiles for high school seniors in 1972 were calculated, expressed in terms of the NLS raw score scale. Then the corresponding TALENT raw scores were determined, using the conversion table developed in the equating study. The resulting values defined the equivalent class intervals for NLS scores and TALENT scores. In using these class intervals, frequencies were prorated between class intervals whenever an interval boundary fell within a particular NLS or TALENT raw score interval. This procedure was used in order to reduce the effect of coarseness of grouping in the raw score data.)

College Entrance. College entrance, necessarily derived from questions on the follow-up questionnaires, was defined as full-time matriculation in a 2- or 4-year college in the academic year following the senior year of high school. Part-time attendance or attendance in vocational or technical schools was not considered college attendance. By this definition, 39% of the high school seniors entered college in 1960 and 43% in 1972.

SAT Taking. As mentioned earlier, the SAT scores for the Project TALENT subjects had to be located in the ETS microfilm files. A search was made to locate these scores, if possible, in the ETS files for the 1958-1959 or 1959-1960 testing years. Of the sample, 18% were found to have taken the SAT at least once. Because College Board statistics were not developed for cohort groups in 1960, there is no directly comparable percentage based on all students from that cohort who took the SAT.

For the NLS sample, taking the SAT was recorded by the participating schools. The accuracy of this procedure was checked in a study by the NLS project staff (Hilton & Rhett, 1973). In the present study, 31% of the sample had SAT scores, a figure very close to the 33% estimated from the number of persons in the class of 1972 who took the SAT, as reported by the College Board's Admissions Testing Program, divided by the number of high school seniors estimated by the National Center for Education Statistics.

SAT-Verbal and SAT-Mathematical Scores. For the Project TALENT sample, up to five sets of SAT-verbal and SAT-mathematical scores were recorded for each individual, as well as the dates of testing. The analyses used the last scores prior to high school graduation. The mean SAT-verbal score for those for whom SAT scores were available was 473.6; the SAT-mathematical mean was 496.2.

For the NLS sample, the schools were asked to record the last SAT scores before graduation. Thus, the two sets of data are comparable. For the NLS sample, the average SAT-verbal score was 453.3 and the average SAT-mathematical score 485.3, mean scores very close to the comparable figures of 453 and 484 published by the Admissions Testing Program for that year (1971–1972).

Age, Sex. In both surveys, ages were computed in months from date of birth. The average age of the 1960 sample, as of June 30 of the year of graduation, was 18 years and ½ month compared with an average age of 18 years and 2 months for the NLS subjects. Sex was obtained from an item in the student questionnaire administered in each survey.

Socioeconomic Status. We used four variables from the two surveys to determine socioeconomic status and made them roughly comparable by combining categories. (These variables might be called socio-educational, rather than socioeconomic.) The four variables are father's education, mother's education, father's occupation, and mother's occupation. Evidence that supports this choice of variables was obtained by Stricker (1976).

The four categories for education are:

1. Did not know or did not respond to the item.
2. Some high school or less.
3. High school graduate.
4. Some college, college graduate, and graduate school.

The occupational classifications are:

1. Did not know or did not respond to the item.
2. *Blue collar*, which includes skilled workers or craftsmen, semi-skilled workers or operatives, service workers, protective workers, laborers, all classifications of farmer, and household workers.
3. *White collar*, including proprietors, salesmen, clerical workers, and military personnel.
4. *Professional and managerial*, including technicians and officials.

5. For mothers, a fifth category was included: *Homemaker* or house-wife.

Family Configuration.   Family configuration was obtained from items in each survey that, in effect, asked the respondents to indicate what their ordinal position was. Specifically, the Project TALENT Student Information Blank (SIB) asked the respondents how many living brothers, half brothers, foster brothers, or stepbrothers were older than they were and, in a second question, how many were younger. Parallel questions inquired about sisters. The respondents were instructed to include children "not now living in your home," but not to count their own twin brother or twin sister (if any).

The National Longitudinal Study included the relevant questions in the second Follow-Up Questionnaire. The items asked only about brothers and sisters and gave no instructions about how to count twins, siblings not in the home, half brothers, and so on. How the absence of these instructions affected the results, if at all, is difficult to estimate.

High School Curriculum.   High school curriculum has three categories: (a) general, (b) academic or college preparatory, and (c) vocational or technical.

For the NLS, this information was obtained from Question 2 of the Student Questionnaire; and for Project TALENT, from Question 91 of the SIB.

Expected College Major.   Creating this variable required extensive collapsing of categories. The final categories are as follows:

1. Science and mathematics, including biological sciences.
2. Social sciences and humanities, including sociology, prelaw, foreign languages, and fine arts.
3. Engineering.
4. Other fields, including business administration, education, agriculture, nursing, home economics, and journalism.
5. Nonmatching categories (categories included in one of the surveys but not the other; for example, the NLS category of Computer Science).

ANALYSIS PLAN

The analysis plan was designed primarily to facilitate key comparisons between student characteristics in 1960 and 1972 for the three main groups: high school seniors, college entrants, and SAT takers. Each of the student characteristic variables served as a basis for dividing each of the three main groups into subgroups. The particular statistics calculated for each subgroup differed for the three main groups. The following discussion of the statistical analyses has been organized on the basis of the main group or groups for which the particular calculation was made. The italicized heading for each result corresponds to the column heading for that statistic in the tables.

Statistics calculated for all main groups:

N. This is the estimated number of students in the designated subgroup and the designated main group. This result was called "Weighted *N*" for high school seniors, "Estimated *N*" for college entrants, and "*N*" for SAT takers. All *N*s are reported in thousands. Because reported percentages were calculated using *N*s including all digits, they will tend to differ slightly from percentages calculated from the reported *N*s.

Percent of Cohort. This result was obtained by dividing the number of students in a subgroup by the number of students in the corresponding total group. (For college entrants and SAT takers, students with missing data on a student characteristic were excluded in calculating "% of Cohort.")

Reading Mean. This is the mean reading score for members of the designated subgroup. These results make it possible to identify shifts in the composition of each of the three main groups with respect to each of the student characteristics and to determine the amount of change in reading scores from 1960 to 1972 for every subgroup.

Statistics Calculated for College Entrants and SAT Takers:

Percent of Stratum. This result was obtained by dividing the number of students in a subgroup (stratum) by the number of students in the corresponding subgroup of high school seniors. These results make it possible to discern trends between 1960 and 1972 in college going and in SAT-taking patterns for the subgroups defined on the basis of student characteristics. They describe changes in the patterns of *self-selection* with respect to college entrance or SAT taking. (To be sure, patterns of self-selection are heavily influenced by college policies, for example, with respect to tests required for admission.) When used along with results on "% of Cohort" for high school seniors, they make it possible to assess the relative importance of changes in the high school senior population and of changes in self-selection for various subgroups in producing changes in the college entrant or SAT-taking group.

Statistics calculated for high school seniors only:

Actual N.   This is simply a count of the number of sample students on which the various results for high school seniors were based.

Reading SD.   The standard deviation of reading scores was calculated to provide some information on within-subgroup variability.

Statistics calculated for SAT takers only:

SAT-Verbal Mean.   Mean of SAT-verbal scores.

SAT-Verbal SD.   Standard deviation of SAT-verbal scores.

SAT-Math. Mean.   Mean of SAT-mathematical scores.

SAT-Math. SD.   Standard deviation of SAT-mathematical scores.

Results for "SAT-verbal mean" were of decisive importance in estimating the effect of changes in self-selection on the SAT score decline and in providing evidence on a possible shift in the SAT-verbal scale between 1960 and 1972. The other three results, although not of direct concern in this study, were considered to provide useful descriptive information on the various subgroups.

CHANGES IN READING COMPREHENSION SCORES FROM 1960 TO 1972

Introduction

In this section we used equated scores on the reading tests taken by Project TALENT participants in 1960 and by National Longitudinal Study participants in 1972 to explore four research questions:

1. Has the reading ability of high school seniors changed?
2. Has the reading ability of college entrants changed?
3. Has the reading ability of SAT candidates changed?
4. Does an SAT-verbal score earned in 1972 represent the same ability level as the same score earned in 1960?

We then addressed the question of what effect changes in the distribution of reading ability in the high school senior and SAT-taking populations had on the average score of the SAT-verbal test. Because different reading tests were administered to the 1960 and 1972 student groups, the rigor of the comparisons reported in this chapter depended directly on the use of appropriate statistical methods for developing interchangeable scores on the two tests. Although a number of difficult technical problems were encountered in implementing the equating design,[1] we are confident that the final equating is satisfactory. We must acknowledge, however, that the equated scores do not and cannot achieve the precision that would have been attained had the same test been used in both studies.

Reading Ability of High School Seniors

Reading ability as represented by the mean scores of these two national samples of high school seniors declined between 1960 and 1972. The results may be expressed briefly by stating that the mean score declined from 10.5 to 9.7 on the NLS scale as shown in Fig. 4.1 and Table 4.1. This decline amounts to about 16% of the standard deviation of scores for high school seniors.

Table 4.1 gave us the opportunity to explore further the drop in average reading score. The rows or "strata" of this table represent levels of reading ability. The six strata were defined as follows: The top tenth of the group tested in 1972 was classified in the highest group, the next tenth was classified in the second group, and the remaining fifths of the class were assigned to correspondingly lower levels. On the basis of the results of the equating of 1960 and 1972 reading scores, the 1960 students were assigned to the level that best described their reading performance. Thus, each row or stratum of the table can be construed as containing students from the two samples who are substantially equal in reading ability.

---

[1]One problem arose because the reading tests administered in the two studies—although fairly similar—differed in length. The TALENT test was longer than the NLS test (30 minutes vs. 15 minutes). When data collected as part of the present study were used, we found that TALENT scores were more reliable and more highly correlated with SAT-verbal scores than the NLS scores. Because the precise equating of TALENT and NLS scores is very important for the present study, we decided to modify the TALENT scores so as to bring the correlation with SAT-verbal to approximately the same level for both tests, and to equate the modified scores. The modified TALENT scores seemed satisfactory and are used throughout this study. (The procedure used is described in more detail in the full report.)

Another concern was the accuracy of individual TALENT scores, particularly very low scores. On the basis of marked inconsistency of certain scores with other information in the 1960 data file, it was decided to treat about 2½% of the cases in the 1960 sample as having missing data on the reading test. (The method by which the cases were identified is described in the full report. In brief, outliers were identified by multiple regression.)

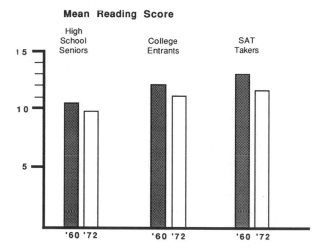

FIG. 4.1.   Mean reading score for high school seniors, college entrants, and SAT takers in 1960 and 1972.

TABLE 4.1
Reading Score Levels of High School Seniors

| | | | | High School Senior | | |
| | | | | | Reading | |
Cohort	Score	Actual N	Weighted N[a]	% of cohort	Mean	SD
TAL 1960	43.65–55	2780	255	14.3	17.8	1.1
NLS 1972	16.19–20	1442	288	10.0	17.6	1.1
TAL 1960	40.46–43.65	2356	216	12.2	15.3	0.5
NLS 1972	14.33–16.19	1504	290	10.1	15.3	0.6
TAL 1960	35.38–40.46	3905	358	20.1	12.9	0.8
NLS 1972	11.43–14.33	2956	575	20.0	12.8	0.9
TAL 1960	29.40–35.38	3683	337	19.0	10.0	0.8
NLS 1972	8.56–11.43	3042	576	20.0	10.0	1.0
TAL 1960	21.77–29.40	3554	325	18.3	6.9	1.0
NLS 1972	5.13– 8.56	3243	577	20.0	7.0	1.1
TAL 1960	(–7)–21.77	3106	284	16.0	2.4	2.4
NLS 1972	(–5)– 5.13	3649	576	20.0	2.4	2.1
TAL 1960	No test	972	89			
NLS 1972	No test	843	133			
TAL 1960	Total	20358	1864	100.0	10.5	5.1
NLS 1972	Total	16681	3015	100.0	9.7	5.0

[a]In thousands

The column in Table 4.1 headed "Weighted N" shows the estimated number of high school seniors in each ability stratum for the years 1960 and 1972. The section of Fig. 4.2 headed "High School Seniors" presents the results for "Weighted N" graphically. (In the figure, the results for the two highest strata are combined.) The graph makes it evident that in 1960, the proportions of students in the higher strata are noticeably larger than the proportions of students in the lower strata.

In 1972 (as a consequence of the way in which the strata were defined), each stratum includes one fifth of the students. Because the strata represent comparable ability levels in the 2 years, these results indicate that there was a decline in reading ability between 1960 and 1972 for high school seniors.

Between 1960 and 1972, the number of high school graduates increased from 1,864,000 to 3,015,000 (Frankel & Beamer, 1974; Simon & Frankel, 1973). Despite the decline in ability levels, there were actually more seniors even at the highest level, which increased by 13% from 255,000 to 288,000, as shown in Table 4.1. But the increase was much greater at the lower levels—the lowest group more than doubled, increasing from 284,000 to 576,000.

The change in the distribution is expressed in percentages in the column labeled "% of Cohort." These percentages show that 14% of the 1960 cohort did as well as or better than the top 10% of the 1972 cohort, and only 16% did as poorly as or poorer than the bottom 20%. This approach may give a clearer idea of the extent to which the ability level has changed than simply comparing mean scores.

The means and standard deviations of the reading scores provide evidence on the average reading ability for each stratum. The small dif-

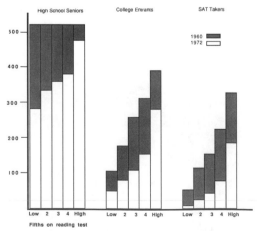

FIG. 4.2. Number of students whose reading score would place them in each fifth of 1972 high school seniors.

ferences between the 1960 and 1972 results indicate that the strata were, indeed, matched on ability level.

We do not know, from the data of this study, why the much larger 1972 cohort has a much larger proportion of students who scored low on the reading test. Some possible factors are shown in the next section. We note here, however, that the change is consistent with a change in the holding power of the high schools, that is, fewer low-scoring students are dropping out of school. The percentage of the age cohort who reached the senior year of high school increased from 67% in 1960 to 79% in 1972 (*Digest of Education Statistics*, 1975 Edition, Table 10). Our tentative opinion is that a substantial fraction of the drop in mean reading score can be attributed to this factor, as described in the full report, but further research would be needed to evaluate this effect.

Reading Ability of College Entrants

The reading ability of college entrants also declined between 1960 and 1972. Expressed as a mean score on the NLS scale, the decline is from 12.8 in 1960 to 11.9 in 1972. The decline in mean score for college entrants is, then, slightly more than that for high school seniors. These means can be seen in Fig. 4.1.

Reading Ability of SAT Candidates

For SAT candidates, the mean score on the NLS scale declined from 14.2 for the 1960 group to 12.4 for the 1972 group. This decline can be seen in Fig. 4.1. The decline in mean score is more than twice as large as the decline for high school seniors, and twice as large as the decline for college entrants.

The column "% of Cohort" of Table 4.2 presents the percentage of students at each ability level from 1960 to 1972. The shift is more marked for students who took the SAT than for college entrants. The percentage of SAT takers in the top stratum decreases from 34% in 1960 to 20% in 1972. In the second stratum, the drop is from 21% to 17%. The percentage in the two lowest strata (the lowest 40% of 1972 high school seniors) increases from about 8% to about 19%.

The "*N*" column in Table 4.3 shows the dramatic increase in the number of students taking the SAT between 1960 and 1972. These figures are shown graphically in Fig. 4.2. More students took the SAT at all levels of reading ability. In the top stratum, the number taking the SAT increased from 108,000 for the 1960 cohort to 177,000 for the 1972 cohort, whereas the bottom fifth increased from 7,000 to 54,000, and the next to the bottom fifth increased by 103,000. These increases at the low end of the reading ability scale result in the larger proportion of SAT takers at the lower ability levels.

TABLE 4.2
Reading Score Levels of Students Who Took the SAT

Cohort	Score	N^a	% of stratum	% of cohort	SAT takers Reading mean	SAT-verbal Mean	SAT-verbal SD	SAT-math[b] Mean	SAT-math[b] SD
TAL 1960	43.65–55	108	42.4	34.2	17.9	547	87	551	103
NLS 1972	16.19–20	177	61.4	19.5	17.7	567	84	573	97
TAL 1960	40.46–43.65	67	31.0	21.2	15.3	499	88	511	101
NLS 1972	14.33–16.19	154	53.1	16.9	15.3	504	80	527	94
TAL 1960	35.38–40.46	75	20.8	23.6	13.0	438	81	474	96
NLS 1972	11.43–14.33	226	39.3	24.9	12.9	453	78	489	96
TAL 1960	29.40–35.38	41	12.1	13.0	10.2	389	76	432	91
NLS 1972	8.56–11.43	176	30.5	19.4	10.1	404	69	446	96
TAL 1960	21.77–29.40	18	5.4	5.6	7.1	341	74	401	84
NLS 1972	5.13– 8.56	121	21.0	13.4	7.1	358	68	408	93
TAL 1960	(–7)–21.77	7	2.6	2.3	2.7	337	104	385	94
NLS 1972	(–5)– 5.13	54	9.4	5.9	3.2	311	61	361	86
TAL 1960	No test	11	12.7			476	114	490	113
NLS 1972	No test	27	20.7			454	115	484	105
TAL 1960	Total	326	17.5	100.0	14.2	474	108	496	110
NLS 1972	Total	935	31.0	100.0	12.4	453	108	485	113

^{a}In thousands

TABLE 4.3
Reading Scores of High School Seniors Grouped by Age

	High school seniors				
				Reading	
Age	Actual N	Weighted N^a	% of cohort	Mean	SD
17½ or less					
1960	2971	272	14.6	11.7	4.8
1972	927	166	5.5	11.0	5.0
17½ + to 18					
1960	7900	723	38.8	11.3	4.8
1972	6395	1171	38.8	10.5	4.7
18 + to 18½					
1960	6003	550	29.5	10.7	4.9
1972	6246	1162	38.5	10.1	4.8
18½ + to 19					
1960	1824	167	9.0	8.5	5.1
1972	1817	314	10.4	8.0	5.2
Above 19					
1960	1180	108	5.8	6.2	5.0
1972	1173	184	6.1	5.2	4.5
No response					
1960	481	44	2.4	7.8	5.6
1972	125	19	0.6	4.5	4.1
Total					
1960	20359	1864	100.0	10.5	5.1
1972	16683	3015	100.0	9.7	5.0

^{a}In thousands

The column headed "% of Stratum" shows the proportion of each ability stratum taking the SAT. The proportions show increases for all strata, even the top level. In 1960, 42.4% of all high school seniors in the top stratum took the SAT, whereas in 1972 the percentage rose to 61.4%. Very few students in the lower strata took the SAT in 1960, but substantially more did in 1972. The SAT, then, is reaching more college-aspiring students in all strata. But the increase is substantially greater for students in lower ability strata.

SAT SCALE DRIFT

Our data permitted the calculation of mean SAT-verbal and mean SAT-mathematical scores for students taking the SAT in each of the six strata. Means and standard deviations for SAT-mathematical scores are included in this report as a matter of interest. Because this study is focused on changes in verbal ability, no attempt is made to discuss the results for SAT-mathematical. The primary objective of this phase of the analysis was to find out whether there has been a drift in the SAT-verbal score scale so that a given score represented a higher (or lower) level of ability in 1972 than in 1960.

The interpretation of the observed differences in means, however, presents a number of difficult technical problems. The questions of strict parallelism between the two reading tests and of the accuracy of some of the individual scores were noted earlier in the introduction to this chapter. The mean SAT-verbal scores for each stratum may be considered to represent a regression of SAT-verbal scores on reading scores, and Thorndike (1971) has shown that important problems arise when a regression approach is used to evaluate differences between groups. Thus, although the sample of 1,657 students in the equating study should have provided an adequate basis for equating of the kind used in this study, caution must be exercised in interpreting the differences in mean SAT scores.

A carefully designed and executed study of SAT scale drift between 1963 and 1973 has recently been completed by Modu and Stern (1976) with results relevant to the interpretation of our findings. The following table brings together the data on SAT-verbal means from Table 4.2 and the Modu-Stern results. The "Adjusted 1972" means apply the Modu-Stern estimates of scale drift from 1963 to 1973 to the 1972 means.

Stratum	1960 (TALENT)	1972 (NLS)	Adjusted 1972 (Based on Modu-Stern)
Highest Tenth	547	567	562
Second Tenth	499	504	496
Second Fifth	438	453	444
Third Fifth	389	404	393
Fourth Fifth	341	358	345
Lowest Fifth	337	311	297
Total	474	453	444

When the SAT-verbal means for 1960 and 1972 are compared, a puzzling reversal occurs. Although the overall mean is 21 points higher for the TALENT sample than for the NLS sample, the means for all strata except the lowest show a substantial difference in the opposite direction. Within strata, the TALENT sample shows consistently lower means than the NLS sample. The column head "Adjusted 1972," however, indicates that if the scale drift found by Modu and Stern based on the period 1963 to 1973 is used to adjust the NLS (1972) means, the results for the second through the fifth strata become satisfactorily consistent for the two samples, although the present results suggest that the drift is, if anything, slightly greater for the period 1960 to 1972 than the shift found by Modu and Stern.

The difference of 15 scaled score points between the 1960 results and the adjusted 1972 results for the highest stratum remains puzzling. The standard error of the difference of the two means can be estimated, with some approximation, as 5.7 scaled score points, large enough to warrant consideration. Although imprecision of equating may have contributed to the difference, it seems probable that the main source of the difference is attributable to differences in the measurement characteristics of the two reading tests. According to this hypothesis, SAT-verbal scores for top stratum students identified by the TALENT test regressed more than did SAT-verbal scores for top stratum students identified by the NLS test.

The difference for the lowest stratum is less difficult to interpret. Multiplying the actual N (3,106) by the percentage of the cohort in the sample (2%) indicates that only 81 students in this stratum took the SAT. Clearly, a relatively small number of outliers in the TALENT score distribution that were not rejected by the procedure used could have raised the TALENT mean appreciably. The fact that the SAT-verbal mean score for the lowest stratum is only 4 scaled points lower than the mean for the next higher stratum is consistent with this interpretation. (The corresponding difference for the NLS sample is 47 scaled score points.)

IMPLICATIONS FOR THE SAT-VERBAL SCORE DECLINE

The fact that reading scores declined more than twice as much for SAT takers as for high school seniors generally makes it clear that changes in the ability level of the high school seniors can account at best for only part of the SAT-verbal score decline.

Using data already presented, we estimated the extent to which the change in the ability level of high school seniors contributed to the decline, and the extent to which the changed patterns of SAT taking contributed to it. An appendix to this chapter provides a complete description of the method we used, which is called partitioning analysis. The application of partitioning analysis was based on three sets of data presented in Tables 4.1 and 4.3: the estimated number of high school seniors in each of the six ability strata in 1960 and 1972, the percentage of high school seniors in each ability stratum who took the SAT in 1960 and 1972, and the mean 1960 SAT-verbal score for students in each stratum. The results of the partitioning analysis provided answers to three questions as follows:

1. What would the SAT population be like if both the distribution of ability in the high school population and the SAT-verbal scale had remained constant, but the percentage of students at various ability levels who took the SAT changed as they in fact did between 1960 and 1972? Our estimate is that the mean verbal score of an estimated 627,000 SAT takers would be 454. The effect of the change in SAT-taking pattern alone is thus to drop the SAT-verbal mean from 474 to 454, a drop of 20 points.

2. What would the SAT population be like if the percentage of students at various ability levels who took the SAT stayed the same and the SAT-verbal scale remained constant, but the ability level of high school senior populations changed as it in fact did between 1960 and 1972? Our estimate is that the mean verbal score of an estimated 465,000 SAT takers would be 462. The effect of the change in ability level of the high school senior population alone is, therefore, to drop the SAT-verbal mean by 12 points.

3. What would the SAT population be like if the ability level of high school seniors and the percentage of students at various ability levels who took the SAT had changed as they in fact did but the SAT-verbal scale had remained constant? There would have been 935,000 SAT takers (as there were), but the mean score would have been 442 rather than 453. The net effect of scale drift is, therefore, to understate the decline in SAT-verbal mean by 11 points.

The effect of the change in the percentage of students at various ability levels who took the SAT, therefore, reduced the mean from 474 to 454, or 20 points on the SAT-verbal scale, whereas the effect of change in the ability level of high school seniors was to drop the mean from 474 to 462, by 12 points. When account is taken of scale drift, the overall decline in SAT-verbal is increased from 21 points to 32 points.

The findings of the partitioning analysis suggest that the question of why SAT scores declined can logically be thought of as two questions: Why did the decline in verbal ability of high school seniors occur; and why did the patterns of SAT-taking change?

Further information on the nature of the changes in both the high school population and the SAT-taking population is presented in the next section, with a view to understanding the declines in mean verbal ability.

CHANGES IN OTHER STUDENT CHARACTERISTICS FROM 1960 TO 1972

In the previous section, we described and discussed changes in the measured reading ability of the high school senior population, college entrants, and students who took the SAT. In this section, nine other characteristics of these populations—age, sex, each parent's education and occupation, family configuration, curriculum, and expected college major (if any)—are described as a means of probing further into some changes that may help us to understand shifts in ability.

Changes in the High School Senior Population

Age.   As shown in Table 4.3, the period from 1960 to 1972 saw a marked decrease in the percentage of high school seniors in the 17½-and-younger age group. This decrease may have arisen because fewer children were entering school at a relatively early age or because there was less tendency to accelerate rapid learners. An alternative hypothesis is that the reduced percentage of younger students may have resulted, in part, from a reduced tendency for students who were progressing through school at an average or slower rate to drop out. From this viewpoint, the increased holding power of the schools during this period may have contributed to this result.

The fact that the increase in the percentage of high school seniors who are between 18 and 18½ is almost exactly equal to the decrease in the percentage who are under 17½ suggests that changed attitudes toward acceleration of school progress is the main source of the change in the percentage of younger students.

Table 4.3 also shows that there were small increases in the percentage of students in the two older groups, perhaps reflecting the increase in the holding power of high schools during this period.

Results for mean reading scores show that within the twelfth-grade groups in both years, younger students tend to earn higher scores than older students, presumably because abler students progress more rapidly through school than do less able students. Despite the shift in the age distribution between 1960 and 1972, the score decline within each age group is similar to the overall decline.

Other Demographic Variables.   Similar analyses of other demographic variables suggest that the following events may have contributed to the observed decline of scores for seniors from 1960 to 1972:

1. A small increase in age.
2. An increase in fathers who completed high school but did not continue their education.
3. A decrease in the percentage of only children and first-born children.
4. An increase in the proportion of students who either did not intend to attend college or intended to attend but did not report a choice of major field.

A second set of analyses of the correlates of changes in the college entrant population (described in the full report) led to the conclusion that, in general, a great increase occurred in the proportion of high school seniors who took the SAT, as a result of the more rapid growth in the SAT candidate volume from 1960 to 1972 than the growth in the number of high school graduates. Of greater interest, however, are the results involving changes in the composition of the SAT population brought about by the increases and decreases reported above. When shifts in the number of students in each subgroup are considered, we find the following changes in the SAT population:

1. A marked increase in the proportion of women candidates.
2. A small increase (5%) in the proportion of "general" students and an equal decrease in the proportion of college preparatory students.
3. An increase in the proportion of students from larger families.
4. Increases in the proportion of students planning to major in the social sciences and humanities and certain undergraduate career programs (for example, business, education, and nursing) and a decrease in engineering majors.
5. A substantial decrease in the proportion of SAT takers who attended 4-year colleges.

On both tests, almost every subgroup of students who took the SAT showed some decline in scores. Among the groups that showed only a slight increase or a relatively small decline were students younger than 17½ years, students whose parents had education beyond high school, students who expected to major in science or mathematics in college, or in some field other than liberal arts and engineering, students whose mothers were employed in white-collar or blue-collar occupations, and students who entered 4-year colleges. Almost without exception, the decline in scores for these groups was only half as large as the average decline. One change appears to have made an appreciable contribution to the SAT score decline: a substantial decrease in the proportion of candidates who enter 4-year colleges.

APPENDIX: DESCRIPTION
OF PARTITIONING ANALYSIS

In studying the decline in SAT scores, we asked ourselves these questions: What part of the decline is attributable to changes in the ability of high school seniors? What part to changes in the types of students taking the SAT? What part to the drift in the SAT scale itself?

Our general approach was to partition frequency distributions. The 1960 and 1972 high school seniors were classified into levels according to their reading test scores. The SAT takers were known nonrandom subsets of these frequency distributions. The difference between the frequency distributions of SAT takers in 1960 and 1972 was partitioned into sections from which answers to the preceding questions could be derived. All calculations were done in the metric of the 1960 SAT with the differences between 1972 and 1960 SAT-verbal averages (given equal reading scores) considered as drift in the SAT-verbal scale.

The (equated) reading scores have 20 items; thus, there are 21 possible scores for the number of items right on the test and over 80 possible formula scores. We first grouped scores on the test into m intervals for calculations of frequency distributions. Presumably, m is small enough to be manageable but large enough to avoid serious loss of precision. Given this grouping of reading scores, we can present the following definitions:

N_1 —the number of high school seniors in 1960

N_2 —the number of high school seniors in 1972

N_{1A} —the number of SAT takers in 1960

N_{2A} —the number of SAT takers in 1972

F_1 —an mth-order column vector containing the number of students at each level of reading ability in 1960. This is a frequency distribution of reading ability for the class of 1960.

F_{1A} —an mth-order column vector containing the number of students at each level of reading ability in 1960 who took the SAT.

F_2 —an mth-order column vector containing the number of students at each level of reading ability in 1972. This is a frequency distribution of reading ability for the class of 1972.

F_{2A} —an mth-order column vector containing the number of students at each level of reading ability in 1972 who took the SAT.

P_1 —an mth-order column vector containing the proportion of students at each level of reading ability who took the SAT in 1960.

P_2 —an mth-order column vector containing the proportion of students at each level of reading ability who took the SAT in 1972.

X_1 —an mth-order column vector containing the average SAT-verbal score for each level of reading ability in 1960.

X_2 —an mth-order column vector containing the average SAT-verbal score for each level of reading ability in 1972.

The frequency distribution of reading scores is, therefore, represented as a column vector of length m. F_1 and F_2 represent the distributions of high school seniors in 1960 and 1972, respectively, whereas F_{1A} and F_{2A}

represent the subsets of F_1 and F_2 who took the SAT. We are now prepared to manipulate these distributions.

The average SAT-verbal scores can be represented using this notation as $\bar{X}_{1A} = N_{1A}^{-1} F'_{1A}X_1$ in 1960 and as $\bar{X}_{2A} = N_{1A}^{-1} F'_{2A}X_2$ in 1972. Because the SAT-verbal means were computed from these same persons, these formulas are essentially the computational procedures for grouped data. We are interested in partitioning the difference between these means into sections associated with the high school populations, SAT-takers, and the drift in the SAT scale.

According to the preceding definitions, the change in the distribution of reading ability for high school students is $\triangle F_1 = F_2 - F_1$, and the change in the proportion of students at each ability level taking the SAT is $\triangle P_1 = P_2 - P_1$.

The change in the average SAT-verbal score for persons of a given reading ability is $\triangle X_1 = X_2 - X_1$. Before proceeding, it is important that we consider further the mean SAT score vectors, X_1 and X_2. The corresponding elements in X_1 and X_2 represent persons of nearly equal reading ability as defined by the reading tests. If the reading tests were strictly parallel to the SAT-verbal, we would expect the corresponding means to be nearly identical, that is, $\triangle X_1 \cong 0$. The difference between these vectors is not zero because of a number of factors: sampling error, equating error, classification error, and so forth. We believe that the effect of these errors is too small to explain the observed differences between the means. We attribute most of the differences to scale drift, the slow upward growth of the SAT scores over 12 years.

What is important here is the assumption that persons with similar reading test scores are expected to have the same SAT-verbal scores, regardless of whether they are members of the class of 1960 or 1972. To keep the SAT scale in a common metric over these 2 years, we will apply the vector X_1 to the frequency distribution F_{2A} in order to develop an SAT-verbal mean adjusted for scale drift. That mean is $\bar{X}_{2A'} = N_{2A}^{-1} F'_{2A} X_1$. The frequency distribution of SAT takers in 1960 can be written as a product of the frequency distribution of high school students and the fraction taking the SAT; that is, $F_{1A} = F_1 \otimes P_1$ and in 1972 as $F_{2A} = F_2 \otimes P_2$, where $\otimes$ indicates element-by-element vector multiplication. An mth-order unit vector 1 is useful for calculating the number of objects in a frequency distribution: Consider $N_{1A} = F'_{1A} 1$ and $N_{2A} = F'_{2A} 1$. Using $\triangle F_1 = F_2 - F_1$ and $\triangle P_1 = P_2 - P_1$, the frequency distribution F_{2A} can be partitioned:

$$
\begin{aligned}
F_{2A} &= (F_2 \otimes P_2) = (F_1 + \triangle F_1) \otimes (P_1 + \triangle P_1) \\
&= (F_1 \otimes P_1) + (F_1 \otimes \triangle P_1) + (\triangle F_1 \otimes P_1) + (\triangle F_1 \otimes \triangle P_1) \\
&= G_{11} + G_{1\triangle} + G_{\triangle 1} + G_{\triangle\triangle}
\end{aligned}
$$

That is, the frequency distribution of SAT takers in 1972 can be partitioned into four parts:

G_{11} = $F_1 \otimes P_1$, which is identical to F_{1A}, the 1960 frequency distribution of SAT takers.

$G_{1\triangle}$ = $F_1 \otimes \triangle P_1$, which is the part of the frequency distribution associated with a change in the pattern of SAT taking.

$G_{\triangle 1}$ = $\triangle F_1 \otimes P_1$, which is the part of the frequency distribution associated with the change in the high school population.

$G_{\triangle\triangle}$ = $\triangle F_1 \otimes \triangle P_1$, which is the part of the frequency distribution associated with both change in high school population and change in the proportion taking the SAT.

G_{11} is a frequency distribution, thus must have non-negative elements. $G_{1\triangle}$, $G_{\triangle 1}$, and $G_{\triangle\triangle}$ are pseudodistributions and may have negative elements. Using $N_{2A} = F'_{2A} 1$, we can compute:

$$N_{2A} = (G_{11} + G_{1A} + G_{\triangle 1} + G_{\triangle\triangle})'1$$
$$= N_{11} + N_{1\triangle} + N_{\triangle 1} + N_{\triangle\triangle}$$

where $N_{11} = N_{1A}$, the number of SAT takers in 1960, and N_{1A}, $N_{\triangle 1}$, and $N_{\triangle\triangle}$ are pseudo Ns (possibly negative) associated with the pseudodistributions. We can write the 1972 mean SAT-verbal score (adjusted for scale drift) as:

$$\bar{X}_{2A'} = \frac{1}{N_{2A}} F'_{2A} X_1$$

$$= \frac{1}{N_{2A}} (G_{11} + G_{1\triangle} + G_{\triangle 1} + G_{\triangle\triangle})' X_1$$

$$= \frac{1}{N_{2A}} (N_{11} \bar{X}_{11} + N_{1\triangle} \bar{X}_{1\triangle} + N_{\triangle 1} \bar{X}_{\triangle 1} + N_{\triangle\triangle} \bar{X}_{\triangle\triangle})$$

$\bar{X}_{11} = N_{11}^{-1} G'_{11} X_1 = \bar{X}_{1A}$, the mean of the 1960 SAT takers,

$\bar{X}_{1\triangle} = N_{1\triangle}^{-1} G'_{1\triangle} X_1$, the effect on the 1960 mean of the changing pattern of SAT taking,

$\bar{X}_{\triangle 1} = N_{\triangle 1}^{-1} G'_{\triangle 1} X_1$, the effect on the 1960 mean of the changing high school population, and

$\bar{X}_{\triangle\triangle} = N_{\triangle\triangle}^{-1} G'_{\triangle\triangle} X_1$, the effect on the 1960 mean of the changing pattern of SAT taking in the high school population.

We can now examine the three following questions:

1. What would be the number and average score of SAT takers on the SAT-verbal if the SAT-taking pattern changed as it did but the high school population stayed the same as in 1960?

The distribution would be $F_1 \otimes P_1 + F_1 \otimes P_1 = F_1 \otimes P_2$; thus, the number of SAT takers would be $\hat{N}_{12} = (F_1 \otimes P_2)' \, 1 = N_{11} + N_{1\Delta}$, and their mean score would be

$$\bar{X}_{12} = \frac{1}{\hat{N}_{12}} \, (F_1 \otimes P_2)' \, X_1 = \frac{N_{11} \, \bar{X}_{11} + N_{1\Delta} \, \bar{X}_{1\Delta}}{N_{11} + N_{1\Delta}}.$$

2. What would be the number of, and average score of, SAT takers if the high school population changed as it did but the proportion at each level of reading ability taking the SAT stayed the same as in 1960?

The distribution would be $F_1 \otimes P_1 + \Delta F_1 \otimes P_1 = F_2 \otimes P_1$; thus, the number of SAT takers would be $\hat{N}_{21} = (F_2 \otimes P_1)' \, 1 = N_{11} + N_{\Delta 1}$, and their mean score would be

$$\hat{X}_{21} = \frac{1}{\hat{N}_{21}} \, (F_2 \otimes P_1)' \, X_1 = \frac{N_{11} \, \bar{X}_{11} + N_{\Delta 1} \, \bar{X}_{\Delta 1}}{N_{11} + N_{\Delta 1}}.$$

3. What is the average scale drift?

The average score adjusted for scale drift is $\bar{X}_{2A'} = \dfrac{1}{N_{2A}} F'_{2A} \, X_1$;

thus, the average effect of scale drift is the difference between the adjusted and unadjusted means, which is:

$$\bar{X}_{2A} - \bar{X}_{2A'} = \frac{1}{N_{2A}} \, F_{2A} \, X_2 - \frac{1}{N_{2A}} \, F'_{2A} \, X_1$$

$$= \frac{1}{N_{2A}} \, F'_{2A} \, (X_2 - X_1) = \frac{1}{N_{2A}} \, F'_{2A} \, \Delta X_1.$$

Numerical Calculations

We divided the samples of high school students in 1960 and 1972 into six strata according to reading ability, and students for whom reading test scores were not available were placed in a seventh stratum. The strata of reading scores were so defined that the top stratum contained the top 10% of the 1972 students for whom scores were available, the second stratum contained the next 10%, and the lower strata contained 20% each. Having set the cutoff points from the 1972 sample, we allocated the 1960 sample into strata using the same cutoff points; thus, the number in each stratum is not constrained.

The basic data, contained in columns (1) through (8) of Table 4A.1 are taken from Tables 4.1 and 4.2 of the text. The columns are:

(1) $= F_1$ the frequency distribution of all high school students in 1960

(2) $= F_{1A}$ the frequency distribution of SAT takers in 1960

(3) $= F_2$ the frequency distribution of all high school students in 1972

(4) $= F_{2A}$ the frequency distribution of SAT takers in 1972

(5) $= P_1$ the proportion at each level of reading ability to take the SAT in 1960 ($P_1 = $ (2) $\div$ (1).)

(6) $= P_2$ the proportion at each level of reading ability to take the SAT in 1972 ($P_2 = $ (4) $\div$ (3).)

(7) $= X_1$ the mean SAT-verbal score for SAT takers in 1960

(8) $= X_2$ the mean SAT-verbal score for SAT takers in 1972

The remaining columns are computed from (1) through (8):

(9) $=$ (3) $-$ (1) $= \triangle F_1$

(10) $=$ (6) $-$ (5) $= \triangle P_1$ and

(11) $=$ (1) $\otimes$ (5) $= G_{11} = F_{1A}$

(12) $=$ (1) $\otimes$ (10) $= G_{1\triangle}$

(13) $=$ (9) $\otimes$ (5) $= G_{\triangle 1}$

(14) $=$ (9) $\otimes$ (10) $= G_{\triangle\triangle}$

As a numerical check, (4) $=$ (11) $+$ (12) $+$ (13) $+$ (14).

As noted earlier, (11) $= G_{11}$ is a frequency distribution. The other G vectors, $G_{1\triangle}$, $G_{\triangle 1}$, $G_{\triangle\triangle}$, are the gains (or losses) in particular strata of the frequency distribution in moving from F_{1A}, to F_{2A}. The effect of these partitions on the number of students is calculated by adding the frequencies in the columns, the results of which are shown at the base of those columns.

The average value of the SAT score without scale drift is derived by calculating the sum of products of these frequencies and the vector (7) $= X_1$. The effects on the means are shown at the base of the corresponding vectors.

The calculation for deriving means of hypothetical groups is given at the bottom of the table.

Note that the vectors G_{11}, $G_{1\triangle}$, $G_{\triangle 1}$, and $G_{\triangle\triangle}$ are computed for expository and interpretive purposes. The estimated populations can be computed directly by:

TABLE 4A.1
Partition of SAT Scores (All Frequencies in 1000s)

Reading level	(1) F_1	(2) F_{1A}	(3) F_2	(4) F_{2A}	(5) P_1	(6) P_2	(7) X_1	(8) X_2	(9) ΔF_1	(10) ΔP_1	(11) G_{11}	(12) $G_{1\Delta}$	(13) $G_{\Delta 1}$	(14) $G_{\Delta\Delta}$
Top	255	108	288	177	.424	.614	547	567	33	.190	108	48	14	6
2	216	67	290	154	.310	.531	499	504	74	.221	67	48	23	16
3	358	74	575	226	.208	.393	438	453	217	.185	74	66	45	40
4	337	41	576	176	.121	.305	389	404	239	.184	41	62	29	44
5	325	18	577	121	.054	.210	341	358	252	.156	18	51	14	39
Bottom	284	7	576	54	.026	.094	337	311	292	.068	7	19	8	20
No test	89	11	133	27	.127	.207	476	454	44	.080	11	7	6	
Sum	1864	326	3015	935					1151		326	301	139	169
Average SAT-verbal	474	474		442							474	433	435	401

Estimated populations   *Number*   *Mean*

	Number		Mean
1960 SAT statistics	326		474
If only SAT taking changed	$326 + 301 = 627$	$\dfrac{326(474)+301(433)}{627} =$	454
If only high school seniors changed	$326 + 139 = 465$	$\dfrac{326(474)+139(435)}{465} =$	462
If both changed but no scale drift	935		442
Scale drift		$\dfrac{1}{N_{2A}}\, F'_{2A}\,(X_2 - X_1)$	+11
1972 SAT statistics with scale drift	935		453

1. SAT-taking change only:

$$N_{12} = (F_1 \otimes P_2)'1$$

and

$$\bar{X}_{12} = N_{12}^{-1} (F_1 \otimes P_2)'X_1.$$

2. High school population change only:

$$N_{21} = (F_2 \otimes P_1)'1$$
$$\bar{X}_{21} = N_{21}^{-1} (F_2 \otimes P_1)'X_1.$$

3. Both changed, but no scale drift:

$$\bar{X}_{2A'} = N_{2A}^{-1} F'_{2A} X_1.$$

ACKNOWLEDGMENT

This chapter was excerpted from a 92-page report prepared for the Advisory Panel on the Scholastic Aptitude Test Score Decline (Beaton, Hilton, & Schrader, 1977), jointly sponsored by the College Board and Educational Testing Service, June 1977. The original report is out of print.

CHAPTER FIVE

Merging Data from Three Data Bases with Common Members: An Example Involving SAT Scores, ASVAB Scores, and HS&B Data

Thomas L. Hilton
William B. Schrader
Albert E. Beaton
Educational Testing Service

This chapter describes a study in which data from three major data bases were retrieved: (a) the files of the ETS Admissions Testing Program, which includes SAT scores, (b) the High School and Beyond (HS&B) public release tape for the 1980 senior cohort, and (c) the data files of the Armed Services Vocational Aptitude Battery (ASVAB) that reside in Monterey, California. In addition, a line of relationship between the High School and Beyond test and ASVAB was developed. Although not done in this study, the same could have been done for the Scholastic Aptitude Test (SAT) and either the HS&B tests or ASVAB or both.

The chapter describes the complex steps involved in a relatively simple task: matching individual subjects in one file with the same subjects in another. The task was made difficult by the urgent need to preserve the anonymity of the human subjects involved. Also described are the risks one takes in attempting to equate the tests used in one survey to the tests used in a second when the two sets of tests are not parallel.

—*Thomas L. Hilton*

This chapter describes several tasks accomplished by ETS in order to enhance the value of the HS&B data base to the United States Army Recruiting Command as follows:

1. Retrieval of SAT scores for seniors in the HS&B sample. These scores were then merged by the National Opinion Research Center (NORC) with other data in the HS&B public use file.

2. Equating of scores on the HS&B test battery to the Armed Forces Qualification Test (AFQT) categories. This task used certain scores on the

AFQT earned by HS&B seniors who had taken the test. These scores were obtained from the Department of Defense by NORC and merged into the HS&B public use file that was made available to ETS.

3. Generation of tables summarizing the responses to 11 HS&B Senior Questionnaire items concerning military service. These tables are not included in this volume.

The retrieval of the SAT scores and the AFQT scores and the relating of an HS&B composite to AFQT scores are described in detail in the following pages.

TASK I: SAT AND ASVAB DATA RETRIEVAL

Data Collection

The SAT score retrieval made use of certain student questionnaire data that were collected as part of the base-year survey of HS&B. In this survey, 36 sophomores and 36 seniors in each participating high school were randomly selected for participation. These students met separately on a "data collection day" sometime between February 1, 1980, and May 15, 1980. They first completed the student questionnaire and then were given the test battery in one session.

Item 9 of the Senior Questionnaire asked whether the respondent had taken the SAT "this year, or last year (or both)." The response frequencies were as follows:

Yes, both this year and last year	3,218
Yes, this year	3,549
Yes, last year	3,483
No, did not take	16,004
Multiple response	22
Missing data	1,964
Total	28,240

Thus, there was a total of 10,250 SAT scores that might have been found if all questionnaire responses were valid.

In addition, Item 9 asked whether the sample member had taken the ASVAB. The response frequencies were as follows:

Yes, both this year and last year	671
Yes, this year	3,505
Yes, last year	2,926
No, did not take	18,450
Multiple response	11
Missing data	2,677
Total	28,240

These frequencies indicate that a total of 7,102 scores might have been found.

SAT Score Retrieval

Data tapes listing all seniors in the HS&B sample, whether they partici-pated in the first follow-up or not, were mailed to ETS in Princeton where the SAT scores were retrieved from the computerized files of the SAT program. The data tapes listed only information identifying the subjects and their response to Item 9; no other questionnaire responses were included. The tapes were processed under strict test security conditions.

Two decisions have a bearing on the scores retrieved:

1. When more than one set of SAT scores were identified, only the latest set was retained.
2. Special search methods were used only for those subjects who indicated in the Senior Questionnaire that they took the SAT but whose scores were not identified by computer.

Procedure for Retrieving SAT Scores

Selecting a procedure for retrieving SAT scores was a minimax problem. The primary goal of the steps taken was to maximize the number of SAT scores found in the ETS history files but, at the same time, to minimize the number of false positives, that is, apparent matching of an individual in the HS&B file with an individual in the SAT history file when, in fact, two different individuals were involved. It also was necessary to minimize the amount of computer time required, for large costs could accumulate rapid-ly, and also to minimize the number of cases that had to be looked up by searching through the files case-by-case to resolve uncertain matches.

The procedure selected was a three-step process as follows:

1. A primary match consisting of last name, first initial, middle initial, sex, and day and month of birth. This produced a file of primary key matches, including many cases requiring further matching. For example, there were 18 John Smiths with the same birth date. Only one of the 18 was the desired test taker. Names not meeting this primary match were printed on a roster for later visual examination.

2. Confirmation of the primary match by a programmed procedure to be described shortly. This step produced two lists: (a) those cases that were confirmed by the program, and (b) those cases not meeting this secondary match. These latter cases were added to the roster described in Step 1.

3. Search for cases on roster. The on-line system used by the College Board Admissions Testing Program to retrieve data on examinees was used to produce score reports for the names on the roster. This listing included demographic information and all SAT scores for each case. Each possible match was then visually examined in accordance with a set of rules with regard to what constituted a match and the nature of the discrepancies that were tolerable. For example, different home addresses were accepted if all other information in the two lists, including high school attended, was in agreement.

The computerized matching method selected for Step 2 is shown graphically in Fig. 5.1. The first match was on the subjects' Social Security Number. If all nine positions of the number of an HS&B subject agreed with a number in the SAT file, the match was accepted as valid and the latest SAT scores were recorded. If the nine positions did not match but seven of them did, then the first name, middle initial, and last name were examined. If they agreed, then the match was accepted as valid. If they did not agree because the middle initial was missing, then the student's address was examined and the case was accepted if the address met the criteria shown in Fig. 5.1.

For those cases that failed to meet the criteria for Social Security Numbers (SSN) because one file or both files had a missing SSN, a more stringent test was made: The case was accepted only if both the name and the address and phone number matched in accordance with the criteria shown in Fig. 5.1.

Thus, there were a number of ways in which SAT scores might not have been identified:

1. Students may have taken the SAT but may not have completed the HS&B Student Questionnaire or, if so, they may have failed to respond positively to Item 9.
2. Students may have taken the SAT after completing the Senior Questionnaire.
3. The student may have reported an SSN seriously in error, that is, more than two of the nine positions were discrepant.
4. The student may have made a small error in his or her SSN and have used a different first name or last name or middle initial in filling out either the SAT registration material or the HS&B identification booklet, or may have omitted or made an error in relevant parts of his or her address.

None of these possibilities was expected to result in a substantial loss of cases.

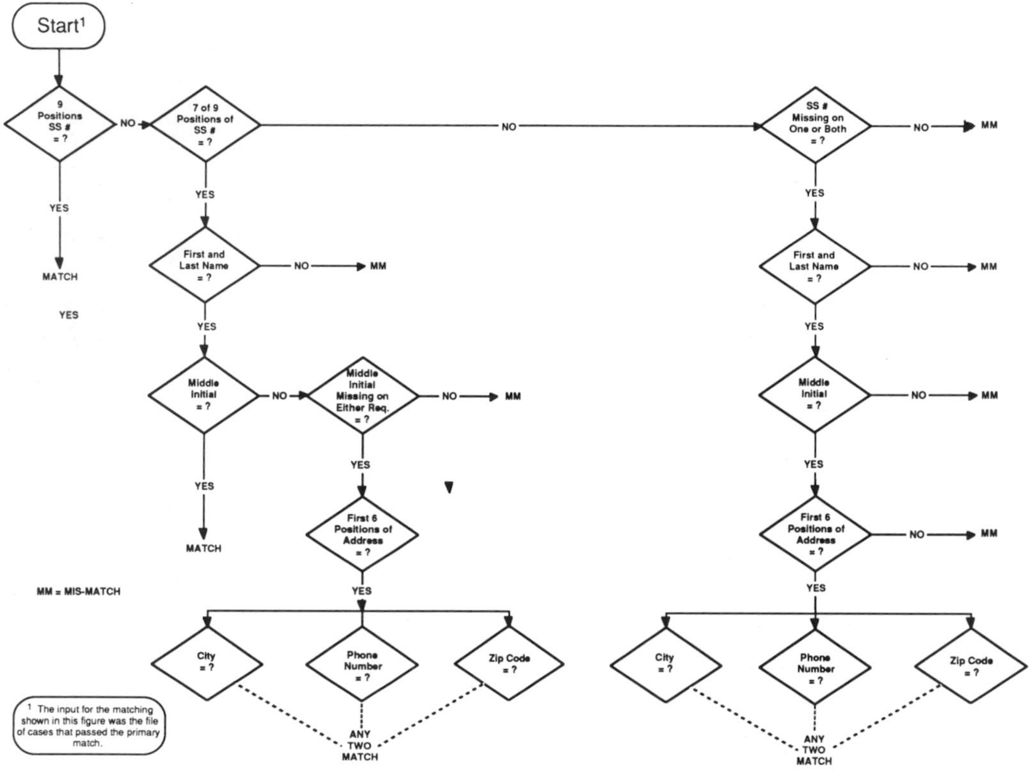

FIG. 5.1. SAT confirmatory matching criteria.

Results of SAT Score Retrieval

The primary key match resulted in a list of 7,821 subjects who said in the Senior Questionnaire that they took the SAT and who met the primary key. Then, the second step described earlier verified 5,767 of the cases, leaving 2,255 cases for Step 3 (the visual search). This resulted in the identification of 738 more cases, giving a total of 6,304 SAT scores retrieved. Thus, scores were retrieved for 61.5% of the students who said they took the SAT.

Two factors substantially reduced the number of computer matches: (a) the complete absence of SSN for approximately one fifth of the HS&B seniors who took the SAT and (b) the tendency of many students to use nicknames in filling out one form but their given name on the other, for example, Bill on the HS&B form but William on the SAT form.

In addition, it is likely that an appreciable number of seniors responded positively to Item 9 but did not, in fact, take the SAT. They may have confused it with some other testing conducted in the school.

To evaluate the adequacy of the retrieval, the mean and standard deviation of the retrieved scores were computed using the sample weights provided by NORC for population estimates. These estimates were compared with the published means for 1980 seniors. The results are as follows:

	Estimated		Actual	
	$\bar{X}$	SD	$\bar{X}$	SD
Verbal	424	111	424	110
Math	465	117	466	117

In addition, intercorrelations, means, and standard deviations were calculated for SAT, ASVAB, AFQT, and HS&B scores for 513 students who took ASVAB between August 1979 and June 1980 and who had complete data on all tests included in this analysis. Results are shown in Table 5.1. The correlations of SAT-V and SAT-M with the other variables appear to be consistent with reasonable expectations. We regard these results as substantial evidence that the retrieval was performed in a satisfactory manner.

Retrieval of ASVAB Scores

At the same time that tapes were provided to ETS for the retrieval of SAT scores, NORC provided the Department of Defense with an identification tape showing which students reported that they took the ASVAB. The ASVAB score retrieval was handled in a somewhat different way.

TABLE 5.1
Intercorrelations, Means, and Standard Deviations of ASVAB Scores Used in Defining AFQT, AFQT Percentile, and Six HS&B Scores (weighted N = 246,140)[a]

Test	AFQT				HS&B					
	WK	AR	SP	%ile	VOC	READ	MATH	VIS	MOS-C	PICT-NO
AFQT: WK	1.000	.606	.418	.847	.774	.737	.646	.403	.316	.172
AFQT: AR	.606	1.000	.508	.831	.522	.569	.725	.464	.327	.208
AFQT: SP	.418	.508	1.000	.750	.372	.400	.515	.643	.357	.138
AFQT %ile	.847	.831	.750	1.000	.712	.711	.763	.602	.382	.204
HS&B: VOC	.774	.522	.372	.712	1.000	.711	.612	.372	.286	.179
HS&B: READ	.737	.569	.400	.711	.711	1.000	.640	.428	.325	.186
HS&B: MATH	.646	.725	.515	.763	.612	.640	1.000	.511	.376	.239
HS&B: VIS	.403	.464	.643	.602	.372	.428	.511	1.000	.347	.115
HS&B: MOS C	.316	.327	.357	.382	.286	.325	.376	.347	1.000	.251
HS&B: PICT-NO	.172	.208	.138	.204	.179	.186	.239	.115	.251	1.000
Mean	19.04	12.44	10.54	42.35	9.27	8.54	14.53	5.39	41.84	11.22
SD	6.33	4.09	4.41	25.95	6.33	5.24	8.00	4.00	16.60	3.88

[a]Based on students who took ASVAB between 8/79 and 6/80

According to Helen Hagan (personal communication, September 1, 1982) of the Defense Manpower Data Center, Monterey, California, where the data were retrieved, the ASVAB scores were obtained from two separate files: the military applicants file and the high school file. The procedures used with the two files were different. In the belief that the Social Security Numbers in the military applicant file are reasonably accurate and complete, the SSNs were matched with the SSNs in the HS&B file and when all digits agreed the case was accepted as a match. No further matching was attempted with this file. This search yielded 2,807 cases.

For the high school file, the SSNs were matched and full agreements were accepted, but the process did not stop there. For those cases that failed the SSN match, the following items were compared: (a) first initial and first five characters of last name, (b) month and year of birth, and (c) first two digits of ZIP code of home address.

This search yielded 4,616 cases. Output obtained later at ETS indicated that 776 individuals were common to both files. Thus, ASVAB scores were retrieved for 67% of the 7,102 seniors who reported in the Senior Questionnaire that they took the test.

TASK II: RELATING AFQT SCORES TO A COMPOSITE OF HS&B SCORES

The analysis plan for this study called for utilizing HS&B test data to define ability strata that would resemble as closely as possible the AFQT Categories used in personnel studies by the Army Recruiting Command. In order to accomplish this task, two basic steps were needed, as follows: (a) to define a weighted composite score based on HS&B tests that would have a high correlation with AFQT scores, and (b) to identify score levels on the HS&B composite that would stratify the HS&B sample approximately into AFQT categories.

The resulting categorization of the HS&B sample should contribute substantially to the value of the special tabulations of HS&B items related to service in the Armed Forces.

Tests Defining AFQT Scores

In defining the composite, consideration was given to the kinds of abilities measured by the three tests that determine the AFQT score and by the tests available in the HS&B data file. The AFQT score is the sum of the raw scores on three tests. On the basis of information provided in the discussion of the content of the test battery in the *ASVAB-5 Specimen Set*, the three tests may be described as follows:

Word Knowledge. "Measures verbal comprehension which entails the ability to understand written and spoken language. It is represented most heavily in what is often termed as reading skill. Vocabulary is only a factor which characterizes reading skill; but it provides a 'good' measure of verbal comprehension."

Arithmetic Reasoning. "Designed to measure general reasoning. It is concerned with the ability to generate solutions to problems. It is different from numerical operations in that a student must construct a solution by some principle in order to solve the given problem."

Space Perception. "Measures an individual's spatial aptitude. This infers an ability of an individual to visualize and manipulate objects in space. This ability seems to be important when performing in engineering, mechanics, and a variety of technical courses" (Department of Defense, 1976, p. 3).

Corresponding HS&B Tests

There are four tests in the HS&B battery administered to high school seniors that appear to measure similar abilities to those measured by AFQT. These may be described as follows:

Vocabulary. This test, which uses the synonym format, was designed to minimize academic or collegiate bias and to be appropriate in difficulty for high school seniors. It includes two separately timed parts.

Reading. Based on short passages (100–200 words) designed to measure a variety of reading skills (analysis, interpretation) but focusing on comprehension. Some attempt was made to include items relevant to minority group students.

Mathematics. Composed of quantitative comparison items, in which the examinee responds by indicating which of two quantities is larger, that the two quantities are equal, or that the data are insufficient to determine the relative size of the two quantities. It measures basic competence in arithmetic processes while minimizing the time devoted to calculations. Like Vocabulary, this test is divided into two separately timed parts.

Visualization. This test, which originally appeared in the Project TALENT survey battery, measures visualization in three dimensions.

Format of AFQT and HS&B Tests

The number of items and time limits for the AFQT and HS&B tests are as follows:

	Number of Items	Working Time (Minutes)
AFQT		
Word Knowledge	30	10
Arithmetic Reasoning	20	20
Space Perception	20	12
HS&B		
Vocabulary Total	27	9
Reading	20	15
Mathematics Total	33	19
Visualization	16	9

Defining Composite Weights

The composite score on the HS&B tests was defined as a weighted sum of HS&B scores. The weights were multiple regression weights, calculated by standard multiple regression methods, using AFQT percentile as the dependent variable. In the analysis, it was decided to use total scores on Vocabulary and Mathematics rather than part scores, on the assumption that differential weighting of the parts would not be worthwhile, and it was decided to include Reading scores in the analysis, because it was expected that these scores would contribute to effectiveness of prediction.

The sample for all analyses concerned with the definition of the HS&B composite and with the development of the conversion table relating the composite to AFQT percentile included only students who took ASVAB between August 1979 and June 1980. All students included in the analysis sample had complete data on all HS&B tests and all ASVAB tests. Weights developed by the NORC, designed to produce correct estimates for the total 1980 high school senior population, were used for each sample member.

The decision to include only students who have complete data in the multiple regression analysis was based mainly on the desire that the validity coefficients for each predictor be based on exactly the same sample. The number of individuals included in this analysis was 2,514.

The HS&B battery included two tests that did not appear to correspond to any of the three tests on which the AFQT score is based. These two tests, Mosaic Comparisons and Picture Number, were included in the multiple regression analysis in order to find out whether using them would increase the multiple correlation. The criterion measure was AFQT percentile. For the students included in the basic regression analysis, all students who had the same total raw score on the three tests had the same AFQT percentile, presumably because all of the students took the same form of ASVAB.

Results

Table 5.1 shows the intercorrelations, means, and standard deviations of the variables used in the multiple regression analysis. The four HS&B tests yielded a multiple correlation of .8615, which was considered satisfactory. The regression weights for the four variables were as follows:

Variable	Standard Score Regression Weight	Raw Score Regression Weight
Vocabulary Total	.2718	1.1147
Reading	.1893	0.9385
Mathematics Total	.3537	1.1477
Visualization	.2394	1.5549

Addition of Mosaic Comparison to the predictor set increased the multiple to .8620 and the further addition of Picture Number produced no increase in the multiple. It was concluded that the composite should be composed of the four variables that appeared to correspond to tests included in AFQT. The resulting equation used the raw score regression weights for the four selected variables.

Having defined a suitable composite, the next step called for developing a conversion table relating each composite score to the appropriate AFQT percentile. This was done by calculating the percentile of each raw score and then finding the corresponding percentile on the AFQT scale, using linear interpolation. Calculations were performed using the standard program for equipercentile equating developed by ETS. The resulting values were rounded to the nearest integer to produce Table 5.2.

It must be emphasized that the application of the equating program to data for two tests will yield equated (interchangeable) scores if and only if the tests are parallel and the equating data were obtained using a suitable equating design. When judged in relation to the high standards of rigor normally employed in score equating, this study is clearly deficient on both criteria. Obviously, the persons who developed the AFQT and HS&B tests worked independently of each other, and the tests were developed for different purposes. Moreover, no account was taken in designing the data collection for either test that the data might be used for equating purposes. It would be very unfortunate if it were assumed that the approximate and possibly biased results shown in Table 5.2 have the degree of precision achieved by score equating in national testing programs. Rigorous score equating produces conversion tables that permit scores on different forms of the same test to be used interchangeably in making decisions about individuals. By contrast, the conversion table developed in this study is likely to be useful only for survey purposes.

TABLE 5.2
AFQT Percentile and Category Corresponding to
Each HS&B Composite Score[a]

HS&B Composite	AFQT %ile	AFQT Category	HS&B Composite	AFQT %ile	AFQT Category	HS&B Composite	AFQT %ile	AFQT Category
111	99	I	73	67	II	35	18	IVb
110	99	I	72	66	II	34	17	IVb
109	99	I	71	65	II	33	17	IVb
108	98	I	70	64	IIIa	32	16	IVb
107	98	I	69	62	IIIa	31	15	IVc
106	98	I	68	61	IIIa	30	15	IVc
105	98	I	67	60	IIIa	29	14	IVc
104	97	I	66	59	IIIa	28	14	IVc
103	97	I	65	58	IIIa	27	13	IVc
102	97	I	64	57	IIIa	26	13	IVc
101	96	I	63	56	IIIa	25	12	IVc
100	95	I	62	55	IIIa	24	12	IVc
99	94	I	61	53	IIIa	23	11	IVc
98	93	I	60	51	IIIa	22	10	IVc
97	92	II	59	50	IIIa	21	9	V
96	91	II	58	48	IIIb	20	9	V
95	90	II	57	46	IIIb	19	8	V
94	89	II	56	44	IIIb	18	7	V
93	88	II	55	43	IIIb	17	6	V

(Continued)

TABLE 5.2
(Continued)

HS&B Composite	AFQT %ile	AFQT Category	HS&B Composite	AFQT %ile	AFQT Category	HS&B Composite	AFQT %ile	AFQT Category
92	87	II	54	42	IIIb	16	5	V
91	87	II	53	41	IIIb	15	4	V
90	86	II	52	38	IIIb	14	3	V
89	85	II	51	36	IIIb	13	2	V
88	84	II	50	35	IIIb	12	2	V
87	83	II	49	34	IIIb	11	1	V
86	82	II	48	33	IIIb	10	1	V
85	81	II	47	32	IIIb	9	1	V
84	80	II	46	31	IIIb	8	1	V
83	78	II	45	30	IVa	7	1	V
82	77	II	44	28	IVa	6	1	V
81	76	II	43	27	IVa	5	1	V
80	75	II	42	26	IVa	4	1	V
79	74	II	41	25	IVa	3	1	V
78	72	II	40	24	IVa	2	1	V
77	72	II	39	22	IVa	1	1	V
76	71	II	38	21	IVa	0	1	V
75	70	II	37	19	IVb			
74	69	II	36	19	IVb			

[a]HS&B Composite = 1.1147 (VOC) + 0.9385 (READ) + 1.1477 (MATH) + 1.5549 (VIS) + 10.5 (Sum should be truncated at decimal point, not rounded.)

110

In order to find out whether the equating is appropriate for various important subgroups, the equating sample was classified on the basis of sex, race, geographical region, and academic versus nonacademic high school program. The mean and standard deviation of actual AFQT percentiles and of AFQT percentiles estimated on the basis of the equatings were calculated. In addition, a t test of the significance of the difference in means was calculated for each subgroup. Although the usual weights for each individual were used in calculating the means and standard deviations, the actual sample size was used in calculating the t tests. It should be noted that the significant tests are very sensitive, because there is a high correlation between the actual and estimated scores. Based on the total equating sample, which included 2,542 students, this correlation was .8647. However, the t test results cannot be regarded as fully rigorous because no account was taken of design effects arising from the sampling procedures used in the HS&B survey.

Table 5.3 shows the results of this analysis that compares results based on actual AFQT scores for students who took ASVAB as high school seniors with results based on AFQT scores estimated from HS&B scores. These results make it clear that, although the HS&B tests measure abilities that are similar to those measured by AFQT, they cannot be regarded as strictly parallel tests. As a result, the equivalency table shown in Table 5.2 has certain limitations. For example, in the case of males and females, Blacks and Whites, and students who were enrolled in an academic program and those in a nonacademic program, the differences appear to be large enough to raise doubts about the appropriateness of using scores on the two tests interchangeably in making decisions about individuals or in other uses where a high degree of precision is needed.

Consideration was given to developing a set of equating tables, each based on particular subgroups, but it was judged that the sample size was not large enough to warrant this approach. The possibility of redefining the HS&B regression composite by including sex, race, or other variables was also considered, but it was judged that this approach would not adequately approximate the results of separate equatings based on defined subgroups. In addition, the use of variables in defining the composite that would also be used in the survey analysis presented methodological problems that were beyond the scope of the present study.

The evidence that the tests are not parallel raises questions about whether the table of corresponding scores can properly be used for survey studies. On the whole, it appears that the use of the equating results to define AFQT categories is justified. It should, however, be kept in mind that: (a) the abilities measured by the HS&B tests differ somewhat from the abilities measured by AFQT, and (b) the proportion of students classified into the five groups would vary to some extent if a different sample had been used in applying the equating process.

TABLE 5.3

Actual AFQT Scores and Estimated AFQT Scores for Students Classified
by Sex, Geographical Region, Race, and Type
of High School Program
(Based on 2,542 ASVAB takers who had scores on both
AFQT and HS&B tests)

	Actual N	AFQT Scores				$Diff./SD_{actual}$
		Actual		*Estimated*		
		Mean	*SD*	*Mean*	*SD*	
Female	1261	38.79	25.07	40.81	25.05	− .08[b]
Male	1183	46.78	26.17	44.72	26.57	+ .08[b]
New England	104	49.50	24.35	51.94	24.61	− .10[a]
Middle Atlantic	194	52.70	24.67	49.27	24.99	+ .14[b]
South Atlantic	530	36.23	24.64	37.57	25.16	− .05[a]
ES Central	437	37.73	25.02	37.19	24.78	+ .02
WS Central	582	38.80	25.28	39.94	25.16	− .05[a]
EN Central	274	46.03	25.89	45.18	26.62	+ .03
WN Central	95	50.15	26.95	49.49	26.82	+ .02
Mountain	109	40.17	26.10	39.53	27.07	+ .02
Pacific	217	52.62	25.59	50.95	25.39	+ .07
Black	514	21.38	17.32	22.64	17.58	− .07[a]
White	1787	47.64	25.00	47.32	25.24	+ .01
Academic	886	55.01	25.78	56.65	25.26	− .06[b]
Nonacademic	1626	35.42	23.26	34.58	22.84	+ .04[a]
Total Group	2542	42.23	25.95	42.26	25.94	− .00

[a]Difference significant at .05 Level
[b]Difference significant at .01 Level

ACKNOWLEDGMENT

This chapter is a revision of the final report of prime contract
#300-78-0208, subcontract #NORC-4345, entitled "Responses to Ques-
tions on Military Service by 1980 High School Seniors Classified on Ability
and Other Variables," on April 1983, conducted for the United States
Army Recruiting Command (Hilton, Schrader, & Beaton, 1983).

CHAPTER SIX

Pooling Results from Two National Surveys: A Study of National Trends in Spatial-Visual Ability

Thomas L. Hilton
Educational Testing Service

This chapter describes a study in which the results from two major data bases in the United States were compared in such a way as to reveal changes in the spatial-visual skills of high school seniors in the United States from 1960 and 1980. Discussed in the chapter are some of the problems encountered when data from two major studies are collected under somewhat different conditions and in different eras: at a time (1960) when students expected to do whatever their teachers told them to do and at another time (1980), when many over-tested and over-researched students had learned that participation was not required and, in any case, that their scores had no bearing on the academic grades they received. What Schaie refers to as "time effects" must be taken into consideration in interpreting time lag data.

—*Thomas L. Hilton*

In 1960, a 16-item test of spatial relations was given to a national sample of high school seniors in Project TALENT. Twenty years later, the same test was given to a national sample of seniors in HS&B, the second cohort of national longitudinal studies sponsored by NCES. These data permitted the investigation of three key questions:

1. Did the mean spatial-visual relations skills of high school seniors change in this 20-year period?
2. Did the relative standing of males and females change?
3. Did the mean spatial-visual relations skills of high school seniors change more or less than mean reading skills?

113

Students of differential psychology learn early in their training that males have higher scores than females in spatial relations (Anastasi, 1965). There is debate, however, about the onset of this differential and, more so, what the causality is. Maccoby and Jacklin (1974) reported that "On the whole, [visual-spatial tests] show no sex differences until adolescence . . ." (p. 94). The same authors concluded that there is a genetically sex-linked component in spatial ability but that how the component functions is unclear. Furthermore, the authors pointed out that:

> The existence of a sex-linked genetic determiner of spatial ability does not imply that visual-spatial skills are unlearned. The specific skills involved in the manifestation of this ability improve with practice. Furthermore, cross-cultural work indicates that the sex difference can be either large or small, or may even disappear, depending upon cultural conditions affecting the rearing of the two sexes. Where women are subjugated, their visual-spatial skills are poor relative to those of men. Where both sexes are allowed independence early in life, both sexes have good visual-spatial skills. (p. 361)

Why gender differences in spatial-visual skills should emerge in adolescence—assuming that they do—is not clear. Some authors have offered physiological hypotheses involving the hormonal system (Broverman, Klaiber, Kabayashi, & Vogel, 1968). Others have linked the phenomenon to the development of cerebral lateralization (Sherman, 1971). A less complicated hypothesis would be that the emergence of male superiority represents the cumulative impact of their years of experience with games, toys, tools, and equipment, and enrollment in school courses conducive to the development of spatial-visual skills. Furthermore, the gradual onset of superiority sometimes has not been detected because the required long-term longitudinal studies with sufficiently sensitive measures were not conducted.

In view of the research literature, what were the expectations of the author in regard to the three questions listed earlier? First, in regard to mean change for the total sample since 1960, it was expected that, on balance, there would be little change. To the extent that the level of skill represents genetic factors, there should be no change and to the extent that the skill in question reflected experiential factors there would be a trade-off. Casual observation suggests that fewer contemporary students enroll in mechanical drawing and advanced math courses contributing to spatial-visual skills but, on the other hand, that more young people—both male and female—are exposed to mechanical and electronic toys, games, and gadgetry that may lead to spatial skills.

Second, as for the male–female difference, the author's clear expectation was that there would be a convergence of difference as a result of a convergence of sex roles, cultural expectations, and the experiences of males and females both in school and out of school from 1960 to 1980.

Third, the author expected that reading skills would display more decline than spatial-visual skills, simply because reading scores declined substantially from 1960 to 1972 (Beaton, Hilton, & Schrader, 1977) and continued to decline from 1972 to 1980 (Hilton, 1985).

METHOD

Visualization

In 1960, a test entitled "Visualization in Three Dimensions" (V3D) was included in a battery of 15 tests given to approximately 400,000 high school students as part of Project TALENT (Flanagan et al., 1960). The cover page of the test is shown in Fig. 6.1. Each of the 16 items of the test required the subject to select, from five solid objects depicted, the one object that could be made by folding or twisting the flat piece shown

SECTION 6
VISUALIZATION IN THREE DIMENSIONS
Time—9 minutes

Directions: Each problem in this test has a drawing of a flat piece of metal at the left. At the right are shown five objects, only one of which might be made by folding the flat piece of metal along the dotted line. You are to pick out the one of these five objects which shows just how the piece of flat metal will look when it is folded at the dotted lines. When it is folded, no piece of metal overlaps any other piece, or is enclosed inside the object. On this test your score will be the number of correct answers.

Now look at example 1 below.

Example 1:   Sample Question

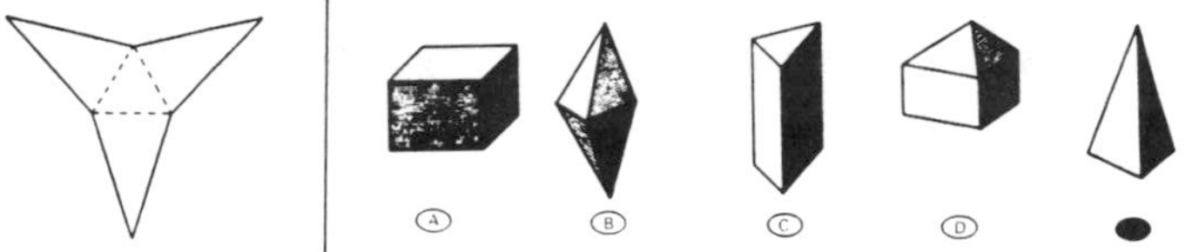

Of the five objects shown, only E could be made from the flat piece shown at the left by folding it at each of the dotted lines. E shows how the flat piece would look after being folded. Therefore, oval E would be marked.

Remember, all folds are indicated by dotted lines; the solid lines show the cuts in the piece, and parts are not folded inside of other parts of any objects (in other words, there is no overlapping).

DO NOT TURN THIS PAGE UNTIL YOU ARE TOLD TO DO SO.

FIG. 6.1. Cover page of visualization in three-dimensions test.

as the stem of the item. The ETS Factor Kit categorizes the Surface Development Test (VZ-3), which is highly similar, as a measure of visualization, defined by Ekstrom, French, Harman, & Dermen (1976) as "the ability to manipulate or transform the image of spatial patterns into other arrangements" (p. 173).

The authors added that "The visualization and spatial orientation factors are similar but visualization requires that the figure be mentally restructured into components for manipulation while the figure is manipulated in spatial orientation" (p. 173). Accordingly, we refer to the skill measured by the V3D test as *visualization* in the remainder of this chapter.

The students in 1960 attended the public and private high schools that participated in Project TALENT. The schools were randomly sampled to be representative of all public, parochial, and private schools in the United States that contained Grade 12. Student participation in the data collection was required. The results to be reported were based on a subsample of the total TALENT sample, which was weighted to be representative of all public and private school students in the United States. Classroom teachers were trained by Project TALENT local coordinators to conduct the data collection.

In 1980, the identical Project TALENT test was included in a battery of six tests given to the high school seniors participating in HS&B. The students attended high schools that were randomly selected to be representative of all public, parochial, and private secondary schools in the United States. In each school, 36 seniors and 36 sophomores were randomly selected for participation, which was optional. Usable test results were obtained from an average of approximately 28 seniors in each school. Approximately 12% of the sampled students were absent on both the survey day and the make-up days, 3% refused to participate, and 3% of the cases were unusable because critical survey material was missing (NORC, 1983, p. 14).

Reading

Both the 1960 and 1980 batteries included tests of reading speed and comprehension, but the format and content of the test differed. However, as part of the score decline study conducted by Beaton, Hilton, and Schrader (1977), the reading tests given in 1960 and the 1972 NLS (Hilton & Rhett, 1973) were equated, and because the 1972 NLS test was identical to the 1980 HS&B test, it was possible to put the 1960 and 1980 reading scores on the same scale. Thus, comparable reading scores were obtainable for the 1960 and 1980 seniors. Because of substantial differences between the items and administrations of the mathematics items in 1960 and 1972, it was not possible to obtain comparable mathematics scores.

RESULTS

The first results, shown in Table 6.1, can be succinctly summarized: the high school seniors in 1980 performed on the V3D test at precisely the same level as the 1960 freshmen. From 1960 to 1980, the mean for the males declined by 1.6 raw score points or .48 standard deviations (*SD*s), and the mean for the females declined by 1.2 raw score points or .38 *SD*s. The mean for the total sample declined by 1.4 or .44 *SD*s. One raw score point is equivalent to one item answered correctly. In one sense, a decline of 1.4 raw score points does not represent a large quantum of learning. But considered in light of the fact that the growth from Grade 9 to Grade 12 on most academic achievement tests is about 2 raw score points (Shaycoft, 1967, Table 4-9), the decline is nontrivial.

As for the second question concerning mean differences between males and females, the discrepancy was 1.2 points or .36 *SD*s in 1960 and .8 points or .26 *SD*s in 1980. Thus, we can say that the raw score difference between males and females decreased in the 20-year period by one third.

TABLE 6.1
Means ($\bar{X}$) and Standard Deviations (*SD*) of Visualization
in Three Dimensions (V3D) Scores in 1960 and 1980

| | *1960* | | | | *1980* | | |
| | *Grade* | | | | *Grade* | | *Effect* |
	9	*10*	*11*	*12*	*12*	*1980–1960*	*Size*[a]
Males							
Sample *N*	3,921	3,876	3,483	2,946	10,977		
Population Est.[b]	822	813	735	619	1,180		
$\bar{X}$	8.1	8.7	9.3	9.7	8.1	– 1.6	.48
SD	3.3	3.3	3.4	3.4	3.3	– .1	
Females							
Samples *N*	4,012	3,914	3,658	3,302	12,055		
Population Est.[b]	827	820	761	678	1,295		
$\bar{X}$	7.3	7.8	8.2	8.5	7.3	– 1.2	.38
SD	2.9	3.0	3.0	3.2	2.9	– .3	
Total							
Samples *N*	7,933	7,790	7,141	6,248	23,865		
Population Est.[b]	1,649	1,634	1,494	1,298	2,561[c]		
$\bar{X}$	7.7	8.2	8.7	9.1	7.7	– 1.4	.44
SD	3.1	3.2	3.3	3.3	3.1	– .2	

[a]Effect size is difference divided by the pooled standard deviation.
[b]In thousands.
[c]In 1980 the sum of the population estimates for males and females does not equal the total population estimate, because 3% of the sample did not identify their sex.

Notice that, for the 1960 sample, the difference between the ninth-grade males and females was .8 scale points, or .26 *SD*s, and between the seniors was 1.2 points, or .36 *SD*s. Because these are cross-sectional results, they reflect both school attrition and individual growth. However, longitudinal results were obtained in a later follow-up of the ninth-graders (Shaycoft, 1967). These results show a gap of .24 *SD*s at the ninth grade and .42 *SD*s at the twelfth grade, with males higher at both grades. Thus, the males in 1960 gained appreciably more in visualization than the females during high school.

The third question was whether visualization skill declined more or less than reading skill. As shown in Table 6.2 and Fig. 6.2, the reading score of the males declined 1.7 points or .32 *SD*s, and the females declined 1.6 points or .32 *SD*s. The difference between the men and women was .1 points in 1960 and 0 points in 1980. Thus, there was essentially no difference between the males and the females in reading in either 1960 or 1980, but both declined by about one third of an *SD* in the time period. Considering that the males declined by .48 *SD*s in visualization and the females by .38 *SD*s, we can say that the decline in visualization was sub-

TABLE 6.2
Means ($\bar{X}$) and Standard Deviations (*SD*) of Reading Scores
in 1960 and 1980

	1960[a]	1980[b]		Effect Size[c]
	Grade 12	Grade 12	1980–1960	
Males				
Sample *N*	9,938	11,362		
Population Est.[d]	910	1,216		
$\bar{X}$	10.6	8.9	– 1.7	.32
SD	5.2	5.3	.1	
Females				
Samples *N*	10,421	12,631		
Population Est.[d]	954	1,353		
$\bar{X}$	10.5	8.9	– 1.6	.32
SD	5.0	5.0	0	
Total				
Samples *N*	20,359	24,892		
Population Est.[d]	1,864	2,661		
$\bar{X}$	10.5	8.8	– 1.7	.33
SD	5.1	5.2	.1	

[a]Source: Beaton, Hilton, and Schrader (1977).
[b]Source: Hilton (1985).
[c]Effect size is difference divided by the pooled standard deviation.
[d]In thousands.

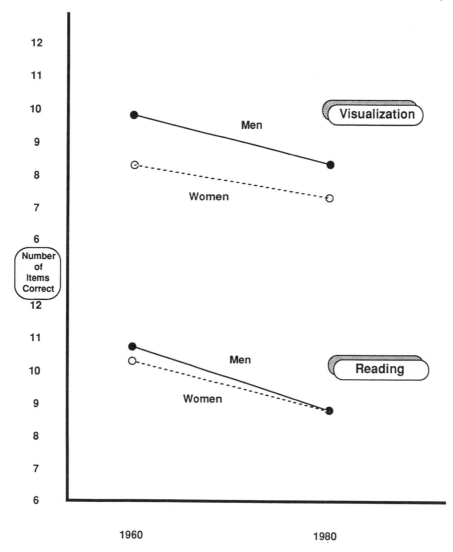

FIG. 6.2. Declines in visualization and reading for men and women.

stantially more than the decline in reading; specifically, the decline in
SD units was 33% more for the males and 16% more for the females.

Total Samples Differences

Possible Artifacts. Why the means in visualization for the total
sample should decline so dramatically from 1960 to 1980 is not clear.
There are several possible explanations, the first of which is that the result

represents an artifact of the survey design and data collection conditions. Examination of the relevant research reports suggests, however, that this is not likely to be the case. Both samples were national probability samples weighted to correct for sampling and for incomplete data. The method of administering the tests differed, but in ways that this author would regard as minor. If anything, the differences would favor the 1980 students: The 1960 testing was toward the end of 2 full days of testing, whereas the 1980 testing was completed within 2 hours. One would think that fatigue and boredom might have had a negative effect on the TALENT students.

The 1980 students were told that their score would be the number of items that they answered correctly—instructions that might have encouraged guessing. On the other hand, the 1960 students were not told how their scores would be computed. The scores reported here are the number of items answered correctly, for both samples. Again, this difference would have favored the 1980 sample, if any.

Another position would be that all students in 1960 were less tested and more compliant and cooperative and, thus, more motivated to do well in testing for research purposes. But possibly offsetting this is the fact that the 1980 students were more self-selected to participate (scores were obtained for only 28 out of the 36 students in each senior class sample). What the net effect of all these factors may have been is impossible to say. The conservative position is that they balanced each other.

Population Changes. A second possible explanation concerns the populations of students sampled. Sixty-seven percent of the relevant age cohort completed high school in 1960, whereas 74% of the 1980 age cohort completed high school. (The number in the relevant age cohort was defined by NCES as the average of the number of individuals who were 17 or 18 in age in the year in question.) Assuming that the students who dropped out had lower visualization and reading scores, the higher dropout rate of the 1960 cohort would to some extent result in higher scores for that cohort. In other words, the 1960 seniors represented a more selected group that could be expected to have higher scores in both visualization and in reading. Beaton, Hilton, and Schrader (1977) concluded that this phenomenon was the main cause of the decline in reading scores from 1960 to 1972.

Racial/Ethnic Composition. Another possible explanation is suggested by the change in the racial/ethnic composition of the two samples. As shown in Table 6.3, the V3D test means are substantially lower for Black students and Hispanic students than for White students. Because the proportion of Black students and Hispanic students increased sub-

TABLE 6.3
Means ($\bar{X}$) and Standard Deviations (SD) of Visualization in Three
Dimensions ($V3D$) Scores for Whites, Blacks and Hispanics[a] in 1980

Subpopulation	Sample N	Population Estimate	$\bar{X}$	SD
Whites	17,264	2,046,000	8.0	3.1
Blacks	2,917	261,000	5.8	2.6
Hispanics	2,601	147,000	6.7	2.8
Total	23,865	2,561,000	7.7	3.1

[a]The Hispanic category includes Mexican-American, Cuban, Puerto Rican, and other Latin American.

stantially from 1960 to 1980, the increase could account for a share, possibly large, of the observed decline. This change in racial/ethnic composition, however, is confounded with changes in socioeconomic status, retention rates, and other possible causative demographic agents, the full analysis of which is beyond the scope of this chapter. The possibility exists, nonetheless, that the general decline in both reading and visualization scores is entirely attributable to these demographic changes. However, in a study of score change from 1972 to 1980, racial/ethnic changes accounted for only a small share of the total change when student behaviors, school characteristics, and home support variables were held constant by analysis of covariance (Hilton, 1985).

Curriculum Changes.   Several studies recently have provided evidence of the strong effect of enrollment in classroom instruction on performance on tests in related areas (see, e.g., Wiley & Harnischfeger, 1974). It seems likely that exposure to certain subjects, such as solid geometry, trigonometry, and mechanical drawing, would enhance performance on the V3D test, and if there was more exposure for the 1960 sample—which is likely—then the difference in test performance might be to some extent explained by curriculum changes from 1960 to 1980.

Sex Distribution.   Another possibility concerns possible changes in the sex distribution from 1960 to 1980. This is difficult to estimate because of missing data in regard to sex identification in the 1980 sample but at most it appears that this change would account for only a small fraction of the observed decline.

In any case there seem to be several possible reasons for the substantial decline in spatial-visual relations. But why the visualization scores should decline substantially more than the reading scores is not explained by the available data. In any future research in this area, the author would give priority to the hypothesis that the differential decline is related to decreases in enrollments in high school courses conducive to the development of spatial-visual skills.

The more puzzling and significant finding is the relative stability from 1960 to 1980 of the higher mean scores for the males. How we interpret this stability depends on what assumptions we make about differential exposure of the sexes to experiences conducive to the development of visualization skills in 1960 as compared to 1980. Is a convergence of one third consistent with changes in exposure or not? The author's interpretation of these results is that the decrease in sex differences does reflect a trend toward uniformity in experience but that substantial differences in the informal and formal educational experience of the sexes remain and, further, that there is no need to hypothesize genetic constraints on the development of visualization skill by males and females. What is clear, however, is that a substantial gap between the sexes in visualization skill existed in 1960, that the skill of both males and females declined appreciably from 1960 to 1980, and that a large gap still existed in 1980.

CONCLUSIONS

In both 1960 and 1980, the same test of spatial-visual ability was given to national probability samples of high school seniors in the United States. The students in 1960 were participants in Project TALENT and in 1980 were participants in High School and Beyond. In addition, a reading comprehension test was given to the 1960 students that subsequently was equated to a similar reading test given to the 1980 seniors. In 1960, the males had substantially higher scores in visualization and slightly higher scores in reading. Between 1960 and 1980, all means scores declined but substantially more so in visualization. However, the gap between males and females narrowed, particularly in visualization. In the absence of a clear explanation, the author attributes the general decline primarily to less student attrition in 1980 and the differential decline to convergence in the experiences of males and females.

ACKNOWLEDGMENT

The author is indebted to Jerilee Grandy and Isaac Bejar for their review of a draft of this chapter.

CHAPTER SEVEN

Estimating Ability in the College-Bound Population from a Self-Selected Sample

Spencer S. Swinton
Educational Testing Service

As is widely recognized, the College Board Scholastic Aptitude Test (SAT) population is self-selected. Nationwide, approximately 30% of high school seniors elect to take the SATs. Consequently, we are severely constrained in what we can say about high school seniors in the United States on the basis of test data from SAT administrations and personal and background data in the Student Descriptive Questionnaire which is completed by most students who take the SATs. If, however, we somehow could weight the SAT data in such a way that the results would be representative of all college-bound high school seniors in the United States, then the SAT data would be substantially more valuable as indicators of educational change in the United States. The possibility of doing this was introduced by the fact that SAT scores were merged into the 1972 NLS file and also the 1980 HS&B senior file. This chapter describes the efforts to develop the desired adjustment procedure.

Among other lessons, the chapter illustrates how changes in the way data are collected from data files can introduce uncertainties in subsequent data analyses.

—*Thomas L. Hilton*

College admissions test scores are not designed, nor should they be, to be used as measures of school effectiveness. Designed to be relatively "curriculum proof," they measure verbal and quantitative reasoning abilities that develop over extended periods of time in the family, peer group, electronic media, and solitary reading and thinking environments, as well as in school. As measures of these broad reasoning abilities, they are highly developed and reliable instruments for those who choose to take them. However, because individuals themselves select whether or not to take these tests, and because this self-selection process varies widely from state to state and across social–economic status and ethnic groups, the high school seniors who take the SAT tests (as well as the American College Testing tests) are a biased sample of all college-bound seniors, and changes in subgroup mean scores from year to year do not necessarily reflect ability changes in the entire college-bound population. Such mean score changes may reflect changing perceptions among different demographic groups of the availability of financial support and of benefits to be gained by attendance at more selective colleges, or changing admission requirements by large state university systems, as much as or more than they reflect changes in student ability. If trends in the developed ability of the group of interest are to be monitored, what is needed is a test administered to a random, not a self-selected, sample of college-bound seniors.

Such a random sample was tested in 1972 in the NLS, and another such sample was available 8 years later from the HS&B study. The same set of reading, vocabulary, and mathematics tests, with strong correlations to the SAT, were administered to both samples.

The fact that SAT scores are available for over half of the college-bound members of these samples who took the NLS tests allows us to address three important questions:

1. Just how biased are SAT mean scores for self-selected subsamples as indicators of ability as measured by the NLS battery for all college-bound seniors?

2. Are data available to allow us to estimate self-selection bias and to reduce its effect?

3. Is the structure of the bias correction equations sufficiently stable over time to enable us to look at annual changes in SAT means and in bias indicators and to estimate ability changes in the overall college-bound population in those 7-year periods of testing famine in which national probability sample data are not available?

METHOD

To address these issues, mean 1972 NLS battery scores were calculated for 24 demographic groups of self-reported college-bound (expected to earn a bachelor's degree or higher) seniors defined by region, ethnicity, and sex. Mean high school grade point average (GPA) and socioeconomic status (SES) were also determined for these groups. In addition, mean SAT scores, high school grade point average (GPA/SAT), and SES (SES/SAT) were calculated for that subset of each group for which SAT scores were available, the subsets ranging from 22% (Hispanic females in the South) to 95% (Asian males in the South) of the college-bound seniors of each group in the NLS sample, with a median of 53% for all groups.

The task we are facing is comparable to that of a fish and wildlife warden who must estimate the size and number of trout in 24 streams on the basis of those caught each April 15th by one fisherman at each stream using Royal Coachman flies. Every 10 years, the warden is allowed to place a seine net across each stream for 1 day, collect, measure, and release the catch, and obtain an unbiased estimate of the populations. In the 9 off years, however, the warden must make allowances for changing water temperatures, speeds and clarities, and the fact that rainbow, speckled, and Dolly Varden trout vary in their proportions in the 24 streams, and in their attraction to Royal Coachman flies.

If these variations are systematic and stable, the game warden can hope to correct for the biases, so that if a sharp change is noticed in one stream's fly catch, it may be possible to decide if this represents a real change in trout population, or is an artifact of changes in stream characteristics that affect only the efficacy of the trout flies. We examine such "stream characteristics" as SES, GPA, and mean class rank in our attempts to extract real change from the "fly catch" of annual SAT scores.

RESULTS

Table 7.1 gives N, mean NLS standardized score for each ethnic group, and mean SAT score for the subset of that group taking the SAT.

This pattern was relatively stable across region, with females generally scoring slightly below males of the same group in mathematics, except for Asian females in the North and Hispanic females in the South, who outscored males in their group. The means for all 24 groups are given in the appendix to this chapter.

The pattern of verbal NLS means was more complex, with females outscoring males in most groups in all regions, but Black females tending to score lower than Black males in the South and West.

The correlation of NLS and SAT mathematics means among the 24 demographic groups was .94 and of NLS and SAT verbal means, .92. These are exceedingly strong relationships, but not unusual for correlations among group means, in which measurement error and individual differences cancel out. These correlations leave 11% of mathematics group variance and 15% of verbal group variance unaccounted for, and are thus not sufficiently strong to justify the use of SAT subsample means as accurate proxies for NLS means in the entire college-bound population.

TABLE 7.1
Mean NLS and SAT Scores by Ethnic Group

	NLS	SAT	NLS	SAT	NLS	SAT	NLS	SAT
Group[a]	N	N	%	%	Math	Math	Verbal	Verbal
Black	527	267	9.2	8.3	−.305	393	−.557	369
Hispanic	184	62	3.2	1.9	−.153	420	−.660	370
Asian	101	74	1.8	2.3	.937	536	1.316	481
White	4933	2814	85.9	87.5	.664	520	1.219	488

[a]An initial group of Native Americans could not be analyzed because of empty cells in the 1980 data set.

For the subsample of individuals who took the SAT, correlations between NLS means and SAT means were .97 for verbal and .96 for mathematics, suggesting that the tests measure quite similar constructs, and that bias due to self-selection of the SAT group attenuates these relationships only slightly.

Note that we are predicting mean scores of only 24 groups: Individual differences tend to cancel out in such a situation; and multiple R^2s, even when shrunk to correct for degrees of freedom, display a propinquity to 1, which is alarming to those who, like the author, are used to the marvelous unpredictability and noisiness of individual data. It must be kept in mind that the object of this exercise is an engineering, rather than a scientific goal; no generalization from the size of the beta weights or the variance accounted for in these group means is intended or warranted in considering disaggregated data for individuals. Given the estimated group means and the proportion of the college-bound cohort falling into each group, we can, however, combine to obtain an estimated overall mean that comes closer to the unobserved mean ability than does the mean of raw SAT scores.

It would be wise not to make too much of the apparent ethnic differences *qua* ethnic differences, however. Table 7.2 shows that mean SES and class rank for the total group and the SAT subsample vary considerably among the groups, and do so in a manner quite consistent with mean test scores. Indeed, as we shall demonstrate, combining these variables in regression equations allows concurrent estimation of group NLS means without recourse to ethnicity.

Class rank is generally considered to be a better indicator of achievement than is GPA, because it partially corrects for differences in grading standards. However, rank does not overcome the problems that students in the same class pursue different curricula, and that high school classes are hardly random samples from a cohort. We began the 1972 analysis with class rank, but because of problems with the 1982 data set, we were forced to use the 1980 HS&B data, which did not contain class rank. We

TABLE 7.2
Mean SES and Class Rank Percentile of Total Sample and
SAT Takers by Ethnic Group

Group	Total Group SES	SAT Group SES	Total Group Class Rank	SAT Group Class Rank
Black	−.286	−.085	53.7	61.3
Hispanic	−.516	−.480	65.7	75.1
Asian	.348	.325	77.7	79.8
White	.413	.558	69.5	79.4

present 1972 results for class rank in Table 7.2, but hereafter use GPA instead.

Table 7.3 gives means for relevant variables in the 1972 and 1980 college-bound groups. These are means of group means, with each of the 24 groups receiving equal weight, and hence minority groups count more heavily than they contribute to the overall population means.

It is clear that group means in the entire population (NLS battery scores) did not move in lockstep with the means of available SAT-taking subgroups, with NLS math means increasing while the SAT math means decreased. The proportion of female SAT takers increased from 49% to 52% in the 8-year period, and the percent of White SAT takers dropped from 87% to 82%. The NLS verbal means dropped .1 standard deviation, and the SAT verbal mean dropped .5 standard deviation.

If we treat SES as a relative ranking, rather than an absolute level, we are led to scale 1980 SES to the 1972 mean and standard deviation. This amounts to assuming that rising parental income and educational attain-

TABLE 7.3
Means and Standard Deviations, 1972 and 1980

	1972 Mean	1972 S.D.	1980 Mean	1980 S.D.
NLS-Math	.29	.58	.36	.48
SAT-Math[a]	468	72.60	458	61.80
NLS-Verbal	.40	1.08	.29	.80
SAT-Verbal[a]	433	67.70	397	52.50
GPA	3.20	.28	3.06	.23
GPA-SAT[a]	3.26	.28	3.19	.22
SES	.01	.43	.09	.36
SES-SAT[a]	.08	.43	.18	.42

[a]These means are based on that subset of each of the 24 groups that elected to take the SAT. 1972 SAT takers ranged from 22% to 95% of their group with a median of 53%.

TABLE 7.4
Correlations Among Group Means (1972 Above Diagonal, 1980 Below)

	NLS-M	NLS-V	SAT-M	SAT-V	GPA	GPA-SAT	SES	SES-SAT
NLS-M		.90	.94	.84	.68	.66	.79	.88
NLS-V	.67		.81	.92	.80	.73	.94	.73
SAT-M	.93	.69		.84	.55	.56	.71	.69
SAT-V	.57	.95	.66		.78	.76	.83	.84
GPA	.71	.49	.65	.40		.94	.68	.62
GPA-SAT	.59	.38	.55	.34	.88		.60	.57
SES	.85	.73	.86	.71	.75	.63		.97
SES-SAT	.77	.68	.80	.66	.71	.59	.96	

ment confer no relative advantage if everyone's SES is rising at the same rate. In particular, it suggests that 1 year of parental college education in 1980 is roughly comparable to parental high school graduation in 1972, or that parental education, like parental income, should perhaps be corrected for "inflation."

Table 7.4 gives correlation coefficients for the 1972 (above the diagonal) and 1980 samples. The most notable difference in the two sets of correlations is the increase of the correlation of GPA with mathematics (M) scores, coupled with a decrease in its correlation with verbal (V) scores. SES shows a similar relationship with NLS and SAT scores, the correlations increasing for mathematics and decreasing for verbal scores. SES/SAT exhibits a similar drop in correlations with verbal scores but inconsistent changes of relationship to mathematics scores.

We can obtain SAT scores, SES, and Class Rank of SAT takers every year for a nonrepresentative sample of each subgroup—the "fly-fishing catch" of the earlier example. The key question is whether we can use this information to estimate NLS means for the whole subgroup. Typically, this sort of problem is addressed by employing multiple regression.

Multiple Regressions

By using only SAT data, mean SES, and class rank of the SAT takers, the prediction of mean NLS scores for all college-bound students can be improved somewhat from that obtained by using unadjusted SAT means ($r_m = .94$, $r_v = .92$). Using these variables in a regression equation for NLS mathematics scores increases the multiple correlation to .96, with standardized coefficients:

NLS/M = .81 SAT + .09 SES/SAT + .20 GPA/SAT.

The verbal multiple correlation becomes .95, with weights:

NLS/V = .55 SAT/V + .38 SES/SAT + .10 GPA/SAT.

This use of background variables improves prediction noticeably in the case of verbal scores, but still does not correct for self-selection, because the mean SES and GPA of the SAT subgroups is serving as a proxy for the values of those variables in the full groups, rather than predicting the degree of nonrepresentativeness of the SAT takers. If the average GPA of all college-bound Hispanic females in the North and in the South is 3.1, but that of the subgroups that take the SAT in the South is 3.5 and in the North 3.3, we would expect the SAT mean to be a greater overestimate of the mean for all college-bound Hispanic females in the former (South) group than in the latter (North), and would wish to further adjust the regression estimate downward for the Southern group. Indeed, the greater the disparity between mean SES or GPA of a self-selected sample of SAT takers and that of all college-bound students in their group, the more negative we would expect the adjustment to be. SES and GPA of only the SAT takers do not provide a basis for such negative adjustments. However, adding to the preceding regressions the mean SES and GPA for all students in the group makes a plausible adjustment for bias, switching the SES/SAT and GPA/SAT coefficients from positive to negative, with rather impressive results. To adjust for gender differences in mathematics, sex is also included in these regressions but adds little to prediction. When GPA for the total group is entered, GPA of SAT takers is no longer needed because SES/SAT then accounts for the required downward adjustment for degree of "skimming" in the SAT subsamples. When these independent variables are taken into account, the multiple correlations exceed .98, and ethnicity is not significant as a predictor.

For mathematics, standardized regression weights are:

$$NLS/M = .73 \text{ SAT/M} + .80 \text{ SES} - .63 \text{ SES/SAT} + .14 \text{ GPA} - .02 \text{ Sex } (R = .98);$$

For the verbal test battery (sum of NLS Reading and Vocabulary):

$$NLS/V = .48 \text{ SAT/V} + 1.16 \text{ SES} - .69 \text{ SES/SAT} + .07 \text{ GPA} - .001 \text{ Sex } (R = .99).$$

All coefficients are highly significant, except the sex coefficient, for estimating NLS/V. Although these standardized regression coefficients would indicate relative importance of the predictors if the predictors were more or less unrelated, extreme collinearity, particularly between SES and SES/SAT, and the fact that the important relationships are distorted in taking group means, suggest taking their relative magnitudes not with a grain, but with a large cake of salt.

The raw regression equations for the 1972 data are:

$$NLS/M = -3.23 + .006 \text{ SAT/M} + 1.07 \text{ SES} - .86 \text{ SES/SAT} + .28 \text{ GPA} - .02 \text{ Sex};$$

NLS/V = − 3.69 + .008 SAT/V + 2.90 SES − 1.75 SES/SAT + .28 GPA − .003 Sex.

To test the stability of the regressions over time, a later similar data set was sought.

Using the 1972 regression equations (including class rank) to predict 1982 NLS group means led to gross overprediction on the order of 1 standard deviation for verbal and for math scores. Inspection of the regression in the 1982 data set revealed that beta weights were quite comparable to those of 1972, but the constants differed.

Comparison of group mean SAT scores in the 1982 data base with national group means revealed that the reported SAT scores were unrepresentatively high. The method of collecting these scores in 1982 differed from the procedure in 1972 and 1980. Rather than matching by student name from SAT records, high school guidance personnel entered SAT scores available in school records in 1982. It would appear that some selection of higher SAT scores took place in this data reporting process. The 1982 data set was thus unusable.

The 1980 HS&B senior data set has SAT scores retrieved and matched from ETS tapes, but does not contain class rank information.

In 1980, the NLS math and verbal raw regression equations based on GPA were:

NLS/M = − 2.93 + .006 SAT/M + .74 SES − .48 SES/SAT + .22 GPA + .03 Sex (R = .95);

NLS/V = − 6.84 + .014 SAT/V + .11 SES − .175 SES/SAT − .08 Sex (R = .96).

Although the multiple R^2s dropped only slightly, from .98 to .95, and .99 to .96, the SES variables, which were highly significant in 1972, were no longer significant in 1980, with the SES regression weight for predicting mean NLS verbal score dropping from 2.90 to .11. SAT/V score increased in importance as a predictor, as did sex. GPA dropped out of the verbal prediction equation altogether.

CONCLUSION

The lack of stability in the regression system suggests that over the time period in question, at least, the proposed estimation strategy is not successful. As was pointed out earlier, inferences to individuals based on highly aggregated data are not appropriate. However, a reanalysis on the individual level to determine if the apparent drop in relationship of SES to verbal ability over this period is real or artifactual is certainly in order.

Although this exploratory study failed to yield a method for correcting annual SAT group means to reflect the means of all college-bound seniors, the method remains promising. Although the regression system including GPA was not stable from 1972 to 1980, the regression system including class rank was quite stable from 1972 to 1982, the failure being due to nonrepresentative SAT data. Complete matching of SAT scores to names in the 1980 data set could well yield an acceptable correction. Were this to be the case, annual updating of the non-SAT variables with a simple postcard survey of SES, class rank, ethnicity, sex, and college plans of high school seniors could yield reasonably accurate monitoring of ability changes. Such data collection, if the correction were to prove efficacious, would be both cost-effective and informative.

ACKNOWLEDGMENT

This chapter is based on a presentation that was part of a symposium on "Drawing Educational Implications from Multiple Data Bases," annual meeting of the American Educational Research Association, Washington, DC, 1987 (Swinton, 1987).

..

APPENDIX

Group Means: 1972 Sample

Group	NLSV	NLSM	SAT/V	SAT/M	SES	SES/SAT	GPA	GPA/SAT
1. NWM*	1.20	.83	483	539	.41	.48	3.13	3.19
2. NBM	-.51	-.21	369	403	-.28	.29	2.87	2.91
3. NHM	-.45	-.09	378	449	-.31	-.25	2.99	3.20
4. NAM	.73	.69	391	486	.20	.13	2.90	2.88
5. NWF	1.47	.71	495	507	.34	.44	3.34	3.38
6. NBF	-.30	-.43	412	394	-.12	-.08	2.96	2.97
7. NHF	-.63	-.60	410	359	-.54	-.32	3.07	3.01
8. NAF	2.79	1.14	574	510	.93	.85	4.00	4.00
9. SWM	.96	.72	474	528	.39	.58	3.20	3.26
10. SBM	-.76	-.32	366	402	-.46	-.36	3.05	3.18
11. SHM	-1.04	.05	391	462	-.74	-.61	2.98	3.12
12. SAM	2.09	1.27	565	622	.22	.23	3.66	3.72
13. SWF	1.13	.55	482	495	.39	.60	3.47	3.52
14. SBF	-.77	-.45	349	371	-.45	-.28	3.19	3.20
15. SHF	-.72	.08	360	400	-.54	-.61	3.23	3.30
16. SAF	1.37	.72	446	498	.42	.34	3.67	3.63
17. WWM	1.24	.74	510	567	.46	.64	3.22	3.41
18. WBM	-.08	.04	386	453	.00	.07	2.87	2.75
19. WHM	-.59	.09	410	443	-.28	.01	3.01	3.33
20. WAM	.83	1.07	471	561	.08	.11	3.21	3.28
21. WNF	1.45	.42	500	490	.52	.66	3.36	3.47
22. WBF	-.76	-.56	347	361	-.21	-.11	2.98	3.04
23. WHF	-.24	-.13	356	386	-.42	-.47	2.97	3.14
24. WAF	1.09	.80	467	542	.14	.12	3.37	3.39

Group Means: 1980 Sample

Group	NLSV	NLSM	SAT/V	SAT/M	SES	SES/SAT	GPA	GPA/SAT
1. NWM*	1.49	.94	465	527	.40	.48	3.13	3.21
2. NBM	.09	.25	381	419	-.04	.07	2.71	2.88
3. NHM	-.03	.31	348	425	-.27	-.33	2.84	2.84
4. NAM	.87	1.30	452	559	.71	.68	3.33	3.37
5. NWF	1.46	.71	458	482	.34	.41	3.34	3.38
6. NBF	-.36	-.25	353	374	-.29	-.25	2.81	2.90
7. NHF	-.17	.05	363	386	-.28	-.30	2.98	3.16
8. NAF	1.11	.89	457	505	.43	.80	3.28	3.42
9. SWM	1.08	.70	437	498	.36	.43	3.17	3.28
10. SBM	-.69	-.26	330	366	-.36	-.22	2.78	2.87
11. SHM	-.34	.15	368	463	-.20	-.14	2.92	3.13
12. SAM	.76	.35	434	501	.27	.37	3.25	3.18
13. SWF	1.08	.46	445	462	.33	.50	3.36	3.39
14. SBF	-.99	-.51	323	351	-.45	-.29	2.97	3.04
15. SHF	-.38	-.21	353	408	-.22	-.07	2.94	3.19
16. SAF	-.97	.99	305	528	.56	.77	3.50	3.58
17. WWM	1.36	.79	469	544	.49	.67	3.14	3.33
18. WBM	.39	-.06	437	443	.34	.57	2.73	2.89
19. WHM	-.12	.13	406	464	-.34	-.38	2.76	2.89
20. WAM	.52	.99	383	530	.21	.39	3.02	3.11
21. WNF	1.20	.52	462	483	.46	.62	3.26	3.45
22. WBF	-.65	-.16	331	361	-.24	-.34	2.96	3.17
23. WHF	-.24	.05	377	432	-.23	-.32	2.97	3.46
24. WAF	.50	.60	389	483	.09	.15	3.21	3.36

*Key Region: *North, South, West.* (*N* includes Northeast and Midwest)
  Ethnicity: *White, Black, Hispanic, Asian.*
  Sex: *Male, Female*
  For example, NWM = Northern White Males

Aggregating Data from Two Testings of the Same Cohort: Do NAEP Means Predict Later SAT Means for the Same Cohort of Students?

Susan Urahn

Minnesota House of Representatives

The question addressed in this chapter is whether the test performance of one sample from a cohort can forecast the test performance of a different sample from the same cohort several years later. In one instance reported, the early cohort members were the 13-year-olds who participated in the National Assessment of Educational Progress in 1971. Five years later, a different sample from the same cohort took the SAT. The only thing the two samples had in common was that they were born in approximately the same year, 1958.

The chapter demonstrates some of the knotty problems encountered in comparing results from two testing programs conducted for different purposes, including the problems of:

- combining ethnic subgroups to approximate the scores of a larger group;
- standardizing mean scores so that means from one data collection will be comparable to scores from another;
- estimating statistics for one sample from statistics for another;
- dealing with changing self-selection for one sample from a cohort to a later sample from *the same* cohort.

—*Thomas L. Hilton*

Trends in tested ability over time derived from one data base may be predictive of trends in tested ability for the same cohort some years later—trends drawn from different ability measures in another data base.

This study evolved as an attempt to answer a very specific question about the correlation of trends in tested ability among different data bases: What is the correlation between the mean scores on the NAEP reading test and the mean score on the SAT verbal test for the same cohort of students? The answer to that question was to be pursued using available data from existing data bases—a very significant constraint. The constraint eliminated the option of drawing a sample of 18-year-old SAT takers who had also taken the NAEP reading test at age 13 and then proceeding with a fairly straightforward analysis. Instead, three waves of NAEP reading tests taken by 13-year-olds (in 1971, 1975, and 1980) and three waves of SAT verbal tests (SAT-V) taken by 18-year-olds, 5 years later (in 1976, 1980, and 1985) were examined. There was no reason to assume that any of the 13-year-olds tested by NAEP were also in the sample of SAT takers 5 years later. However, because the samples for each pair of NAEP-SAT-V means were born in the same year, it was expected that the standardized means would exhibit some degree of correspondence.

Certainly, there were a number of confounding factors to be figured into the equation, the most pressing being that the NAEP tests are administered to a national sample whereas the SAT test represents a self-selected sample. The only option available to adjust for that discrepancy was comparing scores within racial and gender groups. This and other limitations to the study are discussed later in the chapter. First, problems encountered in comparing scores across the two data bases are discussed, and the results of those comparisons are presented.

DATA

Mean scores for students over a span of 14 years on the verbal component of the SAT[1] and the NAEP reading test[2] form the basis for this comparison.

Racial/ethnic classification of SAT takers is based on student response to the Student Descriptive Questionnaire (SDQ). Students voluntarily respond to the SDQ as part of the SAT registration process. SAT scores

---

[1]The SAT is a multiple-choice test measuring developed verbal and mathematical reasoning abilities. The SAT verbal test has both reading comprehension and vocabulary components. Although the cohort of students taking the SAT is often described as "college-bound seniors," this cohort is representative of neither all high school graduates, nor of all students who enroll in colleges and universities (College Entrance Examination Board, 1982). The self-selection process varies by region, race/ethnicity, and socioeconomic status.

[2]The NAEP is an ongoing, congressionally mandated project. NAEP is the only regularly conducted national survey of educational achievement at the elementary, middle, and high school levels. Since 1969 it has assessed 9-year-olds, 13-year-olds, and 17-year-olds in reading, writing, math, science and computer competence. The sample is selected so that assessment results may be generalized to the entire population of students in the United States. Although assessments were conducted annually through 1980 (and biannually since then), not every subject is assessed each time.

are equated from year to year to allow meaningful comparisons across time.

Racial/ethnic classifications for those who take the NAEP reading test were based on observed identifications made by assessment administrators. NAEP reading test scores are also equated to allow meaningful comparisons across time by means of item response theory (IRT) analysis. This procedure provides a common scale on which performance can be compared across groups and subgroups whether tested at the same time or a number of years apart. Because the IRT analysis had not been applied to the NAEP math test scores, the NAEP-SAT comparisons were restricted to the reading area alone. (See ETS, 1985 for a more complete description of the NAEP program.)

Creating a common metric for comparison of the two sets of scores required means, standard deviations, and sample/population sizes for Black, White, Hispanic, male, and female subsamples at each time point from the two data bases. The availability of these three pieces of information for each subsample depended on the date of assessment.

The NAEP reading assessment was first administered to 13-year-olds in 1971.[3] The SAT verbal test scores needed to pair with that NAEP assessment were from the SAT administered to 18-year-olds in 1976. The NAEP data were no problem to obtain. *The Reading Report Card: Progress Toward Excellence in Our Schools* (ETS, 1985) contains mean test scores for Blacks, Whites, males, and females in each reading assessment since 1971, as well as sample sizes and standard deviations. It was impossible to obtain separate results for Hispanics from the 1971 assessment because Hispanics were combined with Whites; however, Hispanics were categorized separately in the 1975 and later assessments.

The 1976 SAT data were another matter. Although it is possible to obtain SAT-V data for the entire sample, as well as males and females for earlier cohorts of SAT takers, it is much harder to find racial/ethnic breakdowns. Because strong differences of opinion existed over the impact of presenting test scores by ethnicity, SAT scores were not reported by ethnicity prior to 1981 although the data did exist (College Entrance Examination Board (CEEB), 1982). SAT verbal means before 1981 for Black, White, and Hispanic subpopulations were made available for the first time in 1986 (Admissions Testing Program of the College Board, 1986). Because there were no population sizes or standard deviations reported for these groups, the closest available proxies for these were provided from unpublished sources by the College Board Programs. Popu-

---

[3]Each NAEP or SAT assessment was administered during an academic year. For ease of presentation, each assessment is referred to by the last year (e.g., the first year of the NAEP reading, conducted in the 1970-1971 academic year, is referred to as the 1971 assessment).

lation sizes were provided for 1975 SAT racial/ethnic subgroups and standard deviations were computed from a random sample of 1975 SAT takers. It is assumed that standard deviations for the 1975 SAT takers did not differ significantly from those for 1976 SAT takers. The mean for Hispanics used in this analysis is the weighted mean of Mexican American and Puerto Rican scores.

The NAEP reading assessment was administered to 13-year-olds again in 1975. SAT-V test scores from the SAT administered to 18-year-olds in 1980 were needed to pair with the NAEP assessment. Again, complete NAEP data were available, and SAT-V data were somewhat inaccessible. Complete 1980 SAT information was available for male and female subpopulations. As was the case for the 1976 SAT-V data, mean scores for Black, White, and Hispanic groups were available; population sizes and standard deviation scores were not. Subpopulation sizes and standard deviations were taken from the 1981 cohort of SAT takers—the first year for which racial/ethnic data were available. It is assumed that standard deviations and population sizes for 1980 SAT takers did not differ significantly from those for 1981 SAT takers. The mean for Hispanics used in this analysis is the weighted mean of Mexican American and Puerto Rican scores.

The third year of the NAEP reading assessment of 13-year-olds was 1980. SAT verbal test scores from the SAT administered to 18-year-olds in 1985 were needed to pair with that NAEP assessment. For this pair of assessments all data were readily available; the 1985 SAT-V means, standard deviations, and subpopulation sizes were reported in *Profiles, College-Bound Seniors, 1985* (CEEB, 1986).

METHOD

The first methodological problem was creating a common metric with which to compare the SAT verbal scores and NAEP reading scores. Converting mean test scores into standard deviation scores for each racial/ethnic and gender group seemed a reasonable approach.

Standard deviation scores within each ethnic population/sample were computed as follows:

For a given subgroup in a given year

X = mean score (SAT verbal or NAEP reading)

$$\text{SCORE}_{sd} = \frac{X - \bar{X}}{SD_{pooled}}$$

$\bar{X}$ = mean score (SAT verbal or NAEP reading) for the total population or sample in a given year

SD_{pooled} = standard deviation for each ethnic subgroup pooled over the three testing years under consideration

For each ethnic group, the standard deviation pooled over the three points in time was computed using the following formula:

$$SD_{pooled} = \frac{N_1\,(SD_1{}^2) + N_2\,(SD_2{}^2) + N_3\,(SD_3{}^2)}{(N_1 + N_2 + N_3) - 3}$$

N_i, SD_i = mean and standard deviation of a given ethnic sample or population at time i

This particular pooled standard deviation (SD_{pooled}), pooled within ethnic group over time, is appropriate because the primary focus of comparisons is within ethnic groups, across time.[4]

Because the standard deviation scores are computed for each racial/ethnic group within each year, a measure of parity is constructed. Looking at three assessment points yields a measure of how a gender or racial/ethnic group's performance in relation to the performance of all test takers changed over time.

RESULTS

In general, NAEP reading scores for 13-year-olds appear to predict SAT verbal scores for 18-year-olds. How well the NAEP scores predict varies by ethnicity. For Whites, the trends over time are very similar and there is little change (see Fig. 8.2). For Blacks and Hispanics, the trends are certainly in the same direction, but NAEP scores predicted more closing of the gap than appeared in SAT scores 5 years later (see Figs. 8.1 and 8.3).

The relative positions of the NAEP reading standard scores and the SAT verbal standard scores vary by ethnicity. For Whites, the two lines are very similar both in slope and position. For Blacks, NAEP standard scores are higher than SAT-V scores whereas for Hispanics NAEP standard scores are consistently lower than SAT-V scores.

For both NAEP reading and SAT verbal, the gap between Whites and minorities is closing. Between 1971 and 1980 for NAEP and 1976 and 1985 for SAT-V, Blacks and Hispanics gained ground, whereas Whites held their own or declined slightly (see Table 8.1 and Figs. 8.1, 8.2, and 8.3).

For males and females, unchanging NAEP scores between 1971 and 1975 did not predict the SAT-V improvement for males and decline for females (see Figs. 8.4 and 8.5). Between 1975 and 1980, changes in NAEP

---

[4]A separate set of NAEP and SAT-V standardized scores were computed using only the standard deviation for Whites throughout—perhaps more appropriate for any across race comparisons. The resulting scores varied only slightly in magnitude. The relative pattern of scores across racial/ethnic groups did not change.

Standard Deviation Score

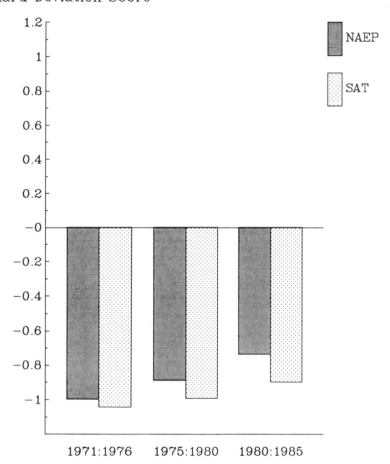

FIG. 8.1.   SAT verbal–NAEP reading score trends for Blacks.

Standard Deviation Score

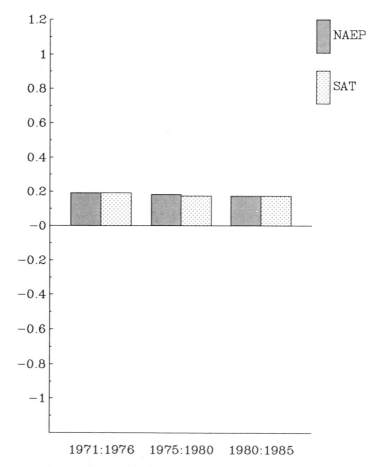

FIG. 8.2.   SAT verbal–NAEP reading score trends for Whites. (1971 NAEP data includes Hispanics.)

Standard Deviation Score

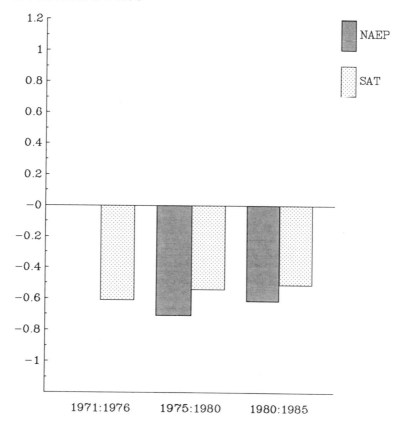

FIG. 8.3. SAT verbal–NAEP reading score trends for Hispanics. (There was no NAEP data for Hispanics in 1971; Hispanics were grouped with Whites that year.)

TABLE 8.1
NAEP Reading (13-Year-Olds)
Means, Standard Deviations, and Subgroup Sizes[a]

1971	Black	White[b]	Hispanic[b]	Female	Male	Total
M_{sample}	219.56	260.12		259.88	247.54	253.71
SD_{sample}	34.05	33.37		35.55	36.64	
N_{sample}	358,200	1,904,010		1,136,563	1,137,386	
1975						
M_{sample}	224.39	260.89	230.32	260.97	248.52	254.75
SD_{sample}	35.20	33.55	35.14	35.05	36.57	
N_{sample}	316,607	2,081,696	129,167	1,234,585	1,284,021	
1980						
M_{sample}	231.94	262.89	235.90	261.38	252.68	257.08
SD_{sample}	33.27	33.47	33.89	34.91	35.51	
N_{sample}	324,449	1,940,907	140,170	1,235,014	1,203,909	
Pooled Standard Deviation	34.17	33.46	34.50	35.16	36.24	

[a]All subgroup sample *N*s are weighted so as to approximate national numbers.
[b]The White subgroup included Hispanics in the 1971 sample.

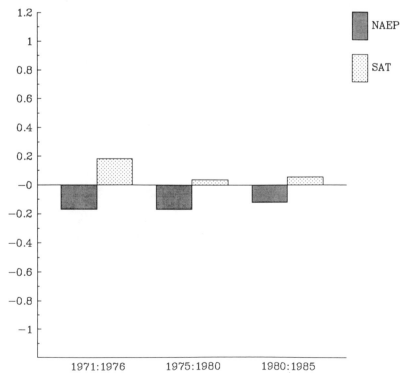

FIG. 8.4. SAT verbal–NAEP reading score trends for males.

Standard Deviation Score

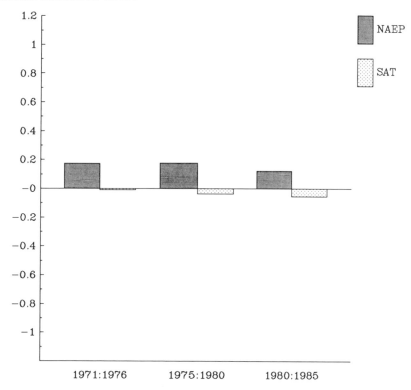

FIG. 8.5. SAT verbal–NAEP reading score trends for females. (No data available for female SAT scores in 1976.)

standard scores (improving for males and declining for females) are reflected 5 years later in SAT-V scores, although the NAEP changes are slightly greater than the SAT-V changes. The tendency of males to outperform females on the SAT verbal and females to outperform males on the NAEP reading is evident. That disparity is increasing very slightly over time for the SAT verbal but decreasing for NAEP reading.

DISCUSSION

The implications of this study are best discussed in two sections: methodological and substantive. First, the substantive. For minorities, Blacks and Hispanics, there was some correlation between NAEP reading scores for 13-year-olds and SAT verbal scores for 18-year-olds. In both cases, the gap between minority and White students is decreasing. However, the

NAEP reading scores for 13-year-old minority students reflect greater strides toward parity than do the SAT-V scores for 18-year-olds. In other words, NAEP scores are forecasting greater improvement than is apparent later in SAT-V scores. This analysis does not yield enough information to understand the reasons for this discrepancy; however, a closer look at the NAEP data may offer some clues.

Steady increases in mean NAEP reading scores between 1971 and 1984 are encouraging, but a comparison of where that improvement has occurred, particularly for minority students, is cause for some concern. NAEP breaks down reading proficiency into five levels—rudimentary, basic, intermediate, adept, and advanced. Patterns in the percentage of students reading at higher levels of proficiency show distinct racial/ethnic differences. Between 1971 and 1980, NAEP scores for only the 17-year-old sample—those closest to taking the SAT test—showed that improvement for Blacks was fairly evenly distributed from the basic to the adept levels (an increase of 13% at the basic level, 24% at the intermediate level, and 9% at the adept level). Hispanic improvement was concentrated more at the intermediate and adept levels (4% at the basic level, 14% at the intermediate level, and 7% at the adept level). Fewer than 1% of Blacks and 2% of Hispanics were reading at the advanced level at any time between 1971 and 1984. Moreover, the average reading proficiency of Black and Hispanic 17-year-olds remained near the level of White 13-year-olds (ETS, 1985). This stands in clear contrast to White 17-year-olds, almost all of whom were reading at least at a basic level of proficiency. Only 4% more Whites were reading at intermediate proficiency in 1984 than in 1971 and only 4% more at the adept level.

These patterns of development in reading proficiency may be part of the reason why improvements in mean SAT-V performance, although steady, were less noticeable than improvements in mean NAEP reading performance for Black and Hispanic students. Students with adept and advanced reading skills are those most likely to succeed in further academic work, and to do well on the SAT verbal test. Mean minority improvements in reading skills will probably continue to be greater than mean improvements in SAT-V performance as long as those reading improvements are less evident at the adept and advanced levels.

The second result that merits some discussion is the relative disparity between standardized NAEP reading scores for 13-year-olds and SAT-V scores for 18-year-olds. For Hispanic students, NAEP scores at 13 were consistently farther below the overall mean than SAT-V scores at 18; for Black students, just the reverse—SAT-V scores were consistently farther below the overall mean than NAEP scores. Is this a function of changes in reading ability or differential self-selection for the SAT?

It is unlikely that differential changes in ability are causing this discrepancy. An examination of 1975 NAEP reading scores for 13-year-olds to HS&B[5] reading scores for high school seniors 5 years later (see Fig. 8.6) is one way to test for that. Here there is no self-selective aspect to the test scores for 18-year-olds. For males and females, the disparity found for 13-year-olds in NAEP reading scores virtually disappears for the 18-year-olds in HS&B reading scores. HS&B standard scores for both males and females were so close to the mean that they do not appear on the graph.

The correspondence between NAEP and HS&B reading varies by ethnicity. For Blacks, NAEP reading scores for 13-year-olds are lower than

Standard Score

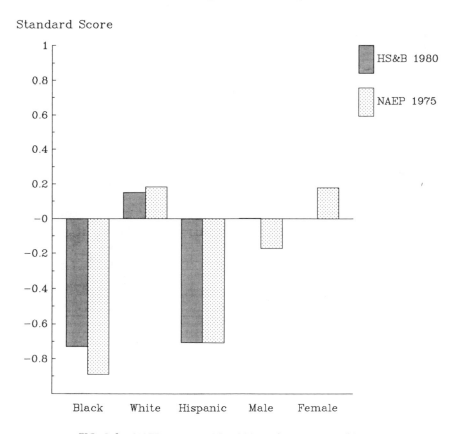

FIG. 8.6.   NAEP 1975–HS&B 1980 reading score profile.

[5]High School and Beyond (HS&B) is a nationally representative sample of students who were high school sophomores and seniors in 1980 (Sebring et al., 1987a, 1987b). Three follow-ups have been carried out for this sample at 2-year intervals (1982, 1984, 1986). Test scores for this study are from those students who were high school seniors in 1980.

HS&B reading scores for 18-year-olds—the opposite of the case for the NAEP–SAT comparison. One explanation for this result may be higher drop-out rates for Black high school students. For White students and Hispanic students, NAEP and HS&B reading scores are very similar.

Within this analysis, there is no control for any change in the rate of self-selection—each group is assumed to have a constant rate of self-selection between 1976 and 1985. It is possible that the Black-Hispanic discrepancy noted may be a result of differential self-selectivity for the SAT test. Proportionately more Blacks than Hispanics may be electing to take the SAT. If this includes a greater number of unprepared Blacks, mean SAT scores could suffer more for Blacks than Hispanics. Given declining Black enrollments over the past 6 years, this is a debatable explanation, but one that cannot be dismissed.

These interpretations have some appeal, but both methodological and data limitations must be considered before placing too much emphasis on any substantive explanations.

Converting the mean NAEP reading and SAT verbal scores to standard deviation scores allowed comparison with a common metric. However, this method was variably effective. For Blacks and Hispanics, it worked fairly well. Both of these groups comprise only a very small part of the total set of NAEP and SAT takers, so measuring changes in distance from the yearly overall mean allowed even slight changes in each group's performance to emerge.

For White students, who comprise a significant majority of both the weighted NAEP sample and the SAT population (over 80% in both cases), the method is less successful. Trying to track changes over time by computing the distance from the overall yearly mean when Whites almost determine that mean may not be a sufficiently sensitive measure. In this case, a better method might be to look at changes in a time series of percentile scores on each test. In a more substantive sense, an overriding concern of educators and policy makers has been the disparity in test scores between Whites and minority students. Tracking the changes in disparity over time is a useful and informative way to view test scores for minority students.

Another factor limiting comparability between these two data bases are methods of determining students' race/ethnicity. For the NAEP assessments, race/ethnicity was assigned by test administrators. For the SAT tests, students' race/ethnicity is self-reported. These two methods could yield differences in classification, particularly for Hispanics (Pennock-Roman & Rivera, 1988). Given the tremendous social and political changes in racial/ethnic issues and attitudes over the 15-year span considered in this study (1971–1985), there is also some potential for change over time, even within these two methods of classification.

Some of the problems with the self-selective nature of the SAT population have already been discussed; however, there are other potentially confounding aspects. A significant part of the SAT score decline throughout most of the 1970s was attributed to compositional changes in the test taking group (Beaton, Hilton, & Schrader, 1977): Growing numbers of minorities and women taking the SAT, traditionally lower scoring populations, brought down mean SAT scores. Compositional changes may also be having an impact on the more recent SAT score improvements. Howe (1985) lists a number of these kinds of changes that could be influencing mean SAT scores: rising high school drop-out rates since the mid-1970s; shifting patterns of college choice, away from colleges more likely to require SAT scores; rising college costs that limit low-income students' college access, and declining Black postsecondary enrollments. In this analysis, focusing on comparisons within racial/ethnic and gender groups minimizes the effect of some changes brought on by self-selection. However, compositional changes other than within racial/ethnic or gender group (e.g., changes in the number of low-income SAT takers) are not controlled in this analysis and could affect the results.

CONCLUSIONS

This chapter might be better described as a methodological exercise than a substantive foray. One method was explored for comparing ability test scores between data bases with non-common members. Although this comparison was constrained by a number of limitations, the substantive results are consistent and of interest.

Given the patterns that resulted, what can be said about SAT-V scores for Blacks and Hispanics in 1989 after examining standardized NAEP reading scores from the 1984 assessment of 13-year-olds? Standardized NAEP reading scores for 1984 are − .636 for Blacks and − .591 for Hispanics. An improvement of 0.10 in standard score units between 1980 and 1984 for Blacks continues a fairly steady trend toward parity in NAEP reading. The pattern of gains in reading proficiency for 13-year-olds appeared at all levels, basic through adept. Black SAT-V scores in 1989 should also continue to show improvement.

Hispanics, however, made few gains between 1980 and 1984 (a mean standardized score change of only .02). The percentage of Hispanic 13-year-olds reading at the adept level decreased. This suggests that Hispanic SAT-V improvement could falter as well. The *Reading Report Card* (ETS, 1985, p. 47) notes that there is "little cause for complacency" even in light of reading gains by traditionally underachieving populations. The possibility raised here of ties between the reading ability of 13-year-olds and performance on the SAT verbal test 5 years later can only reinforce the importance of continuing concern.

ACKNOWLEDGMENT

This chapter is a revision of a paper presented at the Annual Meeting of the American Educational Research Association, Washington, DC, April 20–24, 1987 (Urahn, 1987).

CHAPTER NINE

Pooling Results from Two Cohorts Taking Similar Tests, Part I: Dimensions of Similarity

Thomas L. Hilton
Educational Testing Service

This chapter and the next one concern the problem of drawing conclusions about time lag changes from two administrations of either the same test or similar tests some period of time apart. Even when exactly the same test is administered on both occasions, one cannot be certain that a change in score can be taken at face value. As is shown herein, there may have been differences in the motivation of the test takers on the two occasions, differences in the way the test takers perceived the task, differences in the way in which the tests were administered, or differences in the way in which the test takers recorded their answers (i.e., in the test booklet or on a separate answer sheet).

In addition, detailed information is provided about the items in the 1972 NLS and the three HS&B tests with tables showing which items are common to the four tests and which are unique to one or more of the tests. To the best of our knowledge, this information exists in no other document.

—Thomas L. Hilton

The cognitive tests used in the NLS and in HS&B have a long and complex history, which is recorded, with one exception, only in an assortment of work statements, memoranda, progress reports, and unpublished project reports. The one exception is a preliminary analysis of the tests given in 1980 to the sophomores and seniors in HS&B (Heyns & Hilton, 1982). The purpose of this chapter is primarily to describe the NLS and HS&B test batteries and the conditions under which they were administered. A secondary purpose is to summarize in one place a number of previously unpublished reports that are important background to the development of the two batteries. This history has an important bearing on whether results from the two batteries are comparable.

BRIEF DESCRIPTION OF THE FOUR
BATTERIES AND THEIR INTERRELATIONSHIPS

1972 Senior Tests

In the spring of 1972, 18 randomly selected senior students in each of the sample of 1,044 randomly selected high schools were given a battery of cognitive tests[1] as part of the base year survey of the longitudinal study, which was to continue for an unspecified time. A total of 16,860 students completed the tests. As of this writing, five follow-ups have been conducted. The battery consisted of six tests, which are listed in the left-hand column of Fig. 9.1. These tests and a brief description of each follows (additional descriptive material is included in a later section on the history of the development of the tests):

Vocabulary—Fifteen moderately difficult items consisting of one word followed by five possible synonyms. Test taker selects one word or phrase whose meaning is closest to that of the stem. Time—5 minutes.

Picture-Number—Test of short-term associative memory, from the ETS *Manual for Kit of Factor-Referenced Cognitive Tests* (Ekstrom et al., 1976) in which the test taker first studies pairs of pictures and 2-digit numbers and then is shown the pictures only and is asked to select the number on the answer sheet that was paired with picture. Time—3 minutes to study 15 items in Part 1, and 2 minutes to answer; and similarly for Part 2.

Reading—Relatively unspeeded measure of reading comprehension in which five reading passages are given and test taker answers a total of 20 multiple-choice questions (each with five options) concerning what is stated or implied in each passage. Time—15 minutes.

Letter Groups—Test, from the ETS *Manual for Kit of Factor-Referenced Cognitive Tests*, designed to measure inductive reasoning, consisting of five groups of letters among which four groups share a common characteristic and the fifth group is different. The test taker indicates which group differs from the others. Time—15 minutes.

---

[1]The adjective *cognitive* is used in reference to a broad category of tests that might include basic intellectual skills, achievement, developed ability, and scholastic aptitude.

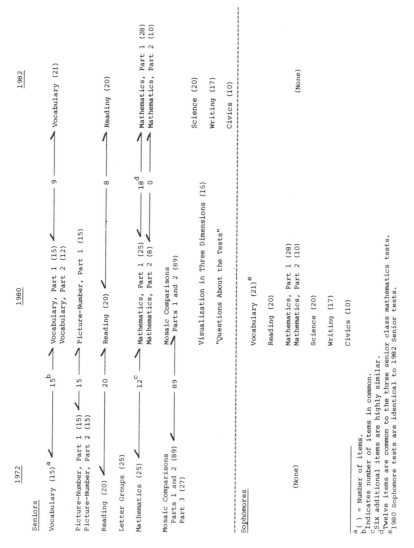

FIG. 9.1.   NLS and HS&B tests.

Mathematics—Twenty-five items in which the test taker indicates which of two quantities is greater, or equal, or that the data given are insufficient to make a decision. The items were selected to not require specific algebraic, geometric, or trigonometric skills. Time—15 minutes.

Mosaic Comparisons—This test, from the ETS Comparative Prediction Battery (French, 1964), was used as a highly speeded measure of perceptual speed and accuracy. One hundred and sixteen pairs of tile-like patterns require the test taker to detect small differences in the design. Time—Part 1 (56 items), 3 minutes; Part 2 (33 items), 3 minutes; Part 3 (27 items), 3 minutes.

Total Testing Time—69 minutes.

The test battery was administered prior to the student questionnaire by a survey administrator in each school, usually a guidance counselor or an experienced teacher. The front page of the test booklet and the instructions for each test and sample items are shown in the appendix to this chapter. (Qualified researchers can borrow full copies of the tests by writing T. L. Hilton, Educational Testing Service, Princeton, NJ 08541.) The students marked their answers in a separate mark-sensed answer sheet, not in the test booklet.

1980 Senior Tests

In the spring of 1980, as part of HS&B, 36 randomly selected seniors and 36 randomly selected sophomores were surveyed in each of 1015 high schools. Both the seniors and the sophomores were given test batteries that roughly paralleled the 1972 test. As shown in Fig. 9.1, the 1980 senior tests were quite similar to the 1972 senior tests. Five of the six tests given in 1972 were repeated; 151 of the 164 items, or 92% of the items in these five tests, were identical. For reasons that are explained shortly, the entire Letter Groups test was dropped, as were parts of two other tests, to make room for a test of spatial relations (Visualization in Three Dimensions) and a self-report measure of the student's reactions to the testing situation ("Questions About the Tests"). Brief descriptions of these two instruments added to the 1980 senior test battery follow.

Visualization in Three Dimensions—This test, which was used in 1960 in Project TALENT (Flanagan et al., 1962), is a measure of the ability to visualize how a figure would look after manipulation in three-dimensional space, by folding a flat figure to make a three-dimensional figure. Each of the 16 items in the test has a drawing of a flat piece of metal in the left-hand column and drawings of five objects on the right, only one of which could be made by folding the flat piece of metal. The test taker selects the one object that could have been made. Time—9 minutes.

Questions About the Tests—This 6-item self-report questionnaire was designed to tap factors that may have prevented the test takers from performing as well as they might have under optimum testing conditions. Included are questions inquiring about the importance of the testing to the students, their concern about doing well, how much they enjoyed participating, and how they felt while taking the tests. Time—5 minutes

The total 1980 senior test battery and the time allowed was as follows:

Vocabulary
    Part 1 — 5 minutes
    Part 2 — 4 minutes
Reading — 15 minutes
Mathematics
    Part 1 — 15 minutes
    Part 2 — 4 minutes
Picture-Number — 5 minutes
Mosaic Comparisons
    Part 1 — 3 minutes
    Part 2 — 3 minutes
Visualization in Three Dimensions — 9 minutes
Questions About the Tests — 5 minutes

Total time —68 minutes

The test battery was administered *after* the questionnaires by the Test Administrator or School Coordinator, who were school staff members with limited survey responsibilities, while the Team Leader and Team Coordinator, who were NORC personnel with broad survey responsibilities, scanned the student questionnaires for completion of "critical items."

In 1982, as part of the first follow-up of the 1980 sophomore cohort, those cohort members who were still in the same schools were asked to take again the same tests they had taken as sophomores and under the same conditions. Sample members who had graduated early, had transferred to another school, or had dropped out were located and given the tests in specially arranged small groups. The front page of the test booklet, instructions, and sample items for the tests that were new to the 1980 and 1982 test batteries are shown in the appendix to this chapter. Certain additional details about the 1980 test administrations are described shortly.

1980 Sophomore Tests

For the sophomores, the basic academic skill tests (Vocabulary, Reading, and Mathematics) were retained—with some changes at the item level and in the lengths of the tests—and three short conventional achievement tests were added. These were as follows:

Science—Twenty items measuring knowledge of general science, biology, chemistry, physics, and the scientific method. Each multiple choice item has a stem and five options. Time—10 minutes

Writing—Seventeen multiple-choice items testing use of capitalization and punctuation, form, and style concerns. Each item has four options. Time—10 minutes

Civics Education—Ten multiple-choice items covering graph reading (1), American history (2), American government (3), and miscellaneous current issues requiring inferential reasoning (4). Each item has four options. Time—5 minutes

Thus, the total 1980 sophomore test battery and the time allowed was as follows:

Vocabulary	7 minutes
Reading	15 minutes
Mathematics	
Part 1	16 minutes
Part 2	5 minutes
Science	10 minutes
Writing	10 minutes
Civics Education	5 minutes
	Total time —68 minutes

1982 Senior Tests

This battery was simply a reprinting of the 1980 sophomore test battery, with changes only on the cover.

All of the original sophomores who were still in the same high schools 2 years later were in the retest sample, but the original sophomores who had graduated early, transferred to another school, or had dropped out were subsampled. Ninety-four percent of the in-school participants and 90% of the out-of-school participants (including transfer students) took the tests. Over 22,400 sophomore cohort members took the tests in both 1980 and 1982.

Common Items

As a result of the modifications of the tests from 1972 to 1980 and the differences between the sophomore and senior test batteries in 1980 and, thus, between the 1980 and the 1982 senior tests (because the 1980 sophomore tests are identical to the 1982 senior tests), there are only a small number of items that are common to the 1972, 1980, and 1982 senior tests. These common items are shown in Table 9.1. All told, 68% of the 1972 items are common to the 1972 senior and 1980 senior tests (assuming that the six 1980 Math items with editorial or format changes can be regarded as identical), but only 19% of the 1980 senior cohort items are common to the 1980 sophomore cohort, and 15% of the 1972 items are common to all three tests batteries. What might be regarded as a fourth battery, namely, the battery given to the 1982 seniors, was identical to that given to the 1980 sophomores.

DIFFERENCES IN ADMINISTRATION AND FORMAT

Although the purposes and general setting of the 1972, 1980, and 1982 test administrations were comparable, there were certain differences that may have significance in interpreting any observed differences in score distributions across the years. Accordingly, each administration is briefly described, and certain dissimilarities are pointed out.

1972 Administration

The test data collection was conducted by survey administrators, usually appointed by the school superintendent of the school district or the principal of the participating high school, as part of the data collection for the base-year survey. Because the survey was undertaken late in the spring of the school year—typically in the month of April—approximately 10% of the schools agreed to participate only if they did not have to conduct the test administration. Another 10% of the schools either refused to participate or could not do so because of early closing dates. Thus, the school participation rate was 80%.

Eighteen seniors were randomly selected for participation by Educational Testing Service from rosters sent to Princeton by each participating school. Five additional students were randomly selected as replacements in the event that any seniors in the primary sample refused to participate. Although no incentive, financial or otherwise, was offered for participation, and participation was voluntary, a high percentage of the students agreed to participate. Usable student questionnaires were obtained from 88% of the students, and 95% of these students participated in the testing (NCES, 1983, p. 38).

TABLE 9.1
Common Items in Senior Test Batteries

	1972 Item No.	Matching 1980 Item No.[a]	Matching 1982 Item No.
Vocabulary	1	1	5
	2	2	New
	3	3	7[b]
	4	4	10
	5	5	11
	6	6	New
	7	7	13
	8	8	15
	9	9	New
	10	10	New
	11	11	New
	12	12	18
	13	13	19
	14	14	New
	15	15	21

Picture-Number—Part I (15 items) is identical in 1972 and 1980. The 1982 battery has no Picture-Number items.

Reading	1	1	New
	2	2	New
	3	3	New
	4	4	New (Defective item, not scored)
	5	5	New
	6	6	14
	7	7	15
	8	8	16
	9	9	17**
	10	10	10
	11	11	11
	12	12	12
	13	13	13
	14	14	New
	15	15	New
	16	16	New
	17	17	New
	18	18	New
	19	19	New
	20	20	New

Letter Groups—No Letter Groups items were used in 1980 or 1982.

(*Continued*)

TABLE 9.1
(*Continued*)

	1972 Item No.	Matching 1980 Item No.[a]	Matching 1982[c] Item No.
Mathematics, Part 1	1	New to '80	New to '82
	2	2	2
	3	3	3
	4	4	4
	5	5	5
	6	6 Edit change only	6 Same as '80
	7	New to '80	New to '82
	8	New to '80	New to '82
	9	New to '80	New to '82
	10	10	10
	11	11 Edit change only	11 Same as '80
	12	12	12
	13	13	13
	14	14 Format change	14 Same as '80
	15	15 Format change	15 Same as '80
	16	16	16
	17	17	17
	18	18 Edit change only	18 Same as '80
	19	New to '80	New to '82
	20	20	20
	21	21	21
	22	22 Edit change only	22 Same as '80
	23	New to '80	New to '82
	24	24	24
	25	New to '80	New to '82
			26 New to '82
			27 New to '82
			28 New to '82
Mathematics, Part 2		1980 Items	1982 Items
		1	1 New to '82
		2	2 New to '82
		3	3 New to '82
	No test	4	4 New to '82
		5	5 New to '82
		6	6 New to '82
		7	7 New to '82
		8 (Defective item, not scored)	8 New to '82
			9 New to '82
			10 New to '82
Mosaic Comparisons	Part 1–56 items	Identical to '72	No test
	Part 2–33 items	Identical to '72	No test
	Part 3–27 items	No test	No test

Note: None of the remaining tests was common to any of the batteries. The 1980 sophomore battery was identical to the 1982 senior battery.

[a]Number in column is the number of the test item that is identical to the 1972 test item in that row; [b]Minor item differences judged to be trivial; [c]The 1982 Math test, Part 1, contained 28 items and took 16 minutes.

The 18 students typically were assembled in a classroom and, in accordance with the 18-page Survey Administrator's Manual, were first given the test battery and, then, following a 10-minute break, the student questionnaire. The Survey Administrator's Manual provided detailed directions for seating and supervision of the students and for arranging make-up sessions.

1980 Administrations

In 1980, 36 sophomores and 36 seniors were randomly selected for participation within each high school. Usable student questionnaires were obtained from 82% of the sample members, and 74% of the sample members participated in the testing (Sebring et al, 1987a, p. 38). The students were assembled in classrooms or in a cafeteria or auditorium. In contrast to the NLS procedure, the tests were administered after the questionnaires, while NORC personnel checked the student questionnaires for completion of "critical items." In some unknown fraction of the schools, presumably small, the sophomores and seniors were given the tests at the same time, despite differences in the timing and instructions for the tests. Some other differences between the ways in which test data were obtained in 1972 and 1980 are discussed in the following sections.

Other Administrative Differences

1. Guessing Instructions.   In 1972, the students were not told how the tests would be scored, that is, that there would be a penalty for guessing, whereas in 1980 the students were told that their score on each section would be the number of correct answers minus a percentage of the number of incorrect answers. Therefore, it would not be to their advantage to guess unless they were able to eliminate one or more of the answer choices. The one exception was the test of Visualization in Three Dimensions, in which the students were told that their score would be the number of correct answers. (The purpose of this exception was to make the instructions for this test parallel to the procedures followed in Project TALENT (Flanagan et al., 1962) from which the test was reproduced.) In both 1972 and 1980, the tests were scored by formula $S = R - W/(n - 1)$, where R is the number right, W is the number wrong, and n is the number of choices in each item, with the exception of Visualization in Three Dimensions, which was scored number right. In a recent study, Angoff and Schrader (1984) demonstrated that formula scores are invariant with respect to directions. The wording of the instructions given to the students in the Angoff-Schrader experiment differed somewhat from that used in the 1972 and 1980 administrations;

the sample characteristics differed as well (college applicants vs. high school seniors). Thus, their results may not be generalizable to the present case. If not, then the absence of formula instructions in 1972 may have favored that sample.

2. Answer Sheets.   In 1972, the students marked their answers on an answer sheet separate from the test booklet. A copy of the sheet is shown in Fig. 9.2. In 1980, however, the students marked their answers in the test booklet by blackening ovals adjacent to the options they selected. (Some examples are shown in the sample items in the appendix to this chapter.)

A second difference was that the 1972 answer sheet required the student to blacken a box, whereas NORC asked students to completely fill in an oval. On the answer sheet, the 1972 students were told to be sure each mark is dark and completely fills the answer box.

Third, the separate 1972 answer sheet did not precisely map the format of the test booklet, that is, the arrangement of item response grids into columns on the 1972 answer sheet did not match the columns in the test booklet. For example, the Mosaic Comparisons items in the test booklet had 12 items in each column, whereas the answer sheet had 14 items in each column.

It is difficult to know exactly what the net effect of these format differences was, but it seems likely that, on balance, the 1980 format saved the respondent a substantial amount of time, particularly on the Mosaic Comparisons Test, which is a speed test. A team at the Air Force Human Resources Laboratory conducted an experiment in which the effect of several similar format differences was examined (Earles, Guiliano, Ree, & Valentine, 1983). They concluded that the net effect was highly significant for speeded tests—amounting to nearly one-half a standard deviation for the most speeded test. The design of their experiment did not permit the estimation of the relative magnitude of the different sources of effects.

3. Administration Date.   Because the contract for the 1972 data collection was awarded later in the academic year than the award for the 1980 data collection, the 1972 test administrations in the schools were conducted approximately 1 month later in the school year than the 1980 administration. Because the tests in question were measures of aptitude or developed ability in contrast to content specific tests and both administrations were conducted late in the senior year—generally regarded as a time of little learning—we suppose that this discrepancy made at most a slight difference in performance. For another reason, however, many— perhaps 25%—of the 1972 students may have been at a disadvantage in

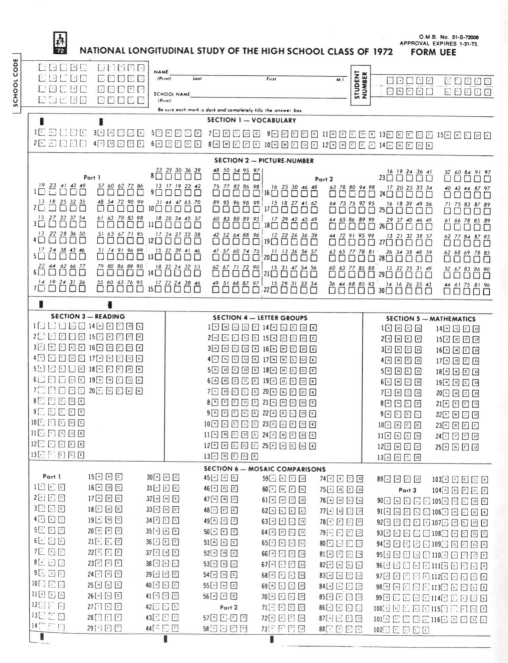

FIG. 9.2.

160

that they were given the tests during the last week of school, a week of many distractions. We would guess that this counter-balanced any advantage that the 1972 sample in general may have had from being tested 1 month later than the 1980 students.

4. *Order of the Tests within the Battery*. As is shown in the following table, the order in which the tests were given in 1972 differed from the order in 1980. What effect this change in order may have had is unknown, although it seems likely that fatigue increases and motivation decreases towards the end of the testing. If so, then the order might have favored the 1980 students, because the tests that were not common to the two administrations (Letter Groups in 1972 and Visualizations in Three Dimensions in 1980) were given fourth in 1972 and last in 1980.

1972	1980
Section 1. Vocabulary	Section 1. Vocabulary (Parts 1 & 2)
Section 2. Picture-Number (Parts 1 & 2)	Section 2. Reading
Section 3. Reading	Section 3. Mathematics (Parts 1 & 2)
Section 4. Letter Groups	Section 4. Picture-Number
Section 5. Mathematics	Section 5. Mosaic Comparisons (Parts 1 & 2)
Section 6. Mosaic Comparisons (Parts 1–3)	Section 6. Visualization in Three Dimensions

5. *Order of Questionnaire and Test Administration*. As was noted earlier, in 1972 the tests were given before the student questionnaires, whereas the order was reversed in 1980. Again, we know of no directly relevant methodological studies investigating the possible effect of such a reversal in order, but it seems likely that completing a long and complicated questionnaire (33 pages for the sophomores and 35 pages for the seniors) just prior to the test administration would have had a deleterious effect on the performance of the 1980 test takers because of fatigue.

6. *Seating and Other Instructions*. In 1972, the survey administrators were given detailed instructions about seating the students so as to make copying and collaboration difficult (e.g., "seat students in alternate rows"), whereas no such instructions were given in 1980. In addition, only in 1972 were instructions given about prohibitions in the testing room (no books, slide rules, etc.) and how routine absences, mistimings, emergencies, and other problems should be handled.

7. *Supervision*. Only in 1972 was the staff instructed to "walk around the room" during the administration of the test. Presumably, in 1980 the school personnel or NORC representatives present were busy checking the student questionnaires during the test administration. Any reduction in supervision in 1980 might have encouraged collaborating, but, on the other hand, any added supervision in 1972 might have resulted in a more controlled testing situation conducive to test performance.

    8. *Timing of Picture-Number Test*.   In 1972, the survey administrators were instructed to tell the students that they would have 3 minutes to study Part 1, and at the end of 3 minutes to tell them to turn to the test page for Part 1. Two minutes later, the students were told to stop. In 1980, the survey administrators were not instructed to tell the students when 3 minutes were up, although the test booklet informed them that they would have only 3 minutes to study Part 1 and then 2 minutes for the test questions. What effect this difference had is uncertain. If it resulted in the 1980 students taking more than 3 minutes to study Part 1, then the effect may have been nontrival.

    9. *Group Size*.   In 1972, the typical testing session included 18 students, whereas in 1980, 36 to 72 students were tested together, depending on whether the sophomore and senior subjects were tested in separate rooms or together. This may have resulted in more distractions in 1980, but it also may have made it easier for students to collaborate if any were so inclined. With one exception we would expect the distractions of the larger group to be the more important factor. The exception was the Picture-Number Test, which may well have had inflated scores in 1980 because of the difficulty of supervising the larger groups. Fetters, Stowe, and Owings (1984) tested this hypothesis by computing the regression coefficients of Picture-Number Test formula scores on test-group size while controlling for the students' self-reported grade average, curriculum, sex, race, and SES. In both 1972 and 1980, the coefficients were positive and significantly greater than zero. Thus, the effect of the larger groups in 1980 may have been appreciable, although Fetters and his associates estimated that, at most, it would account for less than 50% of the higher mean in 1980 (Fetters et al., 1984, p. 7).

Summary

What can we say about the effect of differences between the 1972 and 1980 test batteries in their format and administration? Table 9.2 summarizes our best guess as to which administration would be favored by the difference cited previously. Weighting a slight advantage as 1 and a moderate advantage as 2, the "score" would seem to be 3 to 6 in favor of the 1980 administration. In view of our uncertain knowledge of the true magnitude of the effects discussed, the cautious position would be

TABLE 9.2
Administration Favored by Differences in Administration

	1972	1980
Guessing instructions	*	
Answer sheets		
a. In booklet		**
b. Marking space	–	–
c. Mapping of tests and answers		**
Administration date	–	–
Order of the tests		*
Order of questionnaire and test administration	**	
Seating and other instructions		*
Supervision	–	–
Group size	–	–

– = No difference; * = Possible slight advantage; ** = Possible moderate advantage.

that neither administration had an advantage. A less cautious conclusion is that the 1980 subjects probably had some small advantage and that the advantage may have been greater on some tests than others, for example, tests requiring close supervision and timing.

HISTORY OF DEVELOPMENT OF TESTS

Having briefly described the NLS and HS&B tests and their administration, we turn in this section to recounting the history of their development from 1971 to the present. We do this partly to document a line of developmental research that has important implications for educational research in this country and partly to assist the reader in understanding the purposes and proper uses of the test scores.

The 1972 Tests

That the data collection for the National Longitudinal Study of the High School Class of 1972 should include one or more measures of student ability was originally recommended in a design for the study prepared in 1971 by Research Triangle Institute under contract with the National Center for Education Statistics (Horvitz et al., 1972). The design report described the objectives of the study as follows:

> The survey is expected to provide needed insights into the significant alternative patterns of development experienced by students beyond high school, detailed information on the factors affecting these patterns and methods for relating the occupational and postschool experiences of individuals to their school experience. (p. 6)

Later in the report, the first of 10 main objectives listed was as follows:

1. To identify factors associated with alternative postsecondary school career choices and students' persistence in these choices.

Of six broad categories of factors that determine postsecondary school career paths, the first was "the student's ability, especially in the cognitive area" (Horvitz et al., 1972, p. 19). To measure student's ability, the authors proposed to use the student questionnaire with one exception: this was that the student's intelligence should be measured through "an objective IQ test": the Quick Word Test, a 100-item multiple choice vocabulary test (Borgatta & Corsini, 1967).

A field test of the instruments designed by the RTI staff included the Quick Word Test. The results, however, caused the RTI staff to recommend that the test be eliminated. "The student's own classification of his ability . . . together with his overall grade point average and rank in class should provide a sufficient measure or index of ability" (Horvitz et al., 1972, p. 193). Nevertheless, the Request for Proposals (RFP) for the base-year survey of NLS-72 specified that the Quick Word Test would be used. Moreover, in responding to the RFP, Educational Testing Service not only endorsed the idea of including an objective measure of vocabulary but also recommended that the measurement of student ability be broadened to include "other measures of verbal aptitude and other forms of basic skills which have been shown to be important predictors of academic or vocational training and on-the-job performance" (Hilton, 1971, pp. 4–8). A second reason for considering measures to supplement the QWT was that "legitimate issues can be raised regarding its appropriateness for minority group members from culturally disadvantaged backgrounds" (pp. 4–8).

On January 27, 1972, NCES awarded the contract for the base-year survey to ETS and endorsed the concept of expanding the coverage of the cognitive testing. It is important to note, however, that the primary purpose of the expanded battery of tests continued to be to enhance the prediction of career development choices and outcomes.

A team of 16 ETS professional staff members immediately undertook the design, clearance, pretest, review, revision, and production of the new test battery—a series of tasks completed in an 8-week period (Hilton & Rhett, 1973).

The final composition of the battery represented a balancing of somewhat opposing considerations. The primary objective was to obtain a more comprehensive description of students whose backgrounds, ethnicity, and SES were quite diverse. At the same time, the need for comprehensive measures had to be balanced with the requirement of minimal testing time. Lengthy tests are a nuisance to schools that must schedule time to administer them and to students who must endure them without significant fatigue or loss of interest. For this reason, the battery was held to 69 minutes of testing time plus 36 minutes of administrative time for a total of 105 minutes.

The tests were constructed to measure five distinct factors in a reasonably short period. They were selected on the basis of their efficacy in other ETS programs or projects, two of which were the Comparative Guidance and Placement Program (CGP), a guidance service for 2-year colleges, and Project Access, a project for minority youth.

Many of these tests existed even before the development of CGP and Project Access. Variations of some of the tests had been assembled by ETS in the *Manual for the Kit of Factor-referenced Cognitive Tests* and made available to researchers throughout the country for experimental study. Thus, the tests used in NLS represented instruments already established in psychometric research.

A brief description of each test, abstracted from Hilton and Rhett (1973), and a summary of their psychometric properties follow. (A complete analysis of each test, based on data from the base-year survey, can be obtained from T. L. Hilton, ETS.)

Vocabulary. This is a brief test using synonym format consisting of items drawn from the longer Project Access Vocabulary Test. The items were selected to avoid academic or collegiate bias and to be of an appropriate level of difficulty for the NLS twelfth-grade population. The 15 items selected were those that constituted the then current CGP Vocabulary Test.

Reading. This test is based on short passages (100–200 words) with several related questions concerning a variety of reading skills (analysis, interpretation) but focusing on straightforward comprehension. The Reading Test drew upon items from the CGP Reading Test and items of particular relevance to minority group students taken from the Project Access Reading Test.

Mathematics. The items are quantitative comparisons in which the student indicates which of two quantities is greater, or asserts their equality, or asserts a lack of sufficient data to determine which quantity is greater. This type of item is answered relatively quickly and provides measurement of basic competence in mathematics while at the same time minimizing the amount of time required for actual computation. The test is a shortened version of the CGP and Project Access instruments but omits those items that tap algebraic, geometric, or trigonometric skills.

Letter Groups.   This test of inductive reasoning requires the student to draw general concepts from sets of data or to form and test hypotheses in a nonverbal context. The items consist of five groups of letters among which four groups share a common characteristic and the fifth group is different. The student indicates which group differs from the others. The test was used in exactly the same form in which it appeared in both the Project Access and CGP test batteries.

Letter Groups, as a test of inductive reasoning, measures one of the four aptitudes (verbal, quantitative, reasoning, and spatial/perceptual) that have considerable precedence in representing the varieties of cognitive skills. Tests of inductive reasoning have, in particular, been shown to be useful in research involving minority ethnic groups (Flaugher, 1971; Lesser, Fifer, & Clark, 1965; Stodolsky & Lesser, 1967). This test, in combination with the Mathematics Test that was included in the battery, provided a measure of the reasoning capacity of students. It also may have a verbal component: In a study of persistence in higher education, a confirmatory factor analysis showed it to have a loading on "performance aptitude" that in turn had a correlation of .77 with "verbal aptitude" (Hilton, 1982, p. 9).

Mosaic Comparisons.   This test measures perceptual speed and accuracy through items that required that small differences be detected between pairs of otherwise identical mosaics, or tile-like patterns. A deliberately speeded test, it has three separately timed sections consisting of increasingly more complex mosaic patterns. Mosaic Comparisons, a test in the CGP battery, represented another of the fundamental measures used in many studies of aptitudes among minority groups. Tests like this that represent the spatial/perceptual domain were selected for the 1972 battery to allow minority students an opportunity to perform better than on other cognitive instruments.

Picture-Number.   This test of associative memory consists of a series of drawings of familiar objects, each paired with a number. The student, after studying the picture-number pairs, is asked to recall the number associated with each object. This test appeared in both the CGP and Project Access batteries.

The inclusion of the Picture-Number Test represented acknowledgment of a line of research that suggested that minority populations have relatively higher mean scores in associative memory than in other types of ability (Jensen, 1968; Rohwer, Linch, Levin, & Suzuki, 1968; Semler & Iscoe, 1963).

Results from item and test analysis conducted in 1973 indicate that the 1972 test battery had quite satisfactory test characteristics. Comparison of the performance of White and Black students showed the White means to be uniformly higher by about 1 standard deviation, except on Picture-Number on which the discrepancy was .7 standard deviation. These results and a number of studies supporting the predictive validity of these measures are described in Hilton and Rhett (1973).

The sequential order of the tests was chosen because it interspersed the three more conventional and the three more novel tests, an arrangement that provides interest and motivation for the examinees. Vocabulary was chosen for the first position because of the inherent simplicity of this test's format and directions. At the outset, it was believed that the Vocabulary Test should build the confidence of the students in their capability to perform well. Because it is quite speeded, Mosaic Comparisons was placed last to prevent any anxiety that might be engendered by this speededness from persisting in later test sections.

The 1980 Tests

In the spring of 1978, ETS was given the contract to "revise" the 1972 test battery so as to make the battery suitable for administration to two new cohorts of high school students, namely, the cohorts that became known as the 1980 HS&B Seniors and the 1980 HS&B Sophomores. The expectation of NCES was that some of the items in the 1972 test battery and possibly some of the tests would need to be replaced. The Work Statement transmitted to ETS stressed that it was of the utmost importance that scores be obtainable from the revised instrument(s) that would be statistically comparable to scores on the 1972 battery.

In accordance with this charge, ETS, after weighing the pros and cons of a range of alternative solutions to the increasingly complex requirements of the cognitive tests, submitted a test plan to NCES (Donlon, Hilton, & Schrader, 1978). This plan recommended that the Letter Groups, Picture-Number, and Mosaic Comparisons tests be dropped—primarily because a survey of users of the 1972 public release tape and of the research literature indicated that the tests had been little used—and that two tests be added to the batteries for Grade 10 and Grade 12 (Science, and Career and Occupational Development) and in addition that a spatial relations test (Surface Development) be added to the Grade 10 battery and Abstract Reasoning to the Grade 12 battery.

These recommendations were accepted by NCES, and the revised batteries were field tested by NORC, with ETS conducting the test analyses (Hilton & Schrader, 1980b). When, however, the results were submitted to the National Planning Committee for "High School and Beyond"[2],

---

[2]The members of the National Planning Committee were Robert F. Boruch, Bruce K. Eckland, Barbara Heyns, David S. Mundel, Robert C. Nichols, Ellis B. Page (Chair), Sally B. Pancrazio, and David E. Wiley. Edith M. Huddleston, NCES, was the original Project Officer for "High School and Beyond."

the design of the batteries was challenged. As described in some detail elsewhere (Heyns & Hilton, 1982), the Committee recommended to NCES that:

> the draft batteries be altered substantially to allow for the measurement of school effects and cognitive change in a longitudinal framework. The concerns of the Committee were twofold: First, conventional measures of basic cognitive skills are not designed to assess patterns of change over time, and there was strong feeling that the preliminary batteries would not be sufficiently sensitive to cognitive growth to allow analysts to detect differential effects among students (Haertel & Wiley, 1978). Second, the Committee recommended including items that would be valid measures of the skills or material a student might encounter in specific high school classes. (p. 91)

Accordingly, after considerable discussion and consultation, the batteries were revised to, in brief, make the 1980 senior tests primarily a vehicle for measuring cross-sectional change from 1972 to 1980 and the 1980 sophomore tests a baseline for the measurement of longitudinal change from 1980 to 1982. The final form of the tests is described in the first section of this chapter. This form is the result of a complex sequence of decisions and represents a compromise between several competing motivations: to preserve comparability with the 1972 battery but to introduce new measures more sensitive to school achievement; to maximize validity but to minimize testing time; to achieve a common scale for the sophomore and senior tests but to target measurement at each level.

Whether each of the changes made was justified remains to be seen. The results of the item and test analysis are described in the following section.

PRELIMINARY ANALYSIS OF DATA

Examination of Field Administrators' Reports

As a first step in the psychometric analysis of the test batteries, the ETS staff obtained from NORC copies of the reports by the NORC field staff who supervised the administration of student questionnaires and the test batteries in each participating high school.[3] Approximately 2,000 field supervisors' reports, covering the 1980 sophomore and senior adminis-

---

[3]We are indebted to Calvin Jones, NORC, for his able assistance in making these data available.

trations, the 1982 senior administrations, and various special administrations conducted for transfer students and dropouts, were received from
NORC. The ETS staff examined these one by one to identify those that
cited any problems that might have affected the test scores. A total of
97 reports included remarks suggesting that there may have been events
and conditions that might have reduced the validity of the test results
(see Table 9.3).

Practically none of the reports indicated unequivocally that the answer
sheets for a particular high school should be rejected. Eighteen of the
supervisors reported incidences such as bomb scares (2), typhoon warn-
ings (1), and shootings—of a teacher and three students on the morning
of the data collection (1). A number of schools had fire drills during the
data collection (typically, they did not say whether it was during the test
administration). Twenty-seven schools reported that the data collection
was conducted in a cafeteria or an auditorium or a library where students
were constantly moving in and out or were noisy or that the band was
playing in the next room or outside, or that the PA system was constantly
blaring, or that some "kids were making a ruckus in the back of the
room." Ten supervisors volunteered the information that the seniors and
the sophomores were surveyed in the same room at the same time.

The results of this examination of field supervisors' reports were carefully considered by the project staff in consultation with other senior staff
experienced in the effect of testing conditions on student performance.

TABLE 9.3
Summary of Unusual Circumstances Reported[a]

| | 1980 Sophmores and Seniors | 1982 | | |
		In School	Out of School	Total
Confusion, chaos, bomb scare, fire alarm, burglar alarm, shootings, and tornado alert	9	7	2	18
Noise, distractions, and interruptions	10	6	2	18
Lack of cooperation, students unruly, and hostility	7	0	2	9
Sophomores and seniors together	10	–	–	10
Drug usage in room	1	–	1	2
Problems judged to be inconsequential	22	16	2	40
Total	59	29	10	97

[a]The 97 reports summarized here were screened from approximately 2,000 reports
received from NORC.

Two factors precluded certain corrective steps that might be taken. The first was that the ETS staff could not link the supervisors' reports to data on the public release data tape without making elaborate arrangements to protect the privacy of the schools. The second was the absence of any kind of objective rules by which to reject the data from a particular school. For example, how distracting is a bomb scare in comparison to a band rehearsal next door? In view of these factors and the knowledge that editing of the data by other means would be considered, it was decided not to pursue the rejection of data on the basis of the supervisors' reports.

Editing of the Test Data

Prior use of the HS&B data by ETS staff in various studies has indicated that, in general, the public release file is relatively free of data processing errors and that the students' questionnaire responses and test responses by-and-large seem to have validity (see, e.g., Hilton, Schrader, & Beaton, 1983). The test scores appear to correlate with other test scores about as one would expect of valid measures of student ability. For two reasons, however, it was deemed possible that the test data might—for a small fraction of the total cases—be defective. The first reason was based on the field supervisors' reports. As discussed earlier, these reports indicated that, in some small subset of the participating high schools, testing conditions and procedures may have departed sufficiently from the usual conditions and procedures to raise doubt about the appropriateness of using the data from these schools in a definitive study of test score changes from 1972 to 1980 and from 1980 to 1982.

The second reason was based on a preliminary analysis of the test score changes from 1972 to 1980 by Beaton and Hilton (unpublished). These results indicated that the mean scores for the seniors from 1972 to 1980 decreased somewhat in Reading and Vocabulary but increased dramatically for Picture-Number and Mosaic Comparisons.

Several possible explanations can be offered for the large gains, including the possibility that some intervening influence (e.g., television, video games) has contributed to the development of new skills. Before such an interpretation is considered, however, an alternative explanation for the large score gain needed to be considered; this concerned the nature of the test administration and the unique attributes of the tests that showed large gains. As described earlier in this chapter, the Picture-Number test, designed to measure short-term memory, requires that the test taker study pairs of pictures and numbers, and not turn back to them after turning the page to the section where only pictures are given. Making sure that the test takers do not turn the page back requires close supervision. Lapses in the supervision could result in inflated scores.

The Mosaic Comparisons test also requires conscientious supervision, because it is a highly speeded test. If time limits are not strictly observed, inflated scores will result from this test also.

Examining the test data for defective scores would be highly desirable in any case because of their important role in the study. Such an examination was done by Beaton, Hilton, and Schrader in 1980 when data from Project TALENT and the 1972 NLS cohort were used to examine the SAT score decline from 1960 to 1972 (Beaton, Hilton, & Schrader, 1977).

The objective of the editing was to maximize the rejection of defective scores and minimize the rejection of nondefective scores. The problem is that one cannot assume that the scores on all the tests given within a particular school are defective simply because the scores on a particular test are seriously inconsistent. The Mathematics test, for example, may have been administered with care, and the Mosaic Comparisons test may have been carelessly timed. If, however, the results of other editing checks point to a particular set of data as defective, then we would accept the hypothesis. Thus, we pursued a conservative multiple criterion approach to the editing. In order to make the 1972 senior test data comparable to the 1980 senior data, we decided to edit the 1972 data using similar procedures to those used for the 1980 data.

At the school level, the problem was to identify schools with mean test scores having unusually large deviations from predictions based on other test scores. We also anticipated that examination of the students' responses to Questions About the Tests might also raise questions about the validity of the responses for a particular school. School-by-school analysis of the questions relating to distractions might identify schools in which standard testing conditions were not maintained.

At the individual level, the problem was to identify students whose test performance in general or whose performance on a particular test was seriously discrepant from what would be predicted on the basis of other student data. For example, students whose performance may have deteriorated toward the end of the test battery (through fatigue or some disturbing condition or influence) could be identified by predicting expected performance on the basis of performance on the earlier tests in the battery.

In the following paragraphs, the results of a fairly large number of editing studies are briefly summarized.

1. First-Half Mean Versus Second-Half Mean. If the administration of a particular test was mis-timed, then the mean score on the items in the last half of the test should deviate from what would be predicted on the basis of performance on the first half of the test. Accordingly, for

TABLE 9.4
Mean Scores and Correlation Coefficients (r) Between First and
Second Halves of Test Items for 1972 and 1980 Seniors

	1972			1980		
	$\bar{x}$		r	$\bar{x}$		r
Test	1st half	2nd half		1st half	2nd half	
Vocabulary	4.1	1.9	.82	3.7	1.8	.81
Reading	5.9	3.4	.83	5.3	3.1	.87
Math, Common	3.8	2.3	.85	3.6	2.0	.87
Picture-Number	4.3	4.2	.74	5.0	5.8	.91
Mosaic Comparisons 1	15.0	6.7	.25	15.2	11.2	.36
Mosaic Comparisons 2	11.9	4.0	.31	11.7	6.3	.53

each test common to both the 1972 and the 1980 batteries, the mean
scores of each school on the second half of each test were regressed on
the mean scores on the first half of the test. The results, shown in Table
9.4, indicate that for most of the tests the first half and the second half
were highly correlated and that the results for 1972 were generally similar
to the results for 1980. The three exceptions were the higher means scores
in 1980 on the second halves of the Picture-Number Test and Parts 1 and
2 of the Mosaic Comparisons Test. However, the more important
observation for editing purposes was that there were very few school
means that one would regard as outliers. Figures 9.3 and 9.4, for
Vocabulary and Mosaic Comparisons, Part 2, are typical.

2. First-Half Mean Versus Second-Half Attempts.

As the second
possible basis for editing, the regression of mean scores on the first half
of each test on the mean number of items attempted in the second half

TABLE 9.5
Mean Scores and Correlation Coefficients (r) Between Number of Attempts
in First Half of Items and Number of Attempts in Second Half

	1972			1980		
	$\bar{x}$		r	$\bar{x}$		r
Test	1st half	No. of attempts		1st half	No. of attempts	
Vocabulary	4.1	6.8	.23	3.7	7.3	.04
Reading	5.9	9.2	.37	5.3	9.6	.36
Math, Common	3.8	5.7	.29	3.6	5.9	.29
Picture-Number	4.3	5.1	.62	5.0	7.1	.76
Mosaic Comparisons 1	15.0	7.5	.12	15.2	12.7	.24
Mosaic Comparisons 2	11.9	4.7	.07	11.7	7.7	.29

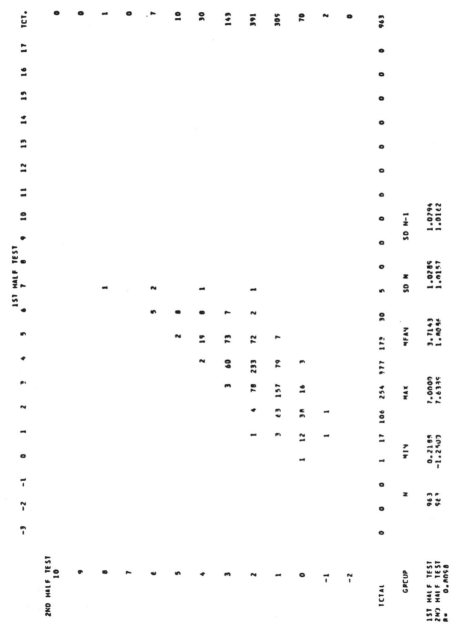

FIG. 9.3. Bivariate distribution of school means on first half and second half of Vocabulary test for 1980 seniors.

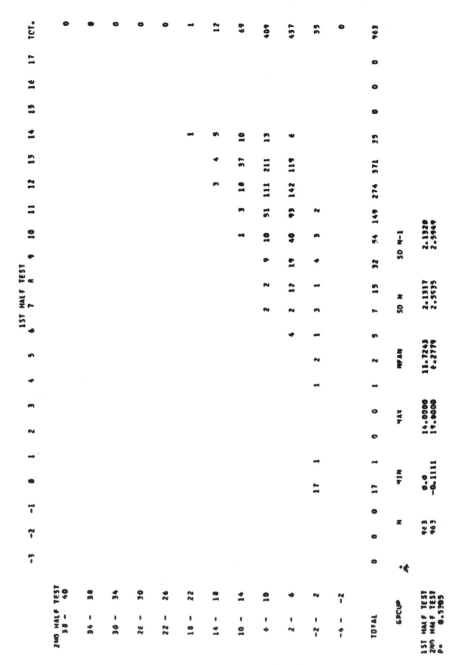

FIG. 9.4. Bivariate distribution of school means on first half and second half of Mosaic Comparisons test, Part 2, for 1980 seniors.

of each test was examined. As shown in Table 9.5, the results indicated that the 1980 sample attempted more items, especially on the Picture-Number and the Mosaic Comparisons Tests but, again, examination of the scatter plots showed relatively few outliers.

3. Mean SAT Scores Versus Second-Half Means.   To investigate whether scores on an independently administered test would provide a basis for detecting outliers, mean scores were computed for those students within each school who took the SAT, and then—for those schools with 10 or more SAT takers—regressions similar to the preceding regressions were computed.[4] The correlations between SAT total and the 1972 and 1980 second-half means ranged from .21 for Picture-Number to .86 for Mathematics, but examination of the residuals from prediction revealed no more than one would expect by chance. Repeating the analysis for SAT-Verbal scores did not appreciably change the results.

4. Distraction Scores.   For the 1980 sample only, it was possible to construct a scale from those items in the Questions About the Tests that seemed to reflect the extent to which each test taker may have been distracted during the test administration. However, this scale score was correlated only .13 with the total score on the Mosaic Comparisons Test—the test that was presumed to be most susceptible to distractions. This low correlation was judged to be insufficient as a basis for editing. Furthermore, examination of the mean test scores for schools in the top tenth percentile with respect to mean Distraction scores revealed no particular pattern of results.

1980 Sophomore and 1982 Senior Data.   In view of the results obtained from the examination of the 1972 and the 1980 senior data, we concluded that similar examination of the 1980 sophomore and 1982 senior test results was not necessary and, in addition, that examination of individual data would not be cost-effective.

Summary

With two exceptions, the various analyses conducted revealed no clear evidence of irregularities. The exceptions are the relatively high mean scores and mean number of attempts on the Picture-Number and Mosaic Comparisons Tests. The high scores on the highly speeded Mosaic Comparisons Test could be attributable to the format change noted in the

---

[4]SAT scores were retrieved for the 1980 seniors as part of a study conducted at ETS for the U. S. Army Recruiting Command. See chapter 5 of this volume.

section on differences in administration, namely, the change from a separate answer sheet to answering within the test booklet next to the stem
of the item. In the absence of other evidence, we will assume that this
is the case.

The explanation of the relatively high scores on the Picture-Number
Test is less clear. Of the several possibilities that have been mentioned,
two seem like the most relevant factors: the likelihood that the 1980
administration was not as closely supervised as the 1972 administration
and the fact that substantially larger numbers of students were involved
in 1980. In any case, in view of the differences, it is recommended that
the Mosaic Comparisons Test and the Picture-Number Test not be used
for cross-sectional comparisons between the 1972 and 1980 cohorts.

ACKNOWLEDGMENT

This chapter is an excerpt from a report entitled "Psychometric Analysis
of the NLS and the High School and Beyond Test Batteries" submitted
to the National Center for Education Statistics as part of Contract
300-83-0247 (Rock et al, 1985).

APPENDIX

NATIONAL LONGITUDINAL STUDY OF THE HIGH SCHOOL CLASS OF 1972

Student Test Book

'72

Prepared for the
UNITED STATES OFFICE OF EDUCATION
BY EDUCATIONAL TESTING SERVICE □ PRINCETON, NEW JERSEY
SPRING 1972

GENERAL DIRECTIONS

This test has six sections. Some sections have more than one part. During the time allowed for each section or part, you are to work only on it. The time limit for each section or separately timed part is printed at the beginning of each section or part, and the supervisor will tell you when to begin and when to stop. If you finish a section or part before time is called, go back and check your work on that section or part only.

Your score on each section will be the number of correct answers minus a percentage of the number of incorrect answers. Therefore, it will not be to your advantage to guess unless you are able to eliminate one or more of the answer choices.

Mark all of your answers on the separate answer sheet, as no credit will be given for anything written in the test book. Make your marks on the answer sheet heavy and black, as in the examples below.

Sample Answers

Be sure that the entire box is blackened.

If you wish to change an answer, erase your first mark completely.

CONTENTS OF TEST BOOK

Section 1	Vocabulary	5 minutes
Section 2	Picture-Number (Two parts of 5 minutes each)	10 minutes
Section 3	Reading	15 minutes
Section 4	Letter Groups	15 minutes
Section 5	Mathematics	15 minutes
Section 6	Mosaic Comparisons (Three parts of 3 minutes each)	9 minutes

Total   69 minutes

SECTION 1

VOCABULARY

Time—5 minutes

-3-**1**

Directions: Each of the questions below consists of one word followed by five words or phrases. You are to select the one word or phrase whose meaning is closest to that of the word in capital letters.

Sample Question

CHILLY :

(A) lazy
(B) nice
(C) dry
(D) cold
(E) sunny

Sample Answer

[A] [B] [C] ■ [E]

In order to find the correct answer you look at the word chilly and then look for a word below it that has the same or almost the same meaning. When you do this, you see that cold is the answer because cold is closest in meaning to the word chilly.

SECTION 2

PICTURE—NUMBER

-5-**2**

Directions: This is a test of your ability to remember picture-number combinations. The section has two parts. In each part you will study a page of fifteen pictures with numbers. On a study page the picture-number pairs will look like this:

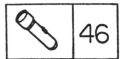  

After studying the page showing both pictures and numbers, you will be told to turn to a page showing the pictures in a different order.

On your answer sheet there are ten boxes with numbers above them for each question. One of the numbers will be the number that goes with the picture. You are to blacken the box with that number above it.

Examples:

1.
| 12 | 24 | 31 | 44 | 51 | | 57 | 65 | 73 | 77 | 92 |
| □ | □ | □ | □ | □ | | □ | □ | ■ | □ | □ |

2.
| 15 | 27 | 34 | 41 | 46 | | 55 | 62 | 75 | 82 | 89 |
| □ | □ | ■ | □ | □ | | □ | □ | □ | □ | □ |

3.
| 13 | 19 | 28 | 34 | 46 | | 58 | 62 | 67 | 73 | 97 |
| □ | □ | □ | □ | ■ | | □ | □ | □ | □ | □ |

The number that goes with the picture of a telephone is 73, so for example 1 you would blacken the box with 73 above it. For example 2 you would blacken the box with 34 above it. For example 3 you would blacken the box with 46 above it.

DO NOT TURN THIS PAGE UNTIL YOU ARE TOLD TO DO SO.

SECTION 3
READING
Time— 15 minutes

Directions: Each passage is followed by questions based on its content. After reading a passage, choose the best answer to each question and blacken the corresponding space on the answer sheet. Answer all questions following a passage on the basis of what is <u>stated</u> or <u>implied</u> in that passage.

(The items consisted of reading passages of approximately 100 words followed by 3, 4, or 5 items each of which had 5 options)

SECTION 4
LETTER GROUPS

Directions: Each question in this section consists of five groups of letters with four letters in each group. Four of the groups have a characteristic in common which the fifth group does not have. Decide which group is different, and blacken the space on the answer sheet that corresponds to the position (A, B, C, D, or E) of your choice.

Note: The common characteristic will not be based on the sounds of groups of letters, the shapes of letters, or whether letter combinations form words or parts of words.

Sample Questions						Sample Answers
A	**B**	**C**	**D**	**E**		
1. NOPQ	DEFL	ABCD	HIJK	UVWX	1.	Ⓐ ■ Ⓒ Ⓓ Ⓔ
2. NLIK	PLIK	QLIK	THIK	VLIK	2.	Ⓐ Ⓑ Ⓒ ■ Ⓔ

In sample question 1, the letters in four of the groups are in consecutive alphabetical order, but group DEFL in column B is not; so space B has been marked in the sample answers. In sample question 2, four of the groups contain the letter L. Letter group THIK in column D is the group that is different, so space D has been marked in the sample answers.

You will have 15 minutes to work on this section.

DO NOT TURN THIS PAGE UNTIL YOU ARE TOLD TO DO SO.

SECTION 5

MATHEMATICS

Directions: Each problem in this section consists of two quantities, one placed in Column A and one in Column B. You are to compare the two quantities and on the answer sheet blacken space

    A if the quantity in Column A is greater;
    B if the quantity in Column B is greater;
    C if the two quantities are equal;
    D if the size relationship cannot be determined from the information given.

	Sample Questions		Sample Answers
	Column A	Column B	
Example 1.	20 per cent of 10	10 per cent of 20	1. A B ■ D
Example 2.	6 × 6	12 + 12	2. ■ B C D

Answer C is marked in Example 1 since the quantity in Column A is equal to the quantity in Column B. Answer A is marked for Example 2 since the quantity in Column A is greater than the quantity in Column B.

You will have 15 minutes to work on this section.

DO NOT TURN THIS PAGE UNTIL YOU ARE TOLD TO DO SO.

SECTION 6

MOSAIC COMPARISONS

<u>Directions</u>: This test consists of pairs of mosaics, that is, patterns of squares like those found on tiled floors or walls. Each mosaic is made up of a number of partially shaded squares. The mosaics in each pair are identical except for one square which differs in shading. The vertical columns of both mosaics are labeled A to C, A to D, or A to E according to the number of columns in the mosaic. Your task will be to locate, for each pair of mosaics, the column that contains the single square which is shaded differently. Then mark the space on your separate answer sheet that corresponds to the letter at the head of that column.

Sample Question   Sample Answer

1.

1.

In sample question 1, the right-hand and left-hand mosaics are identical except for the center square of column B, so answer space B is blackened in the sample answer.

Sample Questions   Sample Answers

2.   3.

2. A B C ■

3. ■ B C D E

In sample question 2, the bottom square in column D is the one that is different, so answer space D is blackened in the sample answers. In sample question 3, the second square in column A is the one that is different, so answer space A is blackened in the sample answers.

There are three parts to this test. All the mosaics in a single part are the same size. During the three minutes allowed for each part, you are to work on that part only. Do not move ahead to the next part until you are told to do so. Remember only one square is different for each pair of mosaics.

DO NOT TURN THIS PAGE UNTIL YOU ARE TOLD TO DO SO.

A-2
(Note: examples are given only of
item types not used in the 1972
test battery)

SENIOR TEST BOOKLET

High School and Beyond is sponsored by the National Center for Education Statistics, an agency of the United States Department of Education.

There are several kinds of tests in this booklet. Each test is timed and has its own instructions. You will be given time to read the instructions before you begin work on the test.

You've probably taken tests like these before, but this time no one in your school will see your test results. The important thing about these tests is that you will be representing thousands of other students like yourself. Your individual answers will be regarded as strictly confidential. They will be combined with answers from other students and will never be identified as yours. Your participation is voluntary.

STOP! DO NOT OPEN THIS BOOKLET
UNTIL YOU ARE TOLD TO DO SO.

STATE:

SCHOOL NO:

STUDENT NO:

Prepared for the National
Center for Education
Statistics by the
Educational Testing Service
NCES Form 2409-12

GENERAL DIRECTIONS
12th Grade

This test has seven sections, and two sections have two parts. During the time allowed for each section or part, you are to work only on it. The time limit for each section or part is printed at the beginning of the section or part and the supervisor will tell you when to begin and when to stop. If you finish before time is called, go back and check your work on that section or part only.

Your score on each section except Sections 6 and 7 will be the number of correct answers minus a percentage of the number of incorrect answers. Therefore, on Sections 1 through 5 it will not be to your advantage to guess unless you are able to eliminate one or more of the answer choices.

Mark all of your answers by filling in the oval next to the appropriate answer.

Use only the lead pencil you have been given.

Make heavy black marks inside the ovals.

Be sure that the <u>entire</u> oval is blackened.

If you wish to change an answer, erase your first mark completely.

This kind of mark will work:
Ⓐ Ⓑ ● Ⓓ

These marks will NOT work:
Ⓐ Ⓑ Ⓒ ●

CONTENTS OF TEST BOOK

Section 1	Vocabulary	
	Part 1	5 minutes
	Part 2	4 minutes
Section 2	Reading	15 minutes
Section 3	Mathematics	
	Part 1	15 minutes
	Part 2	4 minutes
Section 4	Picture-Number	5 minutes
Section 5	Mosaic Comparisons	
	Part 1	8 minutes
	Part 2	8 minutes
Section 6	Visualization in Three Dimensions	9 minutes
Section 7	Questions About Testing	5 minutes

SECTION 6
VISUALIZATION IN THREE DIMENSIONS
Time—9 minutes

<u>Directions</u>: Each problem in this test has a drawing of a flat piece of metal at the left. At the right are shown five objects, only one of which might be made by folding the flat piece of metal along the dotted line. You are to pick out the one of these five objects which shows just how the piece of flat metal will look when it is folded at the dotted lines. When it is folded, no piece of metal overlaps any other piece, or is enclosed inside the object. On this test your score will be the number of correct answers.

Now look at example 1 below.

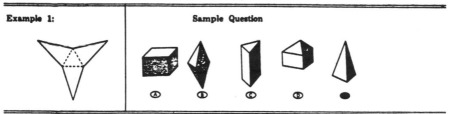

Example 1:   Sample Question

Of the five objects shown, only E could be made from the flat piece shown at the left by folding it at each of the dotted lines. E shows how the flat piece would look after being folded. Therefore, oval E would be marked.

Remember, all folds are indicated by dotted lines; the solid lines show the cuts in the piece, and parts are not folded inside of other parts of any objects (in other words, there is no overlapping).

DO NOT TURN THIS PAGE UNTIL YOU ARE TOLD TO DO SO.

SECTION 7
QUESTIONS ABOUT THE TESTS
Time—5 minutes

Now that you have completed the tests, we would appreciate your telling us how you felt about taking them. The information you fill in will help us to understand better how tests should or should not be used in high schools. We would like to know your own views and reactions; your responses will not affect your test scores in any way and will be treated as confidential information.

1. Today you have taken six tests that were intended to measure different abilities or areas of knowledge. These areas are:

   a. Vocabulary   d. Picture-Number
   b. Reading   e. Mosaic Comparisons
   c. Mathematics   f. Visualization in Three Dimensions

   How important do you think each of these six abilities will be to you in your own future? For each test in the list below, please mark oval A, B, C, or D. Make one mark for each test.

	Of little importance	Fairly important	Very important	Don't know
Vocabulary and Reading Tests	Ⓐ	Ⓑ	Ⓒ	Ⓓ
Mathematics Test	Ⓐ	Ⓑ	Ⓒ	Ⓓ
Picture-Number, Mosaic Comparisons, and Visualization in Three Dimensions	Ⓐ	Ⓑ	Ⓒ	Ⓓ

2. How concerned were you about doing very well on these tests? Mark one.

   Ⓐ Not concerned at all
   Ⓑ Only slightly concerned
   Ⓒ Somewhat concerned
   Ⓓ Very concerned

3. How much did you enjoy taking the tests? Mark one.

   Ⓐ Not at all
   Ⓑ Only to a limited degree
   Ⓒ Somewhat
   Ⓓ A great deal

4. On the whole, how well do you think your scores on the six tests will show your real ability? Mark one.

   Ⓐ My real ability is probably higher than my scores will show.
   Ⓑ My scores will probably be about right.
   Ⓒ My real ability is probably lower than my scores will show.

GO ON TO THE NEXT PAGE.

5. How did you feel while you were taking the tests? Please mark YES or NO after each word or phrase.

		YES	NO
a.	Calm	O	O
b.	Interested in the tests	O	O
c.	Distracted by things going on in the room	O	O
d.	Afraid of not doing well	O	O
e.	Bored	O	O
f.	Eager to do my very best	O	O
g.	Angry or annoyed	O	O
h.	Under a lot of pressure	O	O
i.	Involved in taking the tests	O	O
j.	Under a lot of strain to do well	O	O
k.	Able to concentrate well on the tests	O	O
l.	Uneasy	O	O
m.	Uncomfortable	O	O
n.	Distracted by noises outside	O	O
o.	Confident in myself	O	O
p.	Rather tired	O	O
q.	Feeling that the tests don't matter much	O	O
r.	Often thinking about something else	O	O
s.	Very tense	O	O
t.	Nervous or jittery	O	O

6. If you would like to add any comments or explain any of your answers to these questions about testing, please use the space below:

SOPHOMORE TEST BOOKLET

High School and Beyond is sponsored by the National Center for Education Statistics, an agency of the United States Department of Education.

There are several kinds of tests in this booklet. Each test is timed and has its own instructions. You will be given time to read the instructions before you begin work on the test.

You've probably taken tests like these before, but this time no one in your school will see your test results. The important thing about these tests is that you will be representing thousands of other students like yourself. Your individual answers will be regarded as strictly confidential. They will be combined with answers from other students and will never be identified as yours. Your participation is voluntary.

STOP! DO NOT OPEN THIS BOOKLET
UNTIL YOU ARE TOLD TO DO SO.

STATE:

SCHOOL NO:

STUDENT NO:

Prepared for the National
Center for Education
Statistics by the
Educational Testing Service
NCES Form 2409-11

GENERAL DIRECTIONS
10th Grade

This test has six sections, and one section has two parts. During the time allowed for each section or part, you are to work only on it. The time limit for each section or part is printed at the beginning of the section or part, and the supervisor will tell you when to begin and when to stop. If you finish a section or part before time is called, go back and check your work on that section or part only.

Your score on each section will be the number of correct answers minus a percentage of the number of incorrect answers. Therefore, it will not be to your advantage to guess unless you are able to eliminate one or more of the answer choices.

Answer each question by marking one of the answer ovals as no credit will be given for anything written elsewhere in the test book.

Use only the lead pencil you have been given.

Make heavy black marks inside the ovals.

Be sure that the entire oval is blackened.

If you wish to change an answer, erase your first mark completely.

This kind of mark will work:

These marks will NOT work:

CONTENTS OF TEST BOOK

Section 1	Vocabulary	7 minutes
Section 2	Reading	15 minutes
Section 3	Mathematics	
	Part 1	16 minutes
	Part 2	5 minutes
Section 4	Science	10 minutes
Section 5	Writing	10 minutes
Section 6	Civics Education	5 minutes

(Note: In the following pages, examples
are given only of item types not used
in the 1972 or 1980 tests)

SECTION 4
SCIENCE
Time—10 minutes
20 Questions

DIRECTIONS: Carefully read each question and any material that relates to it. Then, choose the best answer and blacken the corresponding oval.

(No sample was given. Actual items have five options.)

DO NOT TURN THIS PAGE UNTIL YOU ARE TOLD TO DO SO.

—

SECTION 5
WRITING
Time—10 minutes
17 Questions

Directions Carefully read each question and any material that relates to it. Then, choose the best answer and blacken the corresponding oval.

Sample Question

For Example Question find the error in punctuation or capitalization. There is only one error.

Example. All of the letters magazines, and newspapers on his desk were dated
                           A   B
          July 18, 1969.
          C D

The correct answer to this question is A because a comma should be placed after "letters."

DO NOT TURN THIS PAGE UNTIL YOU ARE TOLD TO DO SO.

SECTION 6
CIVICS EDUCATION
Time—5 minutes
10 Questions

Directions: Carefully read each question and any material that relates to it. Then, choose the best answer and blacken the corresponding oval.

(No example was given.   Actual items have four options.)

DO NOT TURN THIS PAGE UNTIL YOU ARE TOLD TO DO SO.

CHAPTER TEN

Pooling Results from Two Cohorts Taking Similar Tests, Part II: Factor Structure and IRT Equating

Donald A. Rock
Educational Testing Service

In the preceding chapter, we introduced the problem of measuring trends (or, in Schaie's language, time lag differences) from tests administered to two different cohorts 8 years apart. In that chapter, we examined the comparability of the content and format of the tests and the administration of the tests. In this chapter, we ask whether there is empirical evidence that the tests are measuring the same dimensions, as reflected in the factor structure of the tests, and we then describe how the scores from the tests were put on a common scale by means of Item Response Theory. A test may measure one construct for one group and a second construct for another, the classic example being a measure involving algebraic word problems. For students whose first language is the same as the language of the test items, the test may be a test of problem-solving skill, but for students handicapped in that language the test may be a measure of language proficiency. Most readers will want to at least skim the previous chapter in order to be familiar with the tests in question and the timing of the administrations.

—*Thomas L. Hilton*

Before the results from two test administrations are used to measure change, it is appropriate to inquire about what the tests are and are not measuring, and whether what is measured is the same across cohort groups and selected subpopulations within cohorts. Logic might dictate that one first define what the tests measure and then evaluate their precision. The order is reversed here because: (a) reliability estimates are going to be needed for the interpretation of the factor analytic results, and (b) we have chosen to "mark" our potential factors with reliable parcels or clusters of items that, in theory, share common content.[1] Independent estimates of coefficient alpha provide some empirical evidence for any subsequent interpretation of these subtests as separate homogeneous entities. With the exception of the biology parcel, the remaining parcels have reliabilities that are in the "ball park" for the number of items included in the parcel. This finding suggests that each of the parcels is relatively internally consistent and, as a consequence, can be assumed to be a measure of a reasonably homogeneous content area. Content areas within a particular discipline, such as the content parcels within the science area, can then be hypothesized as measures or indicators of a science construct or factor in a confirmatory factor analytic solution.

FACTOR STRUCTURE OF THE TESTS

Past empirical and theoretical studies suggest that any one of three possible factor models might fit the present achievement data. The simplest model would be a single underlying achievement factor that would adequately explain the reliable variance within each parcel. If such a model was consistent with the data, one would have to conclude that all parcels were measures of a general knowledge factor. Another model might be a simple two-factor model where each parcel is a different combination of, say, a verbal and quantitative factor. This model is consistent with the usual findings, where verbal and quantitative measures are factor analyzed, and is also similar to the Heyns and Hilton (1982) results with HS&B test data (see previous chapter). A third alternative would be a multiple-factor model where each content area (e.g., science, reading, mathematics, etc.) would define separate but correlated achievement factors. A theoretical model consistent with such a result would be a general knowledge factor that would cut across each discipline area and, in addition, have separate group factors for each discipline area. The general factor would generate or underlie the correlations among the group factors.

All factor analysis computations were based on the weighted data. Two variants of the single-factor model are estimated first. Table 10.1 presents both the percentage of common variance, and the percentage of reliable variance explained by a single-factor model, and then by the two-factor model. The first column, labeled *Common Factor Solution,* shows the

---

[1]In a step in the investigation that is not described in either this or the previous chapter, test development specialists were asked to examine the items in each test and to form subtests based on groups of items showing common content.

TABLE 10.1
Percent of Variance Explained by Selected Factor Analysis Solutions

Populations	Common-Factor Solution[a] — One Factor	Psychometric Solution[b] — One-Factor Solution	Psychometric Solution[b] — Two-Factor Solution
1972 Seniors	100%	77%	88%
1980 Seniors	100%	79%	90%
1980 Sophomores	97%	81%	86%
1982 Seniors	98%	83%	87%

[a]Principal axes with R^2 on main diagonal
[b]Maximum likelihood solution showing percent of reliable variance

percentage of common variance explained by the first principal axes of the correlation matrix with commonalities on the main diagonal. The commonalities were estimated using the multiple correlation squared. Inspection of Table 10.1 indicates that the first factor explains from 97% to 100% of the common variance, depending on cohort group. Using any of the traditional criteria for determining the number of factors, one would be led to believe that all parcels were simply different methods of measuring a single general knowledge factor. Although Anastasi (1982) has argued that the general knowledge factor increases in size with increases in population heterogeneity, there appears to be more at work here than population heterogeneity.

TABLE 10.2
Two-Factor Total Sample Cross-Sectional Solution for 1972 and 1980
(in parentheses) Seniors

Variable	Factor 1[a]		Factor 2[a]		Internal Consistency Reliabilities		Reliable Unexplained Variances	
Vocabulary odd	82	(84)	0	(0)	66	(69)	1	(0)
Vocabulary even	76	(83)	0	(0)	63	(71)	5	(2)
Reading passage 1	44	(43)	21	(24)	53	(56)	17	(17)
Reading passage 2	43	(41)	28	(30)	52	(53)	9	(9)
Reading passage 3	49	(45)	18	(23)	47	(47)	9	(7)
Reading passage 4	50	(51)	9	(7)	42	(40)	10	(9)
Reading passage 5	43	(39)	23	(18)	54	(44)	17	(15)
Mathematics odd	0	(0)	89	(85)	77	(73)	0	(1)
Mathematics even	0	(0)	88	(88)	75	(76)	0	(0)

RMS = .026 (.027)
Percentage of Reliable Variance . . . 87.8 (90.0)
GFI = 978 (976)
$r_{F_1 F_2}$ = .69 (.72)
[a]Decimal points have been omitted.

The traditional factor analytic approach to explaining *common* achievement test variance, rather than *reliable* test variance, seems to be partially responsible for this unexpected factor space degeneration. The columns under the label *Psychometric Solution* show the percent of reliable variance explained by a maximum likelihood solution (MLH) for the single-factor (Model 1) and the two-factor (Model 2) models. The situation improves considerably with a single general factor explaining from 77% to 83% of the reliable variance depending on the cohort. The two-factor model explains from 87% to 90% of the reliable variance. These percentages of reliable variance are probably slightly overestimated, because coefficient alpha is generally a lower bound estimate of the test–retest reliability. The results of this partitioning of the reliable variance suggest that the two-factor model would provide a good starting point for the confirmatory factor analysis.

1972–1980 Cross-Sectional Comparison of Factor Patterns

Table 10.2 presents the factor-loading pattern coefficients for the two-factor solution for the NLS 1972 and HS&B 1980 seniors. The factor loadings for HS&B 1980 seniors are shown in parentheses. This is a maximum likelihood (MLH) confirmatory factor analytic solution with parameters estimated by the LISREL VI computer program (Joreskog & Sorbom, 1983). Consistent with the factor analytic results in the literature, a verbal and a math factor were defined by the vocabulary and math subtests. Inspection of the factor loadings in Table 10.2 indicates that the two vocabulary parcels and the two math parcels were constrained to have zero loadings on the math and vocabulary factors, respectively. These constraints served two purposes. First, they defined a relatively "pure" verbal factor and a "pure" math factor. Second, they made the model identified which, in turn, allowed LISREL to find a unique solution to the maximum likelihood equations. The reading parcels were left "free" to load on either the verbal or math factor, under the assumption that some of the reading passages with heavy scientific emphasis might also load on the math factor. In fact, there is some tendency to do just that, as indicated by the second passages and, to a lesser extent, the fifth passage. Both passages had a scientific theme.

The internal consistency reliability estimates are coefficient alphas. The last two columns are the differences between the amount of a variable's variance that can be explained by the underlying verbal and math factors and that variable's reliability. For example, 66% of the observed variance in the odd vocabulary items is true or systematic variance. Of the 66%, all but 1% was explained by the verbal factor. Similarly, in 1972, 53% of the first reading passage variance was true or reliable variance. Only 36% (53 – 17) of this reading passage's variance can be explained by the verbal and math factor. Thus, 32% of the first reading passage's reliable variance (17/53) was not explained by the two-factor model. The two variables that seem to have reliable variance that is not explained by the two-factor model are the first and fifth reading passages. This result is true for both the 1972 and 1980 seniors. The first reading passage has a Black literature orientation, whereas the fifth passage has a scientific theme.

The similarities in the factor structure for both senior classes are much more striking than are any of the differences. In general, the pattern of loadings is almost identical, with slight exceptions where the reliabilities might have differed from one cohort to another.

The factor intercorrelations are about the size that one has come to expect between verbal and math factors.

It should be noted that the factor intercorrelation can be considered to be corrected for attenuation. That is, the correlation between the verbal factor and the math factor is not attenuated by measurement errors.

Although the LISREL program produces standard errors and χ^2s for testing the overall model fit, they are not reported here, because we have chosen to standardize the variables and deal with the correlation matrix for ease of interpretation. The χ^2 tests and standard errors associated with standardized variables do not have their usual meaning. To insure that one would not come to substantively differing conclusions if one factored the variance–covariance matrices (rather than correlations), parallel analyses were run on the variance–covariance matrices.

In lieu of the χ^2 measure of the overall goodness of fit of the model, we provide the root mean square residual (RMS), which is the average correlation among the residuals after fitting the model. The RMSs of .026 and .027 for 1972 and 1980 are sufficiently low to suggest a good fit. LISREL provides one other measure of goodness of fit that, like the RMS, is independent of sample size, and that is the Goodness of Fit Index (GFI). The GFI varies between 0 and 1, where 1 is a perfect fit. The very high GFIs of .978 and .976 suggest very good fits for both the 1972 and 1980 seniors.

These results are very similar to the Heyns and Hilton (1982) results, except that they also included the Picture Number and Mosaic Comparison. They did not, however, deal with separate reading passages. They found that verbal, math, and a third, unnamed factor seemed to be sufficient to explain the intercorrelations among the tests.

The possibility of a third model that might fit better was investigated by examining the correlations among the reading passage residuals to see if there was any possibility of defining a separate reading factor. No systematic pattern of residuals suggesting a common reading factor was found. Evidently, any part of the reliable variance in the reading passages that was not explained by the verbal and math factor was probably due to the content specific nature of the passage.

Comparisons of Factor Patterns
for Sophomore and Senior Cohorts

Table 10.3 presents a two-factor (Model 2) solution for the sophomore subtest scores and another for the same group as seniors. The senior factor loadings are shown in parentheses. The same math–verbal two-factor pattern of constraints on the factor loadings was used for both sopho-

TABLE 10.3
Two-Factor Maximum Likelihood Solution for HS&B Sophomores
and Seniors (in parentheses)

Variable	Factor 1[a]		Factor 2[a]		Internal Consistency Reliabilities		Reliable Unexplained Variances	
Vocabulary odd	77	(81)	0	(0)	69	(75)	9	(10)
Vocabulary even	76	(80)	0	(0)	65	(72)	7	(7)
Reading passage 1	61	(64)	0	(0)	44	(45)	7	(5)
Reading passage 2	57	(63)	0	(0)	38	(47)	5	(7)
Reading passage 3	64	(67)	0	(0)	44	(48)	3	(3)
Reading passage 4	67	(70)	0	(0)	50	(56)	6	(6)
Reading passage 5	53	(60)	0	(0)	37	(46)	8	(10)
Mathematics-algebra	0	(0)	84	(86)	70	(74)	0	(0)
Mathematics-arithmetic	0	(0)	87	(89)	77	(83)	1	(3)
Mathematics-geometry	0	(0)	69	(75)	51	(61)	3	(5)
Science-biology	47	(51)	8	(5)	32	(32)	3	(2)
Science-chemistry	30	(29)	17	(26)	26	(36)	6	(8)
Science-physics	30	(33)	34	(32)	52	(56)	15	(17)
Science-earth science	40	(42)	13	(15)	38	(41)	11	(11)
Science-methodology	60	(68)	10	(5)	46	(51)	0	(0)
Writing-punctuation	35	(46)	30	(21)	62	(64)	23	(21)
Writing-style	63	(74)	13	(3)	74	(78)	19	(19)
Civics-odd	59	(70)	1	(7)	40	(43)	4	(2)
Civics-even	48	(62)	3	(1)	29	(42)	3	(3)

Factor Intercorrelations

			F1	F2		
RMS 026	(.027)	F_1	1		Percentage of Reliable	
GFI 963	(.953)	F_2	827(852)	1	Variance . . 85.8 (87.0)	

[a]Decimal points have been omitted.

mores and seniors. Because there are now 19 observed variables, it was decided that the number of zero constraints would be increased to overidentify the two-factor model. With this in mind, the reading passages' loadings were constrained to zero on the "pure" math factor. That is, they served as additional marker variables that have been constrained by the model to be zero. Thus, the vocabulary and reading passages were the "marker" variables for the "pure" verbal factor, and the three math subtests served as markers for the math factor. The science, writing, and civics subtests were free to load at will.

Inspection of the loadings suggests that even with 19 observed variables measuring six potential achievement areas (vocabulary, reading, math, science, writing, and civics), two factors seem to explain virtually all of the reliable variance. That is, the verbal and math factors explain 85.8% of the reliable variance for the sophomores and 87.0% of the reliable variance for the seniors. With the exception of the writing subtests and the physics subtest, the remaining subtests' reliable variances seem to be explained by a linear function of the verbal and math factors. These conclusions apply equally to both the sophomore and the senior results. It is also interesting to note that physics and chemistry tend to have complex loadings, that is, they load on both the verbal and math factors, whereas the remaining science subtests load primarily on the verbal factor. Biology and scientific method are almost entirely explained by the verbal factor. As expected, the two scientifically oriented reading passages (P_2 and P_5) had the lowest loadings on the verbal factor among the reading passages for sophomores. However, for seniors this difference decreases.

The correlations among the factors are quite high—.827 for sophomores and .852 for seniors. Part of this relatively high correlation may be artifactual in the sense that we identified the model by constraining the reading passages to have zero loadings on the math. If we re-estimate the model (which is still identified) relaxing that constraint, the correlation does go down to .80 for sophomores and .82 for seniors; and the two scientific reading passages have loadings of .15 (P_2) and .26 (P_5) on the math factor. The goodness-of-fit indices showed little change, and the remaining loadings showed little or no change.

The results seem to indicate that what starts out to be six distinct achievement areas can best be summarized as linear functions of a verbal factor and a math factor. With the exception of physics, the science areas reading passages, civics, and of course vocabulary, form a solid verbal factor. This pattern is quite stable as one goes from the sophomore to the senior year—that is, there is no change in the pattern of loadings as one goes from sophomore to senior. The only change, if any, is the increase in the general level of the loadings probably reflecting the increase in variance, which leads to an increase in reliability, which in turn is reflected in larger loadings. This phenomenon is, of course, consistent with a model that argues that the implementation of a treatment (or additional treatment) increases individual differences and the consequences thereof. The "bad news" aspect of these results is that the lack of specificity in many of the test measures suggests a low probability of finding differential curriculum effects on, for example, changes in science achievement over 2 years. The "good news" aspect is that there is no evidence that what we are measuring shows significant changes in structure or meaning over time in the total population. It does not appear that we have a problem of apples at one time and oranges at another.

Comparison of Sophomore and Senior Factor Patterns by Sex Group

Tables 10.4 and 10.5 present the results of the two-factor model that was fitted separately to male and female sophomores and seniors, respectively.

TABLE 10.4
Two-Factor Maximum Likelihood Solution For HS&B Male
and Female (in parentheses) Sophomores

Variable	Factor 1		Factor 2		Reliabilities		Reliable Unexplained Variances	
VOC ODD	77	(78)	0	(0)	69	(69)	10	(8)
VOC EVEN	77	(78)	0	(0)	65	(65)	6	(4)
READ P1	61	(62)	0	(0)	48	(41)	11	(3)
READ P2	56	(59)	0	(0)	35	(40)	4	(6)
READ P3	64	(63)	0	(0)	45	(44)	4	(4)
READ P4	68	(65)	0	(0)	51	(50)	6	(7)
READ P5	54	(53)	0	(0)	40	(35)	10	(7)
M-ALG	0	(0)	85	(82)	73	(66)	0	(0)
M-ARITH	0	(0)	88	(86)	80	(76)	3	(2)
M-GEOM	0	(0)	72	(65)	56	(46)	4	(3)
S-BIO	45	(50)	11	(5)	33	(31)	3	(2)
S-CHEM	35	(30)	19	(9)	32	(17)	4	(3)
S-PHYS	35	(30)	29	(35)	52	(48)	14	(9)
S-E.S.	44	(41)	12	(11)	42	(32)	13	(6)
S-METHOD	63	(57)	10	(9)	49	(44)	0	(2)
W-PUNC	29	(36)	40	(31)	60	(60)	17	(19)
W-STYLE	62	(62)	18	(15)	73	(72)	14	(15)
CIV-ODD	57	(59)	4	(0)	42	(37)	6	(1)
CIV-EVEN	48	(47)	5	(2)	33	(26)	6	(2)

$r_{F_1F_2} = 82$ (83)

RMS = .024 (.021)

GRI = .969 (.975)

Percentage of Reliable Variance . . . 86.8 (88.5)

TABLE 10.5
Comparison of a Two-Factor Solution for White and Black
(in parentheses) 1982 Seniors

Parcels	Factor 1		Factor 2		Reliabilities		Reliable Unique Variances	
VOC ODD	79	(77)	0	(0)	73	(68)	11	(9)
VOC EVEN	77	(75)	0	(0)	68	(63)	8	(6)
READING P1	60	(61)	0	(0)	42	(40)	6	(2)
READING P2	64	(49)	0	(0)	48	(29)	7	(5)
READING P3	66	(61)	0	(0)	48	(37)	4	(0)
READING P4	69	(62)	0	(0)	54	(48)	7	(10)
READING P5	60	(42)	0	(0)	46	(30)	10	(12)
M-ALG	0	(0)	86	(80)	73	(65)	0	(1)
M-ARITH	0	(0)	89	(82)	83	(72)	3	(5)
M-GEOM	0	(0)	76	(52)	62	(38)	4	(10)
S-BIOL	42	(47)	07	(07)	24	(33)	1	(5)
S-CHEM	30	(23)	26	(08)	37	(16)	8	(7)
S-PHYS	21	(33)	37	(30)	47	(49)	16	(14)
S-E.S.	32	(39)	18	(12)	36	(34)	12	(10)
S-METH	64	(57)	05	(11)	47	(38)	0	(0)
W-PUNCT	45	(21)	19	(43)	62	(56)	24	(19)
W-STYLE	72	(49)	02	(21)	72	(72)	18	(27)
CIV-ODD	69	(54)	−08	(05)	40	(34)	1	(1)
CIV-EVEN	61	(54)	01	(06)	41	(33)	2	(1)

$r_{F_1 F_2}$ = 83 (.79)   RMS . . . .029 (.032)   % of Reliable Variance Explained . . .
                           GFI . . . .951 (.935)   85.3 (83.8)

The female loadings are shown in parentheses. Not surprisingly, the factor loading patterns for the sex groups are quite similar to each other at both the sophomore and the senior level and show little or no difference from the total population results. The conclusions derived from the total sample apply equally well here.

Comparison of Sophomore–Senior Factor Patterns by Ethnic Group

Tables 10.6 and 10.7 present comparisons of factor patterns for Black and White and for Hispanic and White sophomores, respectively. Tables 10.8 and 10.9 show the parallel comparisons for 1982 seniors. There is little in the Black–White comparison that suggests that the tests have a different structure and thus a possibly different meaning for the two subpopulations. Although the pattern of loadings is very similar, there is a general level difference in loadings that, once again, seems to reflect the pattern of lower reliabilities for Blacks. One interesting trend is that

TABLE 10.6
Comparison of a Two-Factor Solution for White and Black
(in parentheses) 1980 Sophomores

Variable	Factor 1		Factor 2		Reliabilities		Reliable Unexplained Variances	
VOC ODD	75	(71)	0	(0)	68	(57)	11	(7)
VOC EVEN	73	(70)	0	(0)	62	(55)	9	(6)
READ P1	59	(56)	0	(0)	41	(39)	6	(8)
READ P2	58	(48)	0	(0)	38	(28)	5	(5)
READ P3	63	(59)	0	(0)	44	(32)	5	(0)
READ P4	65	(59)	0	(0)	50	(42)	7	(6)
READ P5	54	(35)	0	(0)	38	(17)	9	(5)
M-ALG	0	(0)	83	(78)	68	(57)	0	(0)
M-ARITH	0	(0)	87	(78)	78	(63)	2	(2)
M-GEOM	0	(0)	70	(46)	53	(27)	4	(6)
S-BIO	39	(48)	9	(5)	25	(25)	4	(0)
S-CHEM	30	(25)	19	(3)	28	(7)	7	(0)
S-PHYS	23	(30)	34	(26)	43	(41)	14	(12)
S-E.S.	32	(49)	17	(−5)	34	(33)	13	(13)
S-METHOD	55	(58)	11	(8)	44	(34)	2	(7)
W-PUNC	33	(22)	30	(39)	60	(56)	25	(22)
W-STYLE	60	(52)	13	(17)	72	(63)	22	(18)
CIV-ODD	57	(50)	2	(3)	39	(27)	4	(0)
CIV-EVEN	45	(43)	5	(3)	29	(17)	4	(0)

$r_{F_1F_2}$ = 80 (80)

RMS = .028 (.031)   Percentage of Reliable Variance . . . 83.4 (87.1)

GFI = 962 (961)

there appears to be a greater influence of verbal on Black students' performance on the sciences subtests than for the Whites (e.g., see Table 10.6). Inspection of the Hispanic–White comparison in Table 10.7 also shows a greater overlap of verbal and the science subtests for Hispanics. It may be that Blacks and Hispanics are more likely to come from home and school environments that offer less opportunity to learn about the scientific concepts addressed by the subtest. As a result, their performance depends to a greater extent on general verbal knowledge. That is, if certain subpopulations either do not have the opportunity or, for whatever reason, are less likely to take advantage of the opportunity to take additional instruction in specialized areas, we would expect their correlational structure on achievement tests to be driven by a general verbal factor.

Tables 10.8 and 10.9 present the factor loading coefficients and accompanying goodness-of-fit indices for White–Black and White–Hispanic senior comparisons, respectively. Generally, the pattern of salient and nonsalient loadings are quite similar to the sophomore results. One

TABLE 10.7
Comparison of a Two-Factor Solution for White and Hispanic
(in parentheses) 1980 Sophomores

Variable	Factor 1		Factor 2		Reliabilities		Reliable Unexplained Variances	
VOC ODD	75	(70)	0	(0)	68	(60)	11	(11)
VOC EVEN	73	(69)	0	(0)	62	(55)	9	(8)
READ P1	59	(57)	0	(0)	41	(42)	6	(9)
READ P2	58	(43)	0	(0)	38	(24)	5	(6)
READ P3	63	(55)	0	(0)	44	(29)	5	(0)
READ P4	65	(56)	0	(0)	50	(34)	7	(3)
READ P5	54	(36)	0	(0)	38	(22)	9	(9)
M-ALG	0	(0)	83	(78)	68	(61)	0	(0)
M-ARITH	0	(0)	87	(79)	78	(67)	2	(4)
M-GEOM	0	(0)	70	(53)	53	(27)	4	(0)
S-BIO	39	(54)	9	(1)	25	(31)	4	(2)
S-CHEM	30	(30)	19	(4)	28	(12)	7	(1)
S-PHYS	23	(26)	34	(33)	43	(47)	14	(15)
S-E.S.	32	(47)	17	(3)	34	(32)	13	(8)
S-METHOD	55	(60)	11	(3)	44	(37)	2	(0)
W-PUNC	33	(36)	30	(25)	60	(55)	25	(21)
W-STYLE	60	(64)	13	(5)	72	(66)	22	(19)
CIV-ODD	57	(59)	2	(-6)	39	(36)	4	(7)
CIV-EVEN	45	(58)	5	(-16)	29	(23)	4	(3)

$r_{F_1 F_2}$ = 80 (84)
RMS = .028 (.028)   Percentage of Reliable Variance . . . 83.4 (84.1)
GRI = 962 (966)

main difference is that the loadings for all groups show slight increases, which, in turn, reflect the increase in between-individual variation (and thus reliability) that is due to continuation of the educational treatment. Although the "treatment" may have increased between-individual variation within each achievement area, it did not appear to significantly increase the differentiation between the verbal and quantitative factor. Inspection of possible patterns among the normalized residuals did not reveal systematic patterns that would suggest the possibility that additional, albeit small, factors were present. However, small correlated residuals were found between the fifth reading passage (science orientation) and the geometry parcel. Similar sized residuals were found between the physics parcel and the earth science scientific parcel. These correlated residuals, although not statistically significant, occurred in all three subpopulations.

Similar to the sophomore cohort finding, there remains the greater saturation of the verbal factor of Hispanic performance on both the

TABLE 10.8
Comparison of a Two-Factor Solution for Male and Female
(in parentheses) 1982 Seniors

Parcels	Factor 1		Factor 2		Reliabilities		Reliable Unique Variance	
VOC ODD	80	(83)	0		74	(75)	11	(07)
VOC EVEN	80	(82)	0		72	(72)	08	(02)
READING P1	64	(64)	0		50	(39)	10	(0)
READING P2	62	(65)	0		44	(48)	06	(06)
READING P3	67	(68)	0		49	(48)	05	(02)
READING P4	71	(70)	0		55	(56)	05	(07)
READING P5	62	(58)	0		49	(44)	11	(10)
M-ALG	0		88	(85)	76	(72)	0	(0)
M-ARITH	0		90	(88)	84	(81)	2	(03)
M-GEOM	0		76	(72)	64	(57)	4	(06)
S-BIO	52	(51)	04	(03)	33	(31)	2	(02)
S-CHEM	40	(27)	22	(20)	43	(26)	08	(05)
S-PHYSIC	44	(33)	21	(33)	57	(52)	17	(09)
S-E.S.	50	(44)	08	(10)	44	(36)	11	(07)
S-METH	70	(67)	04	(03)	54	(47)	0	(0)
W-PUNCT	33	(47)	38	(23)	62	(61)	14	(16)
W-STYLE	70	(71)	20	(06)	78	(76)	14	(17)
CIV-ODD	69	(67)	− 04	(05)	44	(41)	1	(02)
CIV-EVEN	57	(62)	07	(− 1)	45	(40)	3	(02)

$r_{F_1 F_2}$ = 85 (.85)   RMS . . . .023 (.023)   % of Reliable Variance . . . 87.4 (89.2)

GRI . . . .959 (.967)

science parcels and the writing parcels. Obviously, verbal language skills are critical to Hispanics for performance in science as well as writing. As pointed out earlier in connection with the Black–White contrast at the sophomore level, there is some evidence that performance on science for Black seniors is more heavily tied to general verbal ability than is the case for Whites.

A technical note is in order here. From a statistical viewpoint, the preferable method of comparing factor patterns across populations is to analyze the variance–covariance matrices, rather than the correlation matrix. The theoretical advantage of factoring the variance–covariance matrix is that the factor loadings will be less affected by changes in the relative variability of the traits under examination from one population to another. The MLH factor loadings estimated on variance–covariance data are the raw score regression weights of the observed variables on the factors and thus relatively invariant with respect to selection. The problem with the variance–covariance approach is that interpretation of the resulting loadings in their original metric is often meaningless. In this

TABLE 10.9
Comparison of a Two-Factor Solution for White and Hispanic
(in parentheses) 1982 Seniors

Parcels	Factor 1		Factor 2		Reliabilities		Reliable Unique Variance	
VOC ODD	79	(76)	0	(0)	73	(69)	11	(11)
VOC EVEN	77	(75)	0	(0)	68	(66)	8	(10)
READING P1	60	(60)	0	(0)	42	(41)	6	(5)
READING P2	64	(54)	0	(0)	48	(34)	7	(5)
READING P3	66	(58)	0	(0)	48	(34)	4	(0)
READING P4	69	(63)	0	(0)	54	(45)	7	(5)
READING P5	60	(46)	0	(0)	46	(29)	10	(7)
M-ALG	0	(0)	86	(81)	73	(66)	0	(0)
M-ARITH	0	(0)	89	(84)	83	(74)	3	(3)
M-GEOM	0	(0)	76	(60)	62	(40)	4	(5)
S-BIOL	42	(59)	07	(− 08)	24	(29)	1	(2)
S-CHEM	30	(23)	26	(19)	37	(23)	8	(7)
S-PHYSIC	21	(38)	37	(24)	47	(51)	16	(15)
S-E.S.	32	(42)	18	(11)	36	(39)	12	(12)
S-METH	64	(66)	05	(01)	47	(45)	0	(0)
W-PUNCT	45	(63)	19	(03)	62	(57)	24	(15)
W-STYLE	72	(93)	02	(− 19)	72	(74)	18	(14)
CIV-ODD	69	(71)	− 08	(− 14)	40	(39)	1	(4)
CIV-EVEN	61	(67)	01	(− 13)	41	(36)	2	(4)

$r_{F_1 F_2}$ = 83 (.86)   RMS . . . .029 (.029)   % of Reliable Variance Explained . . . 85.3 (86.0)
GFI . . . .951 (.957)

case, all analyses were run twice, once on the correlation matrix and once on the variance–covariance matrix. Both runs were then inspected to insure that the same conclusion would be drawn about the salient loadings within each population.

Inspection of the variance–covariance generated factor loadings revealed the same general pattern of loadings as was found in the standardized solution. However, the original difference between Whites and Blacks and between Whites and Hispanics in the general level of the loadings was somewhat reduced. This is to be expected, because the reduced variances in both the Black and Hispanic population would have less effect on the unstandardized factor loadings.

In summary, there is little if any change in factor structure either cross-sectionally (i.e., when comparing senior cohorts) or in the longitudinal analysis of the sophomore–senior transition. With the exception of writing style, punctuation parcels, and the physics parcel, the remaining parcels seem to possess little or no unique reliable variance beyond that which can be explained by a verbal and/or math factor. Black and Hispanic factor structures are quite similar to White structures, with the exception that performance on the science measures has a larger verbal component for Hispanics than for Whites. A similar, although less pronounced, finding occurs when comparing the Black and White structures. One somewhat surprising result is that there is no increased differentiation between the verbal and math factors when going from sophomore to senior status (as measured by the factor intercorrelation). However, there is increased differentiation between individuals (as measured by increased test score variance) as the transition from sophomore to senior occurs. It is possible that more achievement factors and additional factor differentiation would emerge if populations were defined by curriculum. Individuals in the academic curriculum would be more likely to take additional specialized courses in areas of particular interest or skill. This should lead to more differentiation. In sum, there is little empirical evidence for the notion that the tests or test parcels measure different things for different ethnic or sex groups.

SCORING AND EQUATING
USING ITEM RESPONSE THEORY (IRT)

Item Response Theory was used to score tests within population (1980–1982) and to score and equate tests across populations. IRT methods were used to put mathematics, vocabulary, and reading scores on the same scale for 1972, 1980, and 1982 seniors. Similarly, IRT methods were used to score all the HS&B tests given to individuals as sophomores and repeated as seniors. The three-parameter IRT model was selected over the one- and two-parameter models because of the possibility that guessing and/or speededness might be additional confounding sources of variance. Item response theory describes the probability of answering an item correctly as a mathematical function of ability level or skill. The mathematical function used here, the logistic function, has one parameter for each individual—ability level—and three parameters characterizing each item (Lord, 1980; Lord & Novick, 1968). The item parameters reflect difficulty level (b_i), discriminating power (a_i), and the likelihood of low-ability individuals guessing the right answer (c_i). The function that relates the probability of passing a particular item i for a person of ability θ in terms of the item parameters is:

$$P_i(\theta) = c_i + (1 - c_i)\frac{1}{[1 + \exp - Da_i(\theta - b_i]}$$ (1)

where:

$D \cong 1.7$

b_i = item difficulty corresponding to the value of θ halfway between the guessing parameter and 1.0.

a_i = discrimination parameter reflecting the steepness of the item characteristic curve at its point of inflection.

c_i = "guessing parameter" probability of a person with very low ability getting the item correct.

θ = a person's ability parameter usually standardized with mean 0 and standard deviation of 1.0, and

$P_i(\theta)$ = probability of correct response of a person of ability level θ.

A person's number right true score (NRTS) is the simple sum of that particular person's $P_i(\theta)$s. Thus, the scoring weights each item receives in the summation to arrive at NRTS are a function of the interaction of the item parameters with the person's θ or ability level. That is, the item characteristic functions, $P_i(\theta)$s, provide a different score for a given item, depending on a person's ability level. Inspection of the item characteristic function in Equation 1 suggests that, for high-ability people, the item score for a given item i will primarily depend on how much higher the person's θ is compared to the item difficulty (b_i, also measured in θ units), and how discriminating the item is.

A low-ability person will get little credit on a difficult item, even if he or she were to get it correct, because the model argues that the correct answer was probably guessed. This readily follows from Equation 1. Such a person might have a θ (ability level) that was negative, say -1.5, and the b_i for a difficult item on the θ scale might be 2.0, and, because a_i is always positive, the denominator of Equation 1 would become large in relation to the numerator. The limit here as the denominator gets larger is a scoring weight $P_i(\theta)$ equal to c_i, the guessing parameter.

The fact that the item scores that are summed to get the number right true score are a function of the person's ability level θ, discrimination, difficulty, and guessing parameters suggests that IRT scoring can be beneficial if: (a) people with low ability can get the right answer by guessing; (b) items in the test vary in both difficulty and discrimination (and thus an optimal scoring procedure should take this into account); (c) there are test center administration irregularities with respect to directions or timing that may lead to varying levels of items attempted, and (d) the purpose is to put tests that share some but not all of the same items on the same scale.

The ability of IRT methods to deal with individuals or groups characterized by differences in the propensity to attempt items is particularly pertinent here for appropriate cross-sectional comparisons between the seniors of 1972 and the seniors of 1980. As was pointed out earlier in this report, there was a systematic tendency for the seniors in 1980 to attempt more items than did the seniors of 1972. The most likely reason for this result was the change in 1980 from a separate answer sheet to an answer sheet as part of the test booklet. As described earlier, previous research has shown that a mechanical change of this nature can lead to a significant increase in the number of attempts. At any rate, IRT scoring can minimize the impact of such confounding sources on test score variance, because the individual ability score, θ, is based only on items attempted. Therefore, the number of items attempted is controlled for in the estimation of θ.

Item Response Theory methodology was used to put the 1972, 1980, and 1982 seniors on the same scale in vocabulary, math, and reading. This was accomplished by pooling samples from the 1972, 1980, and 1982 senior data and estimating the item and ability parameters (θ) for the items and individuals. More specifically, items that were not present for a particular administration were treated as items not attempted for an individual at that administration. Thus, a person's ability parameter, θ, would be estimated from the common "core" items (i.e., items common to all three administrations) and the items unique to his or her administration.

The IRT parameters were estimated using the Logist computer program (Wood, Wingersky, & Lord, 1976). Computer runs were based on random samples of 2,000 individuals from each cohort, all of whom had attempted at least 15 items. Once the item parameters were established for the tests based on the subsamples, Logist was applied to the full sample of 1972, 1980, and 1982 seniors to estimate the ability (θ) of each individual in each of the subject areas tested. Because a person's ability estimate, θ, was based on only those items attempted, individuals who attempted only the first three or four items and got them all correct would have a grossly overestimated θ. Plots of observed formula scores against θ were inspected for those individuals who attempted 1 through 10 items. Only a handful of examinees had θs inconsistent with their observed formula scores. No θs were estimated for these individuals. Using the θs and the item parameters from the 1972 senior tests (vocabulary, reading, and math), the probability of passing each of the 1972 test items in each of the subject areas was estimated for each individual, regardless of his or her cohort. The sum of these probabilities is an individual's NRTS. In this fashion, we can estimate the NRTS on the 1972 items for any individual from the 1980 or 1982 senior population.

In a sense, we are asking how individuals from the 1980 and 1982 senior cohorts would score if they had taken the 1972 items. This makes possible the desired cross-sectional comparison of scores across senior cohorts. Having estimated NRTS for all senior cohorts as if they had taken the 1972 test items, the scores were then transformed to a formula scored scale using a simple algorithm. This transformation puts the "formula scored number right true scores" on a scale similar to the formula scored observed scores.

In addition to estimating NRTS for the 1972 test items, NRTS were estimated for each individual on his or her own set of tests. For the longitudinal IRT scaling, item parameters were calibrated separately for sophomores and seniors and then transformed to the senior scale. Tests that were present in 1982 but not in 1972 or 1980 were treated somewhat differently because of their relatively short length from an IRT perspective. For the science and writing tests, the full samples of approximately 24,000 sophomores and 25,000 seniors were used in the item calibration runs instead of subsamples, because additional observations can help to overcome possible instability of estimates caused by small numbers of items. Because of its very short length (10 items) and its diversity of subject material, the civics test was considered inappropriate for IRT scaling.

Cross-Sectional Comparisons of Test Score Change[2]

Figure 10.1 presents a "box and whisker" plot of vocabulary performance for the three administrations to seniors and the one to sophomores. It should be kept in mind that all of these cross-sectional comparisons are based on estimated formula corrected number right true scores on the 1972 test items. The results are based on the data and include every sampled senior who was still in school and sophomores who remained in school at least until the senior testing.

The box and whisker plots show the 10th and 90th percentiles (the ends of the whiskers), the 25th and 75th percentiles (the lower and upper end of the boxes), and the means and medians. The medians are shown in parentheses. Inspection of the vocabulary results for the total sample suggests that, although there is a senior vocabulary mean performance decline from 1972 to 1980, it levels off between 1980 and 1982. An indication of the possible impact of the educational treatment on increasing the diversity of performance can be shown by the comparison of the sophomore–senior variances.

(In the full project report, similar figures were generated for males and females and for the White, Black, and Hispanic sample members, and each figure repeated for the mathematics test. Because the concern of this volume is primarily methodological, the figures are not repeated.)

---

[2]In Schaie's terminology, the differences reported will be a mixture of cross-sectional differences and time lag differences.

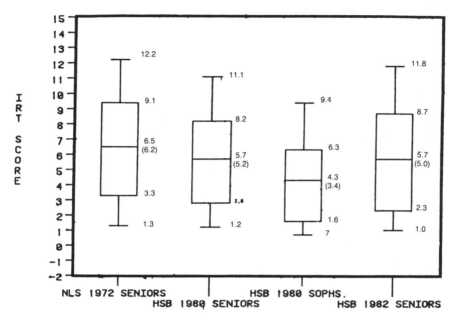

FIG. 10.1. Vocabulary: Total group.

Longitudinal Changes in Test Scores

Table 10.10 presents a comparison of vocabulary test score statistics for sophomore and senior totals and by subpopulations. The entries in the last column of Table 10.10 under the label *gain* are simply the differences between the means $(\bar{X} \text{ (SEN)} - \bar{X} \text{ (SOPH)})$ divided by the sophomore standard deviation. With the exception of Hispanics, all ethnic and sex groups show average gains in vocabulary somewhat over a third of a standard deviation. It is also interesting to note that the Vocabulary score gap between Whites and Blacks and Whites and Hispanics increases as one goes from the sophomore to senior year. We would expect this increasing knowledge gap to be due at least in part to possible curriculum differences. Another interesting finding is that, with the exception of Black females, the vocabulary gap between males and females is reduced as one moves from sophomore to senior status. Once again, this differential gain may reflect differences in curriculum choices. (In the full report, similar tables were presented for the reading and mathematics tests.)

TABLE 10.10
IRT Score Statistics on Sophomore Cohort Tests
Vocabulary[a,b,c]

	HSB 1980 Sophomores				HSB 1982 Seniors				Gain (in SD Units)
	Mean	SD	Skew-ness	Kurt-osis	Mean	SD	Skew-ness	Kurt-osis	
Total Group	8.9	5.2	0.0	− 0.8	10.9	5.6	− 0.2	− 0.8	0.38
Male	9.1	5.1	0.0	− 0.8	10.9	5.5	− 0.2	− 0.8	0.36
Female	8.8[c]	5.3	0.1	− 0.8	10.8[a]	5.7	− 0.2	− 0.9	0.40
White	10.1	4.8	− 0.1	− 0.6	12.2	5.0	− 0.4	− 0.5	0.43
Black	4.9	4.5	0.8	0.1	6.7	5.2	0.5	− 0.6	0.39
Hispanic	5.8	4.7	0.5	− 0.4	7.2	5.4	0.4	− 0.7	0.31
White Male	10.2	4.7	− 0.1	− 0.6	12.2	5.0	− 0.4	− 0.5	0.41
White Female	10.0	4.9	− 0.0	− 0.7	12.2	5.1	− 0.4	− 0.5	0.45
Black Male	5.5	4.5	0.7	− 0.2	7.3	5.2	0.4	− 0.7	0.40
Black Female	4.4	4.5	1.0	0.5	6.2	5.1	0.6	− 0.4	0.39
Hispanic Male	6.0	4.6	0.5	− 0.4	7.3	5.3	0.4	− 0.8	0.27
Hispanic Female	5.4	4.7	0.6	− 0.5	7.1	5.5	0.4	− 0.7	0.36

[a]IRT scores have been estimated on the test items actually administered to the sophomore cohort.

[b]Statistics are based on weighted data.

[c]HSB 1980 sophomores who had dropped out of school by the time of the 1982 followup status determination were excluded from both base year and followup test statistics.

Initial Comparisons of IRT Scale Scores with Observed Formula Scores

The greatest potential benefit from IRT scaling is the ability to estimate how 1980 and 1982 seniors would score if they took the 1972 test battery. Unfortunately, one cannot compare the IRT results with, say, formula score results for the cross-sectional comparisons, because the observed formula score results would be unobtainable. Comparisons, however, can be made between formula scores and IRT scaled scores for the longitudinal sophomore–senior cohort. However, because in the longitudinal analysis the same tests were administered to the same people on two occasions, the advantages of IRT scaling is less clear. In the case of mean changes, the IRT formula corrected scale score means for the total population will be identical to the raw formula scored means, because the "true" score mean is equal to the observed mean. Slight differences between the observed means and the formula corrected NRTS means might occur within some subgroups. However, these mean differences will be negligible. In theory, the variance of NRTS should be somewhat less than the observed formula score variances. This follows from the fact that the true score variance should be less than the observed formula score variance. At the same time, however, there is always an error in estimation of the NRTSs that may inflate the variance of the estimated NRTSs. The end result, with respect to the longitudinal data, is that NRTS and formula scored means are identical for sophomores and seniors, but the NRTS variances are generally equal to or slightly smaller than the observed formula scored variances. Thus, when one looks at mean changes in standard deviation units, the difference in some cases will be larger for NRTS scores.

Although NRTS would be expected to have little or no effect (from test theory assumption) on estimation of means, it was hoped that optimal item scoring weights might increase the differentiation between individuals (especially in the center of the distribution) and thereby increase the correlation with external variables. The NRTS scores tend to pull in extreme scores but increase the differentiation in the middle. Table 10.11 presents correlations between individual IRT gains (1980 NRTS–1982 NRTS) with base-year NRTS scores, base-year SES, and whether or not the individual was in the academic curriculum. The last three columns show the same analysis for observed formula scores.

Table 10.11 suggests that the IRT scale scores lead to some improvement in the gain score correlations. With the exception of the writing test sophomore status, NRTS scores tend to have a less negative relationship with gains than do the observed formula scores. There is, however, almost no difference between the two scoring methods with respect to the correlation with SES and academic curriculum.

Overall, the psychometric analysis suggests that:

- Differences in test administrations in 1972 and 1980, primarily a change in answer sheet format, led to more items being attempted in 1980 than in 1972. It is argued that item response theory being

TABLE 10.11
Correlations of Test Score Gains (1980 to 1982) with Initial Status,
SES, and Academic Curriculum

	Raw Gain in IRT Scores			Raw Gain in Formula Scores		
	With Base-Year Score	With Base-Year SES	With Academic Curriculum	With Base-Year Score	With Base-Year SES	With Academic Curriculum
Vocabulary	−.18	.05	.05	−.23	.05	.04
Reading	−.28	.04	.05	−.28	.05	.05
Math	−.10	.10	.11	−.14	.09	.10
Science	−.31	.04	.02	−.34	.02	.02
Writing	−.36	.00	−.01	−.35	.00	.00

used here may substantially reduce the impact of any effects of this change in administration.

- The test batteries appear to be measuring the same things with the same precision across ethnic and sex groups. Similarly, the 1980 sophomore test batteries factor structure did not change when it was re-administered to the same sophomores 2 years later. The critical finding here is that in this case the test scores at two points in time are valid measures of change along the same dimension. The tests were at the appropriate difficulty level, and the 1980 sophomore cohort battery was sufficiently difficult that gains could be a reasonable expectation.

SUMMARY

Confirmatory factor analysis was conducted to determine what the tests were and were not measuring, and whether what was being measured was the same across cohorts and selected subpopulations within cohorts. The factor analysis was carried out on rationally derived subtest "parcels" whose homogeneity was verified in the aforementioned reliability analysis.

The factor analysis results suggested that there was little if any change in factor structure either cross-sectionally (i.e., when comparing 1972 and 1980 senior cohorts) or in the longitudinal comparison of sophomores with seniors. With the exception of the writing style, punctuation parcels, and the physics parcel, the remaining subtest parcels seemed to possess little or no unique reliable variance beyond that which can be explained by a verbal and/or math factor. Black and Hispanic factor structures were quite similar to White structures with the exception that performance on the science measures had a larger verbal component for Hispanics than for Whites. One somewhat surprising result is that there was no increased differentiation between the verbal and math factors when going from sophomore to senior status (as measured by the factor intercorrelation). However, there was increased differentiation between individuals (as measured by increased test score variance) as the transition from sophomore to senior occurred. It is possible that additional achievement factors and factor differentiation would emerge if populations were defined by curriculum. Individuals in the academic curriculum would be more likely to take additional specialized courses in areas of particular interest or skill. This should lead to more differentiation. In sum, there was little empirical evidence for the notion that the tests or test parcels measure different things for different ethnic or sex groups.

Item Response Theory was used to score tests within populations

(1980–1982), and to score and equate tests across populations. IRT methods were used to put mathematics, vocabulary, and reading scores on the same scale for 1972, 1980, and 1982 seniors. Similarly, IRT methods were used to score all the HS&B tests given to individuals as sophomores and repeated as seniors. The three-parameter IRT model was selected over the one- and two-parameter models because of the possibility that guessing and/or speededness might be additional confounding sources of variance. The IRT analysis allowed one to compare how 1980 and 1982 seniors would score if they took the 1972 vocabulary, reading, and mathematics tests.

ACKNOWLEDGMENT

This chapter is an excerpt from a report entitled ''Psychometric Analysis of the NLS and the High School and Beyond Test Batteries'' submitted to the National Center for Education Statistics as part of Contract 300-830-0247 (Rock et al., 1985).

CHAPTER ELEVEN

Estimating Change in Enrollments from Two National Surveys Eight Years Apart

Thomas L. Hilton
Judith Pollack
Educational Testing Service

This chapter describes an unpublished study entitled *Talent Flow in the 1970s and the 1980s,* which was conducted for the Graduate Record Examination Program. The data were derived from the National Longitudinal Study of the High School Class of 1972 (NLS) and High School and Beyond (HS&B). The two surveys were designed to yield comparable enrollment data, but serious problems resulted from the fact that in NLS the fourth follow-up was conducted 7 years and 5 months after high school graduation, and the most relevant HS&B follow-up (the third follow-up) was conducted 5 years and 9 months after high school graduation. The steps taken to achieve comparable data are described in detail. Also demonstrated in this chapter are the interpretive problems that result when estimates are based on a small number of actual data cases.

—Thomas L. Hilton

The flow of talent in higher education is a matter of national concern. Especially in science and engineering, serious questions can be raised about whether the future production of scientific and technical talent in this country will be sufficient to supply the human resource needs of industry, universities, and the government. Questions also can be raised about the future supply of teachers and researchers in the humanities and the social sciences. According to William G. Bowen, former president of Princeton University, "We need to increase overall production of new Ph.D.'s by two-thirds," and "In the humanities and social sciences, we need to double the current numbers'' (Fiske, 1989, A1). The purpose of this study is to address this and other issues related to the flow of talent in the United States in the 1980s in comparison with the flow of talent in the 1970s.

METHOD

Data describing the flow of talent in the 1970s were obtained from the National Longitudinal Study of the High School Class of 1972 (Hilton & Rhett, 1973; Riccobono, Henderson, Burkheimer, Place, & Levinsohn, 1981; see chapter 3). Data for the 1980s were obtained from a second national longitudinal study, HS&B (see chapter 5 of this volume) that was designed to be parallel to the 1972 NLS cohort and for the most part was successful in doing so (Sebring et al., 1987a, 1987b). However, some features of HS&B created difficult problems in achieving comparability. These problems and the steps taken to resolve them are discussed shortly.

Data Preparation

The HS&B data tape used in the analysis included the 1980 base-year survey, the 1982 first follow-up, the 1984 second follow-up, and the 1986 third follow-up. Thus, the HS&B sample members who continued their postsecondary education without interruption—a small fraction of the total sample—were in their second year of graduate or professional school at the time of the most recent data collection. However, most of the HS&B sample members who enrolled in college were either still in undergraduate school or had dropped out, temporarily or permanently.

Only sample members who responded to all of the relevant instruments of the base year and the first, second, and third follow-ups were included in the sample for analysis, a total of 9,389 subjects.

For descriptive purposes, five stages of educational attainment were defined, following the earlier study of the postsecondary, educational pipeline by Hilton and Schrader (1987). These stages were:

1. High School Program. Four categories were defined on the basis of the number of semesters the student enrolled in science, mathematics, foreign languages, and social studies. Students having 2 years or more in all four areas during their last 3 years of high school formed one group—"Academic: Balanced." Depending on the specific subject or subjects in which the students had less than 2 years of study, students were classified as "Academic: Science," "Academic: Humanities and

Social Studies," or "All Other Programs," including missing data. These categories are described in more detail in Hilton and Schrader (1987). They were judged to be more appropriate for a study of higher education than the traditional "academic, general, and vocational" categories.

2. First College Entered. Students who enrolled in college were classified according to whether their *first* colleges were 2-year or 4-year academic institutions. Students who enrolled in vocational-technical colleges, who did not enroll in college, or who could not be classified constituted the third category.

3. Status in Fall 1982. Students who reported they were enrolled in 4-year colleges in the third fall after finishing high school were identified.

4. Major Field of Bachelor's Degree. Students who had earned bachelor's degrees were classified into "Arts and Science," "Professional Fields," or "Unknown Major" groups on the basis of self-reported major fields. Students who had not earned bachelor's degrees or whose status could not be determined constituted the fourth category.

Arts and sciences include humanities, social sciences, arts, biological sciences, physical sciences, and mathematics. The professional fields include agriculture, architecture, business, journalism, computer science, education, engineering, home economics, law, library science, and theological studies.

5. Type of Postbaccalaureate School. Students who had earned degrees and who reported that they had been classified by their schools as full-time graduate or professional students were identified. They were then classified into one of three groups: "Graduate School," "Professional School," or "Missing Data on School Type." Students who had earned bachelor's degrees but who did not attend graduate or professional school and students who did not earn bachelor's degrees constituted two additional categories. "Professional" included business, health services, medicine, dentistry, law, and theology.

Linking these stages together provided the flow-diagram shown in Fig. 11.1.

The Problem of Comparability of NLS and HS&B Data

In comparing results from the fourth follow-up of NLS and the third follow-up of HS&B, we encountered the problem that the NLS follow-up was conducted in the fall of 1979, approximately 7 years and 5 months after high school graduation, and the "parallel" HS&B follow-up was conducted in the spring of 1986, only 5 years and 9 months after high school graduation. Thus, the NLS counts include graduate school attend-

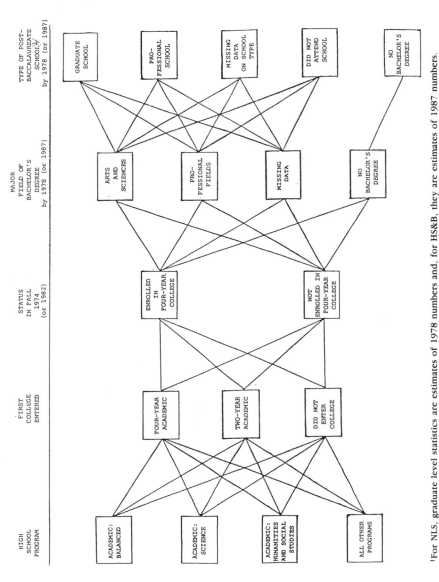

HIGH SCHOOL PROGRAM

FIRST COLLEGE ENTERED

STATUS IN FALL 1974 (or 1982)

MAJOR FIELD OF BACHELOR'S DEGREE by 1978 (or 1987)

TYPE OF POST-BACCALAUREATE SCHOOL¹ by 1978 (or 1987)

ACADEMIC: BALANCED

ACADEMIC: SCIENCE

ACADEMIC: HUMANITIES AND SOCIAL STUDIES

ALL OTHER PROGRAMS

FOUR-YEAR ACADEMIC

TWO-YEAR ACADEMIC

DID NOT ENTER COLLEGE

ENROLLED IN FOUR-YEAR COLLEGE

NOT ENROLLED IN FOUR-YEAR COLLEGE

ARTS AND SCIENCES

PRO-FESSIONAL FIELDS

MISSING DATA

NO BACHELOR'S DEGREE

GRADUATE SCHOOL

PRO-FESSIONAL SCHOOL

MISSING DATA ON SCHOOL TYPE

DID NOT ATTEND SCHOOL

NO BACHELOR'S DEGREE

¹For NLS, graduate level statistics are estimates of 1978 numbers and, for HS&B, they are estimates of 1987 numbers.

FIG. 11.1 Pathways for high school seniors.

217

ance for students who entered graduate school during a time interval almost 2 years longer than that covered by the HS&B questionnaire.

To adjust for this difference in time span, we would have liked to separate out all NLS students whose first graduate or professional school attendance was after March 1978. The wording of the relevant NLS enrollment items, however, is such that we were able to establish attendance for the NLS cohort only for the last year, not 1½ years. The data indicated that 56.2 students per thousand attended graduate or professional school in 1979, of whom 14.8 per thousand, or about a quarter, were attending for the first time during the last year surveyed. Accordingly, we reduced the 1979 graduate and professional school enrollment figures by 25% and refer to the resulting figures as "estimated 1978 enrollments."

The 25% reduction did not completely close the gap in time span between the two follow-ups. What was needed was a way of estimating how many students in the HS&B cohort were enrolled in graduate or professional schools in the fall of the 6th year after high school graduation. (We knew only the number enrolled in the spring of the 6th year and the number who said they had applied for fall admission.) Accordingly, we decided to assume that all who had applied for admission were accepted and actually enrolled in the fall of 1986. We suspected that the actual enrollment rate was somewhat less than 100%, but knowing that the HS&B figures for graduate school enrollment were substantially less than the NLS figures, we preferred to err on the side of overestimation. In other words, we wanted to know what was the maximum number of postbaccalaureate students we were likely to observe. We also recognized that there may have been some sample members who had not applied for graduate school at the time they completed the third follow-up questionnaire but who later did so. As is shown herein, the adjustments to the NLS and the HS&B data brought the graduate-level enrollment figures into remarkable agreement. Nevertheless, the adjusted figures should be regarded as approximations.

Adjustments to Bachelor's Degree Data.   Because the fourth level of the pathways diagram was also subject to the same differences in time span, we made adjustments at that level. First, to reduce the NLS data to a 6-year span, we reduced the 1979 7-year numbers by 5% on the basis of an analysis of NLS data that indicated that 5% of the sample members who received bachelor's degrees did so in the 7th year after high school graduation (CES, 1986).

Second, to adjust the HS&B data, we assumed that all of the HS&B subjects who were seniors in the spring of the 6th year (39 per 1,000 for the total sample) actually completed the school year and received bachelor's degrees. (Again we suspected that the actual completion rate was somewhat less than 100%, but we chose to use 100% for the same reason mentioned earlier and to keep the adjustment sample.)

RESULTS

Total Sample

The comparable estimates for the total NLS population and total HS&B population are shown in Fig. 11.2. The estimated number per 1,000 NLS cohort members is shown under each box, and the comparable number for the HS&B cohort is shown in parentheses. For example, the numbers in the left-hand column indicate that 187 per 1,000 of the NLS cohort were enrolled in high school in what we defined as the *academic balanced* high school program. However, 8 years later, only 144 per 1,000 of the HS&B cohort were so enrolled. The next box down suggests the reason for the decline in the balanced program—namely, the substantial increase in the number of students enrolled in an *academic science* program. This result is consistent with the recent emphasis in our high schools on engineering and science careers. This is also reflected in the third box down, which shows a decline in the number of students specializing in humanities and social studies. In the remainder of this chapter, numbers taken from the flow diagrams are always the estimated number per 1,000 in the cohort.

The numbers on the lines connecting the boxes in the first column with the second column show how many students followed each pathway. For example, 127 NLS students went from the balanced high school program to enrollment in 4-year academic colleges, compared with 103 of the HS&B students, presumably reflecting the fact that a smaller proportion of high school students chose the balanced academic program. The proportion going from the science program to 4-year academic programs increased by 50% from 1972 to 1980. To simplify the flow diagrams, the numbers following each pathway are omitted in the balance of the diagrams in this chapter. The numbers may be obtained from Thomas Hilton.

The second column of boxes concerning the first college entered by the student, if any, indicates that a higher proportion of the 1980 students entered a college but that the ratio of 4-year to 2-year college admissions remained approximately the same (1.65 vs. 1.59). The boxes in the third column concern which students were enrolled in 4-year colleges in the third fall after high school graduation. The comparable figures indicate

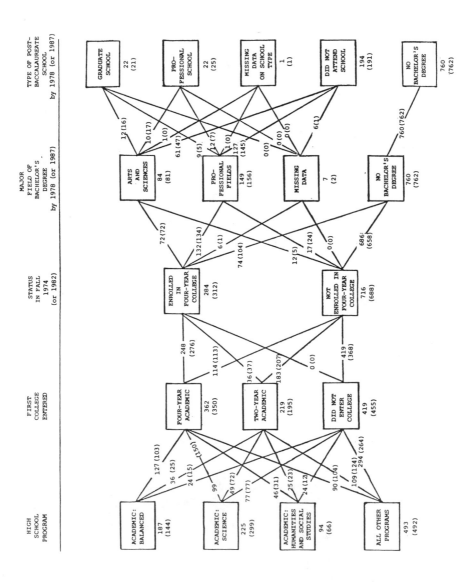

FIG. 11.2. Pathways for 1972 high school seniors and 1980 high school seniors (in parentheses): estimated number per 1,000 sample members (actual 1972 N = 16,740; 1980 N = 9,389).

220

that a somewhat larger proportion of the HS&B sample was enrolled in 4-year colleges.

The numbers in the fourth column indicate that, as adjusted, slightly fewer of the HS&B subjects majored in arts and sciences, slightly more majored in professional fields, and slightly more did not receive bachelor's degrees. The last column is both of most interest and the most problematical. As explained earlier, we reduced the 1972 NLS figures by one quarter in an effort to make them comparable to the HS&B figures. In addition, recall that we counted HS&B seniors who had *applied* to graduate or professional school as having *enrolled* in the schools.[1] When these steps are taken, the initial disparity between the 1972 and the 1980 cohort disappears. In fact, the agreement is striking, even though achieving agreement was not our objective:

	NLS	*HS&B*
"Enrolled" in graduate school	22	21
"Enrolled" in professional school	22	25
Missing data	1	1
No postbaccalaureate school	194	191
No bachelor's degree	760	762
	1,000	1,000

Although the adjustments required several possibly debatable assumptions, we conclude that there are no major differences in enrollments between the 1972 and the 1980 cohorts as far as the total populations are concerned. There were, however, substantial differences between major subgroups of the two cohorts, which are discussed in the following paragraphs.

It is important to keep in mind that in all these frequencies the subjects in question are the members of a single cohort who graduated from high school either in 1972 or 1980. There are no foreign students, nor are there older students returning to graduate or professional school and, lastly, only full-time graduate and professional school students are considered.

Being based on large samples, most of the differences reported, for example, a certain number in a subcategory of the NLS sample and the corresponding category of the HS&B sample, are statistically significant. However, on the bases of *t* tests using estimated standard errors reported by Schmitt (NCES, 1989), we tend to regard differences in percentages

---

[1]On the flow diagrams we label the adjusted 1986 figures as "1987" and the adjusted 1979 figures as "1978."

that are based on less than 50 actual data cases as suspect unless the difference is huge. These differences are usually noted in the text.

Cohort Differences by Gender

Males.   As shown in Fig. 11.3, from the 1972 cohort to the 1980 cohort, the flow diagram for the men changed very little, except for the marked increase in interest in high school science subjects and concomitant decrease in enrollments in humanities and social studies courses, as well as a decrease in the number per thousand enrolling in graduate schools (from 23 to 17). Because the baccalaureate and postbaccalaureate figures are adjusted estimates, we recommend that they be regarded as probable changes that should be confirmed by other data.

Females.   The women displayed an even greater increase in science interest (from 160 to 251) and a marked increase in the number enrolling in college (Fig. 11.4). The number receiving bachelor's degrees increased slightly, but the undergraduate attrition rate for women is still higher than the rate for men. At the postbaccalaureate level, however, the enrollments of women increased, from 22 to 28 in graduate school and from 13 to 17 in professional schools.

Between-Gender Differences.   The men in 1972 were more likely than the women to:

- Enroll in science programs in high school.
- Enroll in 4-year academic colleges.
- Receive bachelor's degrees.
- Enroll in professional schools.

By the 1980s, however, these differences between the men and women had diminished dramatically. Equal proportions of men and women first enrolled in 4-year colleges, substantially more women enrolled in 2-year colleges, approximately equal proportions received bachelor's degrees, a substantially higher proportion of women attended graduate school, but a smaller proportion attended professional school (although more than the 1972 cohort). Similar but less-pronounced results have been reported for cross-sectional data.

Ethnic Trends and Differences

White Students.   Because the White students constitute such a large proportion of the total sample, their flow diagram is not significantly different from that of the total sample and is not shown. We would note,

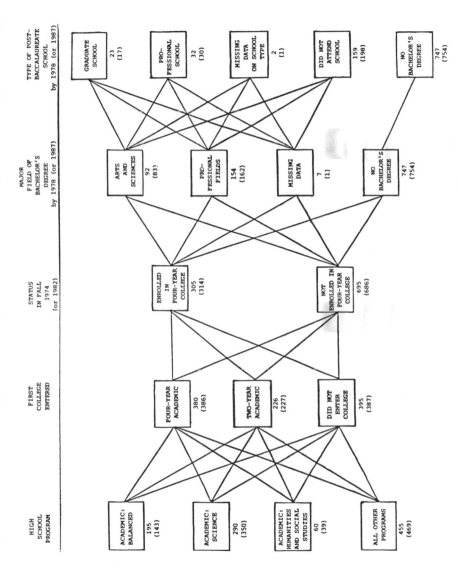

FIG. 11.3. Pathways for 1972 and 1980 male high school seniors: estimated number in each category per 1,000 sample members (1980 in parentheses) (actual 1972 $N = 7,957$; 1980 $N = 4,193$).

223

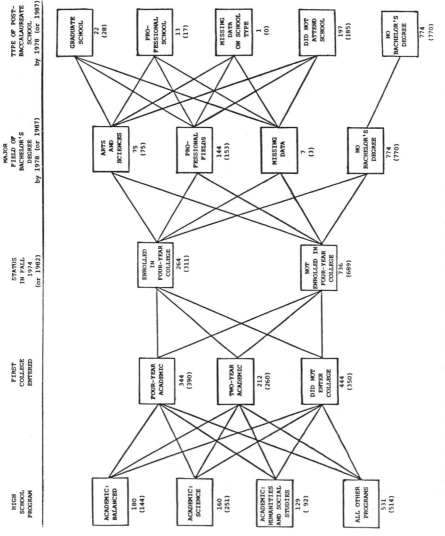

FIG. 11.4. Pathways for 1972 and 1980 female high school seniors: estimated number in each category per 1,000 sample members (1980 in parentheses) (actual 1972 N = 5,196).

however, that—unlike the total sample—enrollment of White students in graduate schools increased slightly, from 23 to 25, suggesting that the enrollment of some other ethnic group must have declined, as becomes apparent shortly.

Black Students.   For the 1972 cohort, in comparison with White students, a higher proportion of the Black students (Fig. 11.5):

• Enrolled in nonacademic high school programs.
• Did not enter college.
• Did not receive bachelor's degrees.

Substantially fewer Black students enrolled in graduate schools (15 vs. 23), and even fewer enrolled in professional schools (12 vs. 24).

By the 1980s, however, the situation had changed substantially. A higher proportion of Black students than White students enrolled in science programs in high school,[2] the proportion of Black students going on to college increased (but still lagged behind the White students), the proportion receiving degrees in arts and sciences decreased substantially (69 to 36), and the proportion receiving professional degrees remained the same. Similarly, the proportions enrolling in graduate school decreased (15 to 6), whereas the proportions enrolling in professional schools remained approximately the same. Thus, the Black students made gains in the early undergraduate years but seem to have lost ground later. The postbaccalaureate school results are, however, based on only 26 actual data cases and must be regarded with caution.

A decline in the college enrollment of Black males has been widely discussed (see, e.g., Daniels, 1989), leading us to expect marked differences between the educational development of male and female Black students in the 1980 HS&B sample. However, this data set does not exhibit such differences, although there are some.

As shown in Fig. 11.6, fewer Black women were enrolled in "Academic: Science" in high school, but more Black women than Black men enrolled in academic colleges (616 vs. 568). More women must have dropped out, taken additional time, or ended their education with an associate's degree, because in the third fall after high school graduation, slightly more Black men were enrolled in 4-year colleges. Almost the same number received bachelor's degrees (139 vs. 140 women). For both genders, the degrees tended to be in professional fields, probably business

---

[2]Actually, the higher proportion of Black students in science programs is an artifact of fewer Black students taking enough foreign languages and social studies to be classified in a balanced program.

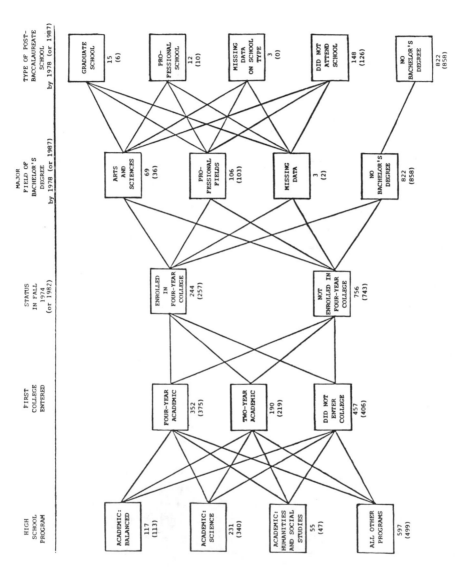

FIG. 11.5. Pathways for 1972 Black high school seniors and 1980 Black seniors (in parentheses): estimated number in each category per 1,000 sample members (actual 1972 N = 1,995; 1980 N = 2,230).

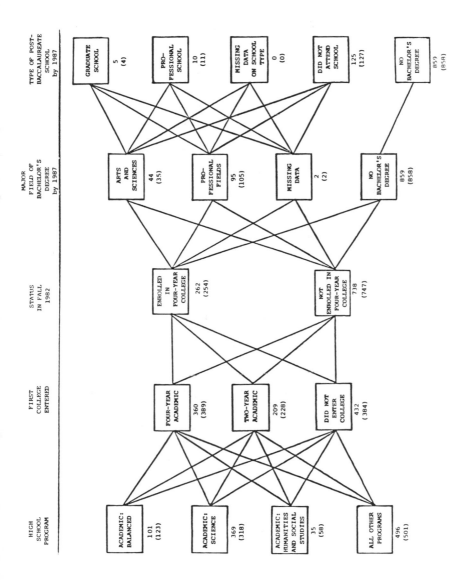

FIG. 11.6. Status at each of five stages for 1980 male and female Black students (in parentheses): estimated number in each category per 1,000 sample members (actual N = 916 males and 1,314 females).

227

administration and education. (We cannot be sure, because no count was kept of individual fields.) Lastly, very nearly the same small number enrolled full-time in graduate or professional school.

Hispanic Students.   The Pathways Study reported (Fig. 11.7) that the Hispanic students in the 1972 cohort, in comparison with the White students, were:

- Much less likely to enroll in a balanced high school program.
- Less likely to enroll in college but, of those who did, more likely to enroll in 2-year colleges (321 for Hispanic students and 217 for White students).
- Far less likely to be enrolled in a 4-year college 2 years after high school graduation (147 vs. 299).
- Far less likely to receive bachelor's degrees (107 vs. 262).
- Less likely to attend graduate or professional school (27 vs. 47).

As with the Black students, however, the statistics changed by the time of the 1980 cohort. In general, the Hispanic students display the same increase in science study that the White students did. Unlike the White students, however, the Hispanic students show a slight decrease in college enrollment, but, of those who did enroll, an increased proportion attended 4-year colleges rather than 2-year colleges. Approximately the same proportion received degrees, although there was a shift from arts and science to professional schools. (In 1979 the split was 48 to 59, whereas in 1986 it was 40 to 72.) In comparison with Blacks, fewer Hispanics had received bachelor's degrees by 1987, but for a different reason: Fewer Hispanic students than Black students enrolled in undergraduate schools. As for postbaccalaureate schools, the numbers for Hispanic students are too small to be trusted, being based on only 26 actual data cases, as in the case of the Black students. The numbers suggest a marked decline in postbaccalaureate enrollments.

High Ability Students

In addressing questions about flow of talent, it is usually more pertinent to have results for the higher ability segment of the total sample. Accordingly, for both the 1972 NLS cohort and the 1980 HS&B cohort, the top quartile in ability was identified by means of the composite test score included in the public release file for each cohort.[3] Obviously,

---

[3]For HS&B the composite is the average of the Reading, Vocabulary, and Mathematics test scores. For NLS it is the sum of the Reading, Letter Groups, Vocabulary, and Mathematics test scores after each was standardized with a mean of 50 and a standard deviation of 10.

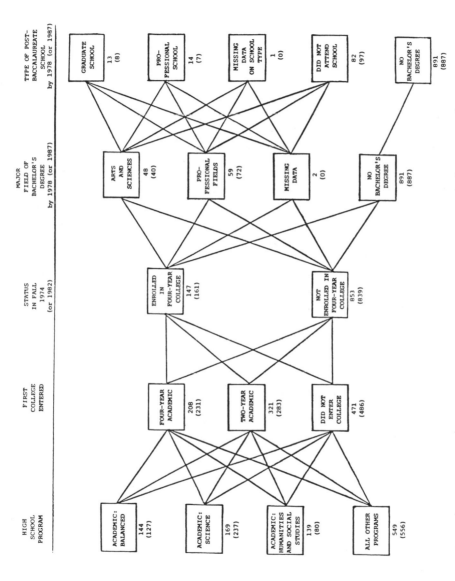

FIG. 11.7. Pathways for 1972 Hispanic high school seniors and 1980 Hispanic high school seniors (in parentheses): estimated number in each category per 1,000 sample members (actual 1972 N = 639; 1980 N = 2,302).

focusing on the top quartile reduces the sample sizes by a factor of 4, so extra caution is necessary in examining the results, particularly in the case of ethnic subgroups.

In 1972, the high-ability group constituted 19% of the weighted sample; in 1980, the number was 22%. (The percentages are not exactly 25% because the unweighted sample distribution is skewed to the left.)

When the top-ability quartile of the 1972 sample is observed (Fig. 11.8), the statistics generally are as expected; nearly twice as many (567 vs. 284) were enrolled in a 4-year college 2 years after high school graduation, over twice as many received bachelor's degrees, and nearly three times as many enrolled in graduate or professional school.

For the 1980 cohort we observe, first, an unusually large swing to science at the high school level (275 to 398) with a concomitant desertion from the balanced academic programs and the programs emphasizing humanities and social studies. As was noted earlier, these results do not necessarily mean students took more science but instead that they did not take enough humanities and social studies courses to qualify for the other programs. Thereafter, however, the results for the 1972 and 1980 cohorts are quite similar, to the point that the parallel figures (adjusted) for graduate school are 55 and 57 and, for professional school, 64 and 66.

High-Ability Ethnic Groups.   Of particular interest is the educational attainment of the high-ability ethnic subgroups, White, Black, and Hispanic. It was necessary, however, to take some special steps in reporting the results. In the Pathways Study of the 1972 cohort (Hilton & Shrader, 1987), the high-ability samples included 3,252 White students, 49 Black students, and 24 Hispanic students. In view of the numbers involved, the decision was made to not report the results for the Hispanic students and to report the results for the Black and White students only as percentages, our opinion being that the implied precision of reporting the number per thousand was not justified. However, in designing the sampling for the 1980 cohort, Black and Hispanic students were over-sampled, resulting in somewhat larger samples, specifically 152 and 208 actual data cases, respectively. We decided, therefore, to report the results in numbers per 1,000 for all students but not to report the numbers following particular pathways. The figures shown in Fig. 11.9 are the result. At the high school senior level, fewer of the Hispanics selected science programs (265 vs. 411 for Black students and 402 for White students). Somewhat more high-ability Hispanic students enrolled in 2-year programs, and slightly fewer subsequently enrolled in 4-year colleges. Approximately the same proportion of high-ability White and Hispanic students were awarded undergraduate degrees, but substantially fewer high-ability Black students were (495, 483, and 319, respectively).

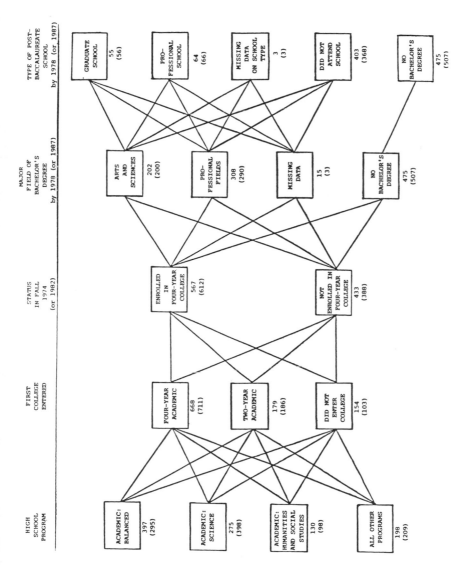

FIG. 11.8. Pathways for high ability high school seniors in 1972 and 1980 (in parentheses): estimated number in each category per 1,000 sample members (actual 1972 N = 3,470; 1980 N = 2,033).

231

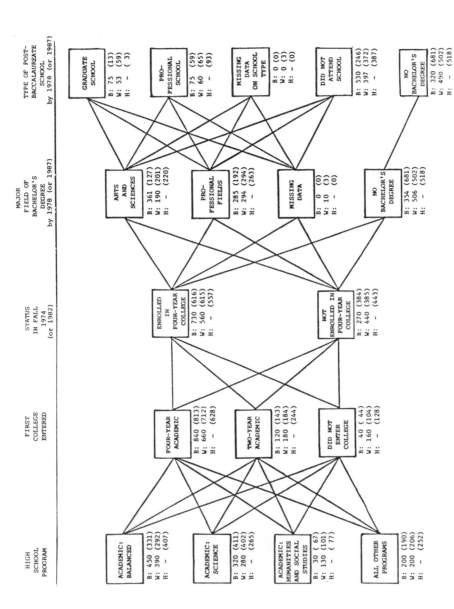

FIG. 11.9. Status at each of five stages for 1972 and 1980 (in parentheses) high ability Black, White, and Hispanic high school seniors (actual 1972 Ns = 49 Black and 3,252 White; 1980 Ns = 152 Black, 1,576 White, and 208 Hispanic). (1972 figures are not reported for Hispanic students because of their small number, and frequencies

The decline, from the 1970s to the 1980s, in the proportion of high-ability Black students who received bachelor's degrees within 7 years of high school graduation from 646 to 319 is possibly the most important finding of this study. The result, which is significant at the .001 level, deserves the most serious consideration.

At the postbaccalaureate level, the results suggest that the status of the White students remained the same but that the graduate and professional school enrollment of the Black and Hispanic students may have declined. However, the numbers of actual data cases for both the Black and Hispanic groups are too small to make defensible estimates.

When data for those selected groups with an adequate sample size are summarized from the viewpoint of academic progress, the following table results:

	Percentage of Group Who:					
	Earned a Bachelor's Degree		Entered Graduate School		Entered Professional School	
Group	NLS	HS&B	NLS	HS&B	NLS	HS&B
All high school seniors	23.3	23.7	2.2	2.1	2.2	2.5
All males	24.6	24.5	2.3	1.7	3.2	3.0
All females	21.9	22.8	2.2	2.8	1.3	1.7
All Whites	24.9	26.1	2.3	2.5	2.4	2.8
All Blacks	17.5	13.9	1.5	.6	1.2	1.0
All Hispanics	10.7	11.2	1.3	.8	1.4	.7
High-ability seniors	51.0	49.0	5.5	5.6	6.4	6.6

DISCUSSION AND CONCLUSIONS

Perhaps of greatest interest to the GRE program and to those concerned with human resources in this country are the results concerning trends in the educational attainment of students in the United States in the 1980s in comparison with the 1970s. In general, we found few changes occurred in the total population despite the fact that substantial changes have been reported in the literature. Schmidt, for example, analyzed the same data bases as the authors did and concluded, "Comparing NLS-72 seniors with HS&B seniors shows that the level of degree attainment has declined for the HS&B seniors" (NCES, 1989, p. 12). Specifically, he estimated that "by 6 to 7 years after high school nearly 25 percent of the NLS-72 seniors and 19 percent of the HS&B 1980 seniors completed the requirements of the bachelor's degrees" (p. 3). Schmitt made no adjustments in the data to take into consideration the fact that the NLS sample had nearly 7½ years in which to obtain the bachelor's degree, and the most nearly comparable

HS&B sample had only 5½ years to obtain the bachelor's degree. When adjustments are made, the differences between the NLS sample and the HS&B population estimates disappear, as far as the total group is concerned.

Black Students. As we saw, however, there were some striking differences between subgroups of the two national samples, particularly between the Black students in the 1970s and Black students in the 1980s. The major difference was in the proportion of Black undergraduates who eventually received bachelor's degrees (32% of those who enrolled in 2- or 4-year colleges vs. 23%).

The decline occurred primarily in the arts and sciences, a trend that augurs ill for Black enrollments in graduate school. In fact, we observed a sharp decline in Black graduate school enrollments for the HS&B sample, but the finding is based on so few actual data cases that we cannot regard the result as reliable even though other evidence is consistent with the finding. This evidence comes from the number of Black students who have taken the GRE annually since 1976. As shown in Fig. 11.10, the number declined by 50%, from 2,800 to less than 1,400. GRE takers are,

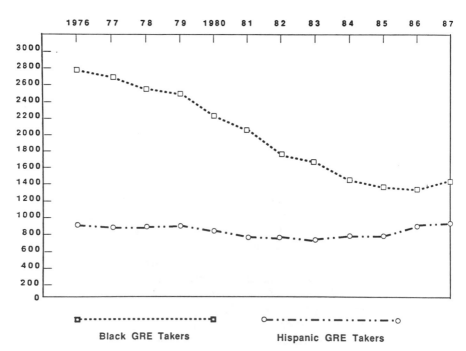

FIG. 11.10. Number of Black and Hispanic GRE takers, age 22, by year (U.S. citizens only)

of course, self-selected, and by no means do all test takers enroll in graduate school, nor do all graduate students take the test, but the trend is consistent.

In the HS&B cohort, the rate of attainment of bachelor's degrees was almost twice as great for White students as for Black students (261 per 1,000 vs. 139 per 1,000). These results for attainment of the bachelor's degree are consistent with a Census Bureau report that "Whites are twice as likely as Blacks to finish college, although there is only a small gap between the two groups in high school graduation rates" (Collison, 1987, p. A27). Taken together, these results point to the conclusion that the declining educational attainment of Black undergraduates is a matter of serious national concern.

Hispanic Students.   The numbers reported for Hispanic students are equally disconcerting. Although certain indicators improved from the 1970s to the 1980s (e.g., more attend 4-year colleges in the 1980s), their college enrollment rate is still less than that of either Blacks or Whites.

Gender Differences.   The major finding in this part of the data analysis is the evidence of substantial gains in attainment for women. In most respects, they achieved equity with men, and they may have surpassed men in the number enrolling full-time in graduate school. Other analyses, however, indicate that they have not achieved equity in mathematics and science (Hilton & Lee, 1988).

High-Ability Students.   Of particular interest in regard to flow of talent are the results for the top-ability quartile of the samples, the main finding being one of little change from the 1970s to the 1980s, except for a swing from the humanities to the sciences. Of more interest are results indicating that the proportion of high-ability Black students who are completing undergraduate school has drastically declined, from 646 to 319 (or 64.6% of the age cohort to 31.9% of the cohort). The decline for high-ability Black students receiving degrees in the arts and sciences is particularly striking, from 361 to 127.

The explanation for the difference is not obvious. We would attribute it to some combination of four factors: the high cost of higher education, the contraction of financial aid, the relative attractiveness of military service (Arbeiter, 1986), and the availability of high-paying positions in industry for able students who have had at least some college. Why should an able Black student go thousands of dollars into debt when a lucrative job in industry is open to him or her? Why the same does not seem to hold for able Hispanic students is puzzling. In any case, the implications for future minority student enrollment in graduate schools are not encouraging.

ACKNOWLEDGMENT

This chapter is an abridged version of a paper presented at the Annual Meeting of the American Educational Research Association, Boston, Massachusetts, April 16–20, 1990.

CHAPTER TWELVE

Merging Data from Two Data Bases Without Common Members—A Proposal

Thomas L. Hilton
Educational Testing Service

When two bases have no members in common, there would seem to be no basis for merging the data in the two files. In this chapter, however, a possible method is described. It rests on the assumptions that, at least over a period of a few years, the personal characteristics of the members of homogeneous subgroups (e.g., Black females) do not change appreciably and that transitional probabilities (e.g., the proportion of Black females making the transition from high school to 4-year colleges) does not change appreciably. Whether the method will be useful in the future remains to be seen. A small exploratory test of the method raised questions about the assumptions underlying it.

—*Thomas L. Hilton*

For the purpose of this chapter, let us assume that we desire to estimate the number of undergraduates who are likely to drop out of 4-year colleges during some time period in the future. A rough estimate can be made from census data, but these are confounded by the fact that census data are cross-sectional. Possibly better data are available for a longitudinal sample—namely, the 1972 National Longitudinal Study. These data, however, are for the time period from 1972 to 1986. It is likely that the numbers are different now, both because the demographic mix of students in the schools has changed appreciably since the late 1970s and because the proportion of each population subgroup who drop out probably has changed (otherwise, efforts at numerous universities to reduce dropouts have been to no avail). Even if the proportion of each population subgroup

237

that drops out has remained approximately the same, the change in the number in each subgroup would change the results for aggregated samples. In this chapter, a possible remedy to the situation is described.

PROPOSED METHOD

Specifically, we propose to update the 1972 NLS data base by merging it with the 1980 Sophomore High School and Beyond data base. (Descriptions of these national surveys appear in several chapters of this book.) In the case of the preceding example, we would apply the drop-out *rates* for the 1972 cohort to the *numbers* of the 1980 cohort beginning college in 1982 and thereby estimate the total number of college dropouts (for the 1980 Sophomore cohort).

This proposal immediately raises the question of how one merges two data bases without common subjects. To do this, we propose to create a new unit of analysis, namely, the "average" individual in identical deeply stratified cells of each sample. An example of a "deeply stratified cell" would be the cell that includes only Hispanic females in the top quartile in ability and the top quartile in SES. The sample members in this cell in the NLS cohort and the parallel sample members in the HS&B cohort would be treated as if they were the same individuals. When we want a particular result for a cell or series of cells, we would compute it from the 1980 data file if the data are available, and, if not, we would compute it from the 1972 file and make adjustments for changes in the numbers in each cell, recognizing—of course—that the transitional probabilities may have changed since 1972. But, in the absence of data to the contrary, our assumption would be that the 1972 file provides the best available estimate of the drop-out proportion or other transitional probabilities in which we may be interested.

Technically speaking, this proposal hypothesizes that the number of individuals in a particular category at a given time (N) is equal to the cumulative sum of the product of the number of individuals in prior categories leading to the category of interest and the probability of the individuals in each prior category making the transition in question. For example, assuming that the students enrolled in the junior year of 4-year colleges in this country were previously either sophomores of 4-year colleges or 2nd-year students in 2-year colleges, we can say that:

$$N_4'' = P_4 N_4' + P_2 N_2' \tag{1}$$

where:

N_4'' = the number of students at time 2 in four-year colleges,

P_4 =   the probability of students in 4-year colleges making the transition from the 2nd to the 3rd year of 4-year colleges,

N_4' =   the number of 2nd year students in 4-year colleges at time 1,

P_2 =   the probability that students in the 2nd year of 2-year colleges will make the transition from 2-year colleges to 4-year colleges, and

N_2' =   the number of 2nd-year students in 2-year colleges at time 1.

Obviously, this example assumes that in any particular year there are no other pathways leading to the junior year of 4-year colleges.

Pursuing the drop-out example, we will not know how many members of the 1980 Sophomore cohort will complete college until the early 1990s (and some fraction of the cohort will complete college after that). But we do know how many of the 1980 high school sophomores started college and thereby are "in line" for graduation. Furthermore, we can compute the number "in line" for hundreds of cross-classifications. The number of female Hispanics of high ability and high SES who started college in 1982 would be one example. From knowledge of the completion rate by 1979 for the identical cross-classification of the 1972 cohort, we can estimate how many members of the identical cell in the 1980 cohort are likely to complete college within 7 years of high school graduation. Then, by aggregating across cells, we can estimate the number for any category, for example, all Hispanics, or for the total 1980 cohort.

Stratification.   How deeply the data should be stratified is an unanswered question. One view is that the nature of complex developmental processes, such as withdrawal from college, differs for individuals with different characteristics, and thus that the more cross-classifications there are, the more likely one is to reduce variance within groups. But increasing the number of stratification variables and categories within strata rapidly reduces the number of individuals in the final cells. At some unknown point, the transitional probabilities must become prohibitively unstable. This question needs further consideration.

Obviously, the validity of the proposed method rests on the assumption that transitional probabilities (e.g., dropout rates) are reasonably stable over periods of several years. Occasional opportunities to check this assumption suggest that it may be generally valid. For example, Table 12.1 from the 1985 *Condition of Education* (NCES, 1985a) lends support to this assumption. The similarity of the percentages in the second and sixth columns is impressive. Additional evidence comes from an article by Tinto (1982). As shown in Fig. 12.1 from the article, bachelor of arts

TABLE 12.1

Postsecondary Education Participation Rates of High School Graduates
Immediately Following Graduation, by Selected Characteristics:
United States, Fall 1972 to Fall 1980

Characteristic	Percent Participating in Fall 1972				Percent Participating in Fall 1980			
	Total[a]	4-Year Institution	2-Year Institution	Other[b]	Total[a]	4-Year Institution	2-Year Institution	Other[b]
All Graduates	53	30	16	7	54	31	18	5
Male	54	31	17	6	49	30	16	4
Female	53	29	15	9	56	32	19	6
White, non-Hispanic	55	32	16	7	55	33	18	5
Black, non-Hispanic	47	26	12	9	47	30	14	5
Hispanic	46	16	21	8	40	16	18	5
Low performer	30	8	12	10	27	9	13	6
Median performer	53	26	20	8	55	29	22	5
High performer	79	60	15	4	81	65	15	3
Low SES	34	14	11	8	35	17	15	5
Male	33	15	12	6	32	16	14	4
Female	35	14	11	10	37	17	15	5
White, non-Hispanic	31	12	11	8	33	15	15	5
Black, non-Hispanic	39	20	10	10	41	24	13	4
Hispanic	41	15	18	8	32	13	14	5
Low performer	27	8	10	9	23	8	10	6
Median performer	36	16	11	9	41	19	19	4
High performer	62	41	18	4	62	44	16	3

Middle SES	51	25	18	8	53	30	19	5
Male	51	26	18	7	48	28	18	3
Female	50	24	16	10	58	31	21	6
White, non-Hispanic	51	25	18	8	54	30	19	5
Black, non-Hispanic	55	34	14	8	53	36	14	4
Hispanic	51	17	25	9	46	18	23	5
Low performer	30	8	12	10	28	10	14	6
Median performer	51	22	20	9	54	28	22	5
High performer	73	49	19	5	80	60	19	3
High SES	79	57	18	4	77	55	19	4
Male	78	56	18	3	73	51	18	4
Female	80	57	17	6	82	61	20	3
White, non-Hispanic	79	57	18	4	78	56	19	4
Black, non-Hispanic	81	53	21	8	70	48	21	2
Hispanic	c	c	c	c	74	45	20	10
Low performer	46	16	22	9	49	18	23	9
Median performer	74	43	25	6	75	44	28	4
High performer	89	76	11	2	86	75	10	3

[a]Details may not add to totals because of rounding and because respondents in 1980 could have indicated that they attended more than one type of postsecondary institution.

[b]Includes vocational, trade, and business schools and schools that could not be classified otherwise.

[c]Small sample size precludes showing percents.

Note: From U.S. Department of Education, National Center for Education Statistics, National Longitudinal Study of the High School Class of 1972 and High School and Beyond, unpublished tabulations (December 1983).

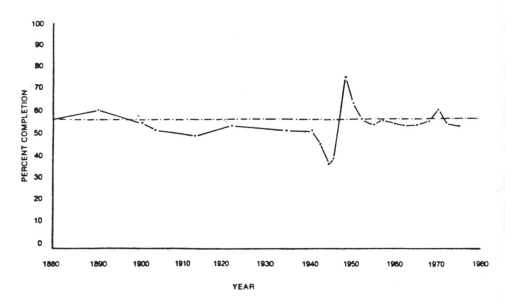

FIG. 12.1.   BA completion rates in higher education, 1880–1980 (with
estimated regression line). Percent completion = No. of BAs or first
professional degrees/no. of first-time degree enrollment four years earlier.
(From "Limits of Theory and Practice in Student Attrition" by V. Tinto,
1982, *Journal of Higher Education*, *53*, p. 694.)

completion rates in higher education have fluctuated around 55% since
1880! (What these data may say about the effect of educational interven-
tion programs is a fascinating subject in itself.)

Which stratification variables should be used is not obvious. My tentative view is that the variables selected should be those that account for
the most variance in the particular transition in question. The outcome
variable might be the number of high school seniors who were enrolled
in academic or college preparatory programs who later enrolled in 4-year
academic colleges. This transition is shown in Fig. 12.2, which was taken
from the GRE Pathways Study (Hilton & Schrader, 1985). A tentative list
of stratification variables might be sex, race/ethnicity, ability quartile, and
SES quartile. Region of the country might be an important stratification
variable, as may urban–rural location of the high school, but let us assume
for the time being that they are not.

If there are two sex categories, seven race/ethnic categories (White,
Black, Puerto Rican, Mexican American, Asian American, Native American, and other or unknown), four ability quartiles, and four SES quartiles,
then the number of final cells would be 224. Whether this number of
final cells is too few or too many is a technical question that will need
consideration, as mentioned earlier. For the moment, let us assume that

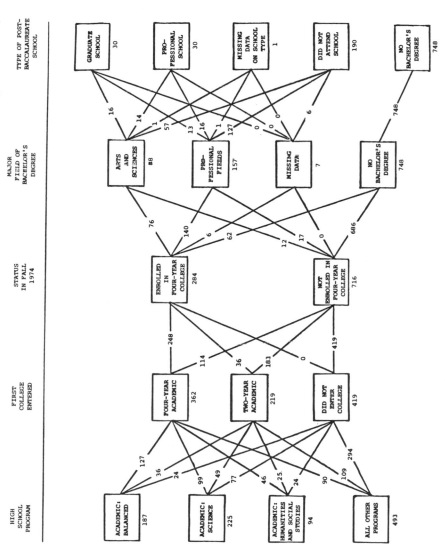

FIG. 12.2. Pathways for 1972 high school seniors: estimated number per 1,000 sample members (actual N = 16,740).

243

TABLE 12.2
Proportion of High School Seniors Naming MSE Majors
Who Actually Enrolled in MSE Undergraduate Majors

	1972 NLS		1982 HS&B	
		Sample		Sample
	p	N	p	N
Whites Males	.44	541	.47	501
White Females	.40	130	.37	162
Black Males	.38	18	.31	32
Black Females	.37	13	.37	35
Hispanic Males	.30	9	.29	23
Hispanic Females	.25	2	.33	14
Total	.42	768	.42	715

the only question is whether these 224 cells can usefully be considered individuals.

RESULTS

As a preliminary test of the proposed model, the transitional probabilities from the category of high school seniors who intended to major in math, science, or engineering (MSE) to the category of college students who were attending 2- or 4-year colleges and intended to major or actually were majoring in the MSE field were computed for the NLS cohort and the HS&B sophomore cohort.

As shown in Table 12.2, the p for the total sample was .42 in 1972 and .42 in 1982. In other words, approximately 42% of the high school seniors who cited a MSE major as their intended college major actually enrolled in college and indicated that they were enrolled in an MSE major or intended to do so. Similarly—10 years later—42% of the HS&B sophomores reported the same experience.

For subgroups of the sample, the probabilities were less similar but still generally parallel, with the exception of the Hispanic female figure that in 1972 was based on only two cases. However, when the 1972 probabilities were used—in accordance with the hypothesized model—to predict the actual numbers making the transition in 1982, the predicted numbers were usually very similar but significantly different from the actual numbers according to a chi-square test. Details of this test are provided in the next chapter. Furthermore, when the number of subgroups was increased in hopes of improving the fit, the difference was still significantly different.[1]

---

[1]The author is indebted to Valerie E. Lee for performing the many calculations required for these tests.

These results suggest that 10 years may be too long a time period to expect transitional probabilities to remain constant. Surely governmental and educational efforts designed, in effect, to increase transitional probabilities, and also labor market conditions, must have some effect on the probabilities. The results also suggest that the model may be valid only for large samples, because otherwise the probabilities become prohibitively unstable. In conclusion, the author still finds the rationale for the model appealing, but obviously more work on it needs to be done. It is also the case that subtle differences in the instruments used in NLS and the two cohorts of HS&B no doubt contributed to differences in cell frequencies and transitional probabilities. These differences are described in the next chapter.

CHAPTER THIRTEEN

Pooling Data from Two Longitudinal Cohorts: Some Problems and Solutions

Valerie E. Lee
University of Michigan

The *1972 National Longitudinal Study* and *High School and Beyond* were designed—among other objectives—to yield parallel data on the educational development of three cohorts of students in the United States: the high school graduating classes of 1972, 1980, and 1982. When, however, researchers try to make fine-grained comparisons of the three cohorts, numerous difficulties are encountered. In this chapter, some of these problems are described, along with steps taken to make comparisons more valid and meaningful.

—Thomas L. Hilton

The *National Longitudinal Study* contains a nationally representative sample of students who were high school seniors in 1972 (Hilton & Rhett, 1973). These students were followed longitudinally at regular 2-year intervals until 1979. Only those students with data at all five time points were selected for the study described in this chapter, resulting in a sample of 12,964. With this sample, the proportion of the high-school senior cohort of 1972 who expressed interest in majoring in mathematics, science, and engineering or who actually chose such majors in college and/or graduate school could be determined at five time points:

- Senior year of high school.
- First college entered, within 2 years of high school graduation.
- Junior year of college.
- College graduation (BS or BA degree).
- Graduate school.

Although the value of regular follow-up data on a large random sample of students is well appreciated, it is recognized that the NLS-72 sample is somewhat out of date. Moreover, more recent data indicate that the actual composition of the high-school senior cohort has changed considerably in the last decade or so. Therefore, it is advantageous to use more current longitudinal data to update the projections that may be drawn from NLS. Fortunately, another large nationally representative longitudinal study was available to add to our knowledge of persistence in the sciences: *High School and Beyond.* In this chapter, the focus is on the cohort of students who were high school seniors in 1982 (Sebring et al., 1987b). For these students, information is available for three time points. Again, only those students with data for all three were selected (*n* = 10,739).[1] The three time points were:

- Sophomore year of high school.
- Senior year of high school.
- First college entered, within 2 years of high school graduation.

There are several characteristics of these two data bases that make them especially useful for making projections of persistence in the sciences for high school and college students. First, they are both comprised of large nationally representative samples of the high school population, affording generalization to the entire population of high school seniors for 1972 and 1982.[2] Second, they are separated by exactly a decade—a convenient time period to investigate both similarities and changes. Third (and crucial), both studies contain parallel data on at least two time points (senior year of high school and first college entered), making possible investigation of specific changes and similarities in *rates* of persistence in the sciences, rather than simple cross-sectional single-time-point comparisons. It is the existence of two similar time points in both data bases that originally encouraged our attempts to link the two in order to make long-term projections.

There are, however, several characteristics of the data that make the physical linking of these two data bases difficult, if not impossible. Although the two surveys were designed to be highly parallel in nature, small changes between them make linkage problematic. First, certain

---

[1]The HS&B sample also contained students who were in high schools as sophomores but who had dropped out by senior year (*n* = 1,684, or 14% of the sample). These students were excluded from these analyses, in order to make the HS&B sample as comparable as possible to the NLS sample, which contained no dropouts.

[2]All analyses with both NLS and HS&B have been run employing design weights, in order to compensate for the oversampling of certain strata and the loss of certain students due to attrition over several follow-ups.

crucial questions were asked slightly differently for the two samples. For example, both location in the survey questionnaire and actual wording of certain items were different across the two studies. This sort of difficulty is to be expected in studies that span a 10-year time period. Second and more important, there were considerable changes in the high school senior student samples over the decade from 1972 to 1982. Not only were there serious demographic changes in the composition of the high school senior cohort (becoming more minority, slightly more female, and somewhat less able), but the environment in which these students existed (educational, social, and economic) changed substantially. These latter changes are likely to have resulted in a considerable increase in interest in the sciences over the decade.

The original aim of this study was to physically link these two data bases. That aim was based on a hypothesis that interest and persistence in the sciences was stable over time for specific stratified subgroups in the high-school population (see chapter 12). An example of the level of subgroup stratification was, say, Hispanic females of high ability, or Black males of below-average SES. Analysis of the feasibility of linking the data bases suggested the need for a specific statistical test of that hypothesis. Using a chi-square goodness-of-fit test[3] to assess the tenability of that hypothesis, it was decided that persistence in the sciences for stratified subgroups was *not* sufficiently stable over time to confirm the original hypothesis of stability of persistence for stratified subgroups. Therefore, the notion of physically linking the two data bases was abandoned. Instead, it was decided to present results in the form of information from both sources. This form of presentation recognizes both the quasi-longitudinal nature of the combined data (i.e., information on six important educational time points) and the specific changes in persistence rates from

---

[3]The goodness-of-fit test was conducted as follows. First, cross-tabulations were performed between high school senior year and first college entered on choice of major ("MSE," "other majors," "everyone else") for both the HS&B-82 and the NLS-72 samples. These were done separately for six groups: White, Black, and Hispanic males and females. NLS results were adjusted for the different distributions in the sample on the race-by-sex group proportions, as well as the differences in the sample sizes. The HS&B sample was considered as the "expected" results, and the NLS sample (adjusted for the differences in demographic distributions) as the "observed." These figures were then used for computation of a chi-square statistic, with 4 degrees of freedom. Because the aim of the goodness-of-fit test is a nonsignificant chi-square statistic, rejection of the null hypothesis of no difference indicates that the fit is not good. The chi-square statistic computed on these stratified groups was 191.1, and the critical value for chi-square ($df = 4$) is 9.488. The hypothesis of comparability was thus rejected.

The same computations were performed for the two samples without adjusting for the differences due to stratified subgroups, and the resulting chi-square statistic ($df = 4$) was 388.8. Therefore, while stratification appeared to help somewhat, neither value is close to "passing" the goodness-of-fit test.

1972 to 1982. The results are presented separately for demographic subgroups and thus demonstrate differential persistence rates by race/ethnicity and by gender.

This chapter focuses on specific methodological problems encountered in conducting this study. It is hoped that this discussion has value both as an example of a specific effort to combine two rather similar data bases that contain information that is reasonably common and as an alternative strategy when actual linkage is not feasible.

Changes in the High School Population 1972 to 1982

The availability of the HS&B and NLS data bases has allowed a series of comparisons of the two. The most comprehensive comparison study was produced by the Educational Testing Service (Rock, Ekstrom, Goertz, Pollack, & Hilton, 1984). Although this study made comparisons of the 1980 senior cohort of HS&B with the 1972 NLS sample (rather than the 1982 HS&B senior cohort that is the focus of this study), its conclusions are relevant. In brief, some of the important changes noted in the Rock et al. report are as follows:

- The high school senior cohort went from being 86 percent White in 1972 to 80 percent White in 1980. This change incorporated an increase of 33 percent in the Black population (from 9% to 12%), and a corresponding increase in Hispanics.
- The proportion of the population that is female rose from 50% to 52%.
- The proportion of the population classified as low socioeconomic status (SES) rose 12% (from 24.5% to 27.4%).
- The proportion of students in the general (as opposed to the college preparatory or vocational) curriculum track increased by 17% (from 32% to 37%), and this was coupled with many other indicators of less academic emphasis in schools and in student behaviors.
- Test scores declined, both for the general population and for specific subgroups.

Although the demographic changes in the population might explain the overall test score decline, the declines within demographic subgroups cannot be explained by this phenomenon. In general, although the test score decline was largest for Whites, it was not inconsequential for minorities. Although the minority disadvantage vis-à-vis Whites thus has declined somewhat, the overall test score decline for racial subgroups is marked. For example, White test scores in mathematics, reading, and vocabulary declined significantly. Male scores declined more than female scores (.26 standard deviation units for males in vocabulary, for example). Declines were relatively greater for higher-SES students.

The analysis for this study have confirmed those changes reported by Rock et al. (1984) (more minorities, more females, less advantaged students, lower demonstrated ability) when comparing NLS-72 with the 1982 sample from HS&B. However, because the focus of the study is persistence in the sciences, differences across the two cohorts that relate to planned science majors are reported. Because there are two common time points in the two data bases—high school senior year and first college entered—concentration is on changes reported only for those two time points. Although several differences could be reported that impact students' science interests, only two have been chosen for focus: (a) the proportion of students of above-average demonstrated ability interested in science for the two samples, and (b) the increase in the college-going patterns for several stratified subgroups (race/ethnicity, gender, and ability). Taken together with the data reported by Rock et al. (1984) and summarized previously, these cross-decade comparisons should supply some explanations for the differences that were observed for the two data bases.

The Problem of How to Define High Ability. Table 13.1 displays comparisons between 1972 and 1982 for the proportions of above-average achieving students who expressed interest in MSE at both their senior year of high school and after they have entered their first college. Definition of the high-ability group was somewhat different for each subgroup listed. For example, above-average Black students were selected as those who have scored above the average *for Black students* on a composite measure of achievement (reading, vocabulary, and mathematics—equally weighted). That means that the "cut point" for constituting these groups was different for each subgroup, and considerably lower for the Black and Hispanic than for the White subgroups. The decision to vary the cut point for each subgroup was made in order to insure substantial numbers of minority students in these above-average ability samples. It also could be argued that such a decision reflects the admissions procedures for minority students in many colleges (i.e., affirmative action). The tests were equated between the two samples, with means determined separately for each data base. Roughly half of each subgroup sample fell above the mean, with minor variations due to slightly negatively skewed distribution, especially for minority groups.

Change in College Attendance Patterns from 1972 to 1982. In order to pursue a major or career in MSE, students must first attend college. Table 13.2 displays comparative college attendance patterns,

TABLE 13.1
Proportion of Above-Average Achieving Students in Total Sample.
Racial/Ethnic, and Gender Subgroups Who Plan Majors in Mathematics,
Science, and Engineering (MSE) in HS&B and NLS Samples

		Senior Year High School	First College
Total Sample	HS&B[a]	.258[b]	.167
	NLS	.204	.119
Whites	HS&B	.270	.177
	NLS	.214	.124
Blacks	IIS&B	.195	.136
	NLS	.134	.081
Hispanics	HS&B	.211	.107
	NLS	.107	.056
Males	HS&B	.360	.211
	NLS	.309	.182
Females	HS&B	.152	.111
	NLS	.095	.052

[a]HS&B sample is 1982 seniors, and does not include students who dropped out of high school between their sophomore and seniors years.

[b]Above-average achieving students are specific for each subgroup. That is, students in each subgroup who scored above the mean *for that group* on a composite achievement test are included in these analyses. Composite scores are IRT-equated achievement scores for NLS and HS&B.

broken out by 2-year and 4-year college and separated for several subgroups. College attendance patterns for the same subgroups presented in earlier analyses are shown at the top of the table, but these racial/ethnic subgroups are further broken down by gender and by the same ability groupings shown in the last analyses (i.e., below- and above-average achievement relative to the racial subgroups as a whole). Clearly, the high school class of 1982 is more likely to be in college 2 years after high school than was the class of 1972—36% more likely. The increased likelihood of attending a 2-year college is very slightly greater than a 4-year college. This trend should be seen in light of the changing character of the high school classes from 1972 to 1982, which contain more minority and more disadvantaged students, more females, and students of somewhat lower demonstrated ability. A striking comparison is between those groups more likely to be in college in 1984 than in 1974: a slightly higher increase for minorities than for Whites, but particularly more females, who have increased their college attendance patterns by 55%. This "female college attendance increase" is particularly concentrated in their proportionate increase in 2-year college attendance, which grew by 76%.

Perhaps the more interesting patterns of increased college attendance are shown in the lower rows of Table 13.2, however, where the racial

TABLE 13.2

Proportion of 1972 and 1982 High School Seniors In 2-Year and
4-Year College Two Years After High School Graduation Separately by
Race and Gender for Below- and Above-Average Achievement Groups

	1982[a]			1972			% Increase in Proportion
	4-Yr.	2-Yr.	Total	4-Yr.	2-Yr.	Total	
Total Sample	.365	.215	.581	.285	.144	.428	+35.7%
White	.386	.218	.604	.291	.144	.434	+39.2%
Black	.315	.188	.504	.264	.091	.355	+42.0%
Hispanic	.249	.231	.480	.124	.209	.333	+44.1%
Male	.333	.191	.523	.292	.146	.438	+19.4%
Female	.398	.240	.637	.274	.136	.410	+55.4%
White Males							
Below-Aver.	.176	.190	.365	.102	.145	.251	+45.4%
Above-Aver.[b]	.604	.217	.822	.485	.149	.635	+29.4%
White Females							
Below-Aver.	.275	.252	.537	.009	.130	.233	+130.5%
Above-Aver.[b]	.622	.208	.829	.460	.149	.610	+35.9%
Black Males							
Below-Aver.	.159	.131	.290	.101	.053	.152	+90.8%
Above-Aver.[b]	.436	.175	.612	.437	.115	.552	+10.9%
Black Females							
Below-Aver.	.256	.236	.492	.133	.103	.234	+110.3%
Above-Aver.[b]	.584	.225	.809	.432	.095	.526	+53.9%
Hispanic Males							
Below-Aver.	.117	.170	.297	.029	.219	.247	+20.2%
Above-Aver.[b]	.307	.263	.560	.188	.277	.465	+20.4%
Hispanic Females							
Below-Aver.	.214	.205	.419	.064	.127	.191	+119.4%
Above-Aver.[b]	.426	.350	.777	.244	.221	.465	+67.1%

[a]HS&B sample is 1982 seniors, and does not include students who dropped out of high school between their sophomore and seniors years.

[b]Above-average achieving students are specific for each subgroup. That is, students in each subgroup who scored above the mean *for that group* on a composite achievement test are included in these analyses. Composite scores are IRT-equated achievement scores for NLS and HS&B.

groups are separated first by gender and then by ability. Clearly, students of above-average demonstrated ability are considerably more likely to be in college both in 1972 and 1982. For White males in the class of 1982, those of above-average ability are 2.5 times more likely to attend 4-year college, and even slightly more likely to attend 2-year college. The same pattern was seen in 1972, where the likelihood for high-ability White males to be in 4-year colleges was almost 4 times greater than for low-ability students in that subgroup. The same patterns are observed for all the race/gender/ability groups.

By far, the more important increases in college attendance patterns are seen for students scoring below average in high school achievement. Although this pattern holds for all subgroups except Hispanic males, it is considerably higher for females than for males. In fact, the proportions of White, Black, and Hispanic females of below-average ability who attended college in 1984 has increased by over 100% (i.e., more than doubled) in each case. The only group of male students who approach these increase figures are Black males of below-average ability. Clearly, the increase in college attendance rates is concentrated in the groups of high school graduates who score below their groups' average in high school achievement. Although the percentage increase figures shown in the right-hand column of Table 13.2 for combined 2-year and 4-year college attendance, the attendance rate increases for 2-year colleges are very slightly greater than for 4-year colleges.

This is not an important difference, however. Surely, the proportionate increases in college attendance for females, for minorities, and particularly for students of below-average demonstrated ability is no surprise to those who are charged with admission and remediation programs in institutions of higher education. However, to those who are perhaps not quite so familiar with the characteristics of the contemporary college population compared to a decade ago, the proportion of the high-school graduate population who make up that 36% increase may be rather startling.

Other Methodological Problems Encountered

Including a section with this title may be seen as a justification for not being able to do what was proposed. This is a tempting motivation. However, this section is included mostly to demonstrate the technical difficulties in carrying out the original aim of this study: to link data bases with noncommon subjects to make long-term projections. Two very similar data bases were selected for a project that was begun as a feasibility study, to serve as a "best case" approach. Both NLS and HS&B were conceived and conducted with very similar aims and approaches. Both samples were nationally representative, which makes the studies considerably more useful in providing information about the high school senior cohort than such selective groups as the annual population of SAT takers. Although both are reasonably large, when attempts to examine the behaviors of specific subgroups are made (e.g., Hispanic females of high ability), size limitations loom large. Being drawn exactly a decade apart provides a useful across-time contrast. Specific attempts were made by NCES to make HS&B very similar to NLS in many respects, primarily so that comparisons such as those made in this study would be possible.

In fact, it is surprising that the number of cross-study comparisons has not been greater.

The pitfalls of such cross-study comparisons are less obvious. In fact, the pitfalls were discovered only as attempts at specific comparisons were undertaken, and these technical differences between the two studies were often found to have a more profound influence on results than would seem obvious. Some of the difficulties that were encountered are illustrative of problems implicit in any attempt to link data bases with non-common subjects. An example follows.

Variable Definition.   The variable of particular focus in this study involves students' responses to a question that was phrased, "Indicate the field that comes closest to what you would most likely study in college" (Jones et al., 1986; Item BB120 and FY127 on the HS&B base-year and first follow-up survey questionnaires). Students were given a 25-level response choice. To define the variable for use in this study, responses that fall into the MSE categories must be grouped together—a simple task. However, by the HS&B second follow-up in 1984, the data for MSE choice in first college entered were drawn, the item was phrased and structured quite differently. That is, students were asked to indicate their possible field of study in their first, second, and possible third college attended during the 2 years since high school graduation. The items (SY18H, SY19H, and SY20H) were phrased as follows: "During the last month you attended, what was your actual or intended field of study or training?"[1] No response pattern was provided, and a verbal response was expected. NORC coded these responses into a series of 6-digit numerical categories. It was up to researchers to create a coding pattern to correspond to the 25-level code from earlier time points. The difficulties involved in such a procedure are magnified by the fact that the same variable was yet again differently coded on the base year and multiple follow-ups from NLS. NCES has provided little guidance on making such codings comparable across the two data bases. However, absolute comparability is essential in a study of this nature, with the onus for comparability falling on individual researchers.

There are many other variables that required comparable recoding, which are not described in detail here. In fact, the definition of "Hispanic" is far from obvious, and this definition was not comparable across the two data bases. In NLS, respondents were asked to choose one of the following racial/ethnic categories to describe themselves:

---

[1]Jones et al. (1986), Section 8.8, p. 20, 22, 25.

American Indian
Black or Afro American or Negro
Mexican American or Chicano
Puerto Rican
Other Latin American origin
Oriental or Asian American
White or Caucasian
Other

How Latin Americans who considered themselves White or Black made a choice is problematic. In 1980, the item was changed to a two-stage response—that is, the respondents first were asked what their race was and then were asked about origin or descent. While this change permitted more precise distinctions within the HS&B data base, it left researchers trying to achieve comparability in a quandary. Should White Cubans, for example, be classified as White or Hispanic?

Being "in college" is also not entirely straightforward. Should both full-time and part-time students be included (that is the choice selected here)? How can one be sure certain vocationally oriented or proprietary schools are correctly classified as "college" (FICE codes were employed to eliminate the marginal schools)? If students transfer from one college to another, or in and out of college, between one follow-up and another (a fairly common occurrence), how can one be sure to have captured the proper college and to have tapped the student's intended major in that college?

Creating comparable ability measures across the two data bases, which include different achievement tests, created a special problem. Fortunately, the researchers who conducted the earlier ETS study (see chapter 11) had created IRT-equated scores for these two studies that were available for use in this study. Had those not been available, the equating of such noncomparable tests would have been very time consuming and tremendously costly. The conclusion reluctantly reached was that creating comparable variables across separate follow-ups on the same study, and especially across different data bases, is quite difficult but absolutely critical to making such comparisons.

The Problem of Defining the Sample.   In any such study that uses a random sample of the population, including the entire sample is necessary to preserve external validity. Only the entire sample is truly representative of the population to which we wish to generalize. A particular problem of longitudinal studies with several follow-ups is the nontrivial loss of cases for subsequent follow-ups. That is, should a study that has four follow-ups use only those students who have full data on all follow-ups? Because both attrition and nonresponse (i.e., missing data) are generally nonrandom (these were tested on NLS and found to be highly nonrandom), there is no easy way to make such decisions. Moreover, when attempts are made to compare across data bases that have different numbers of follow-ups, the difficulty of maintaining large and equally representative samples in both data bases is magnified. For example, the HS&B sample was originally drawn at sophomore year of high school. A number (over 15%) of those students in the original sample dropped out of high school between their sophomore and senior years, and were surveyed and tested by NCES along with their cohort. Although studying these students is an interesting inquiry in itself, they were dropped in these analyses. This decision was made to render the samples from HS&B and NLS comparable and included only those students who were in high school as seniors. However, eliminating those dropouts caused the loss of some important information, especially about minority students. In cross-data base comparisons, one is forced to use comparability as the most important consideration for drawing the samples. But the samples constructed under such limitations are likely to lose their representativeness for their respective age cohorts. Balancing these several considerations is difficult.

Questionnaire Comparability.   This is another important problem in cross-data base comparability. That is, NLS students were asked to indicate their intended college major in a section of the questionnaire that a fair number of students never reached. In an early section of the questionnaire, those students who thought they might seek some sort of vocational training after high school were asked to skip over several pages of the questionnaire to a different section. Those who did not want vocational training were to proceed through the items without skipping pages. Investigation of spaced samples showed that many more than the students who desired vocational training skipped over a section of the questionnaire containing items that were vital to our analyses. Those who construct such questionnaires learned a lesson from NLS, and very few of these "survey detours" exist in the HS&B questionnaires. However, groups of students were lost who should not have been lost in NLS (and neither their background characteristics nor their major choices are known). It is clear that the samples are not quite comparable because of this "detour" problem. Moreover, the loss of students from NLS is very likely to bias the results (i.e., the inadvertently excluded groups are probably not a random sample of the NLS population). There is no way to adjust for such losses, even with reasonably comparable data bases.

A Test of Data Base Comparability. During the early part of this study, the hypothesis about the stability of persistence rates in science for stratified subgroups was investigated. Specifically, the hypothesis was tested on the two most comparable data bases available—the two cohorts of the *High School and Beyond* study. Although this study focused on the HS&B sample that consisted of high school seniors in 1982, a comparable cohort of HS&B 1980 seniors existed. These two data files (the 1980 and 1982 HS&B seniors) seem as parallel as two data bases with noncommon subjects could be. Therefore, a test of the "stable transitional probabilities" hypothesis (between high school and first college) on these two samples was undertaken, using the same chi-square goodness-of-fit test described earlier. Specifically, the comparability of transitional probabilities from senior year in high school to first college was tested across the two data bases. The results from this test revealed two things: (a) the transitional probabilities were not comparable over even a 2-year separation (i.e., they did not pass the goodness-of-fit test); and (b) stratifying by subgroups (here, race-by-gender) did not markedly improve the comparability of transitional probabilities over these two data bases. The reasons for these curious results were pursued.

Upon closer examination, it was discovered that, even over these two highly parallel studies, a factor important to this study was in fact not comparable. That is, the individual item defining probable college major choice for students in their first college in two data bases had been defined quite differently. For the 1982 seniors, field of study was defined as described earlier, and the first college where students had selected a major field was used to define the variable. However, for the first follow-up of the 1980 seniors, the "college major" question was formulated quite differently. Students were not asked to indicate a field of study in each college they attended. Rather, they were asked the following question: "Academic fields typically lead to a four- or five-year Bachelor's degree. Please select below the category which best describes this field or area" (Sebring et al., 1987; Item FE34B). Students were given the same 25-level response code to choose from that was earlier described as the high school major choice variable. However, this major choice variable was drawn from "the most recent month, in the last school attended." Recall that all other data were constructed around students' choice of planned major in their first college, but in HS&B-80 only the last college major choice could be identified. At least 15% of these students attended a second college within 2 years after high school graduation, with much smaller (but nontrivial) proportions in third, fourth, and even fifth colleges. It seems likely that as students change college, they might change majors as well.

The results of this test of the hypothesis, using two highly comparable data bases with noncommon subjects, show that the issue of comparability of individual questionnaire items (i.e., variables) is a major difficulty in the use of different data bases to make long-term predictions. It was after this analysis that attempts to test the hypothesis of stability of transition probabilities for stratified subgroups were abandoned. Instead, the focus was broadened to include both changes over time for the same cohorts and science loss over the course of the educational pipeline for the same students.

Although the original aim of this study was to physically link two data bases with noncommon subjects to make long-term projections, it was concluded that this is an impossible task with the two data bases selected. Small changes in the data-gathering methods over the two studies, usually instituted to improve the quality of the data collected, made technical linkage impossible. However, using reasonably comparable data bases with common time points, the study described in this chapter represents an attempt to construct a useful picture of the persistence of students in the sciences, a picture that captures both the longitudinal (i.e., multiple time points for the same individuals) and the cross-sectional (i.e., equivalent time points for different individuals) nature of the educational environment for students interested in the sciences. Specific pitfalls that were encountered in the course of this study (noncomparable variables, noncomparable samples, order of questionnaire presentation) would cloud findings for almost any study that uses multiple data bases. Nevertheless, it is concluded that nationally representative longitudinal studies, such as those investigated in this study, continue to offer some of the best information available about the educationally related behaviors of America's youth. Despite the inability to link the data bases, they are still excellent sources of data to investigate these questions. The major advantages of both HS&B and NLS are that they are: (a) nationally representative and (b) longitudinal. This means that conclusions drawn from a study such as this one may be generalized to all American high school graduates from those years—conclusions that incorporate change in the same individuals.

CHAPTER FOURTEEN

Drawing Educational Implications from Multiple Data Bases

William W. Turnbull
Educational Testing Service

Four of the chapters in this volume were first presented in a symposium at the 1987 annual meeting of the American Educational Research Association. The late William W. Turnbull served as the discussant of the symposium. His remarks are presented verbatim in this chapter. He not only summarizes the main conclusions of each of the four chapters but also points out their implications for future research and suggests ways in which the topics of each chapter can be pursued further.[1]

—*Thomas L. Hilton*

In some fields of science, it is possible to do small and elegant laboratory studies of causal relationships, where single variables are isolated experimentally. In education, however, we can almost never hold things constant experimentally. Instead, we have to control them statistically in order to tease out the contingent relationships.

This means we must represent all the possible explanatory variables in our data set. No single study ever seems to provide data on all the possibly relevant variables, but sometimes the missing variables may be tantalizingly included in somebody else's data set. Why not just appropriate the missing pieces and complete the picture?

The preceding chapters tell us why not. Borrowing a piece from another data set to complete your own is much like borrowing a piece

---

[1]This chapter originated as Dr. Turnbull's discussion of a symposium entitled *Drawing educational implications from multiple data bases,* annual meeting of the AERA, Washington, DC, April 1987.

from somebody else's jigsaw puzzle to complete your own. Even though
the borrowed piece represents part of the sky or the river or the house
in each puzzle, it turns out that when you try to use it in your own the
color is off or the shape is not right, and no amount of pounding will
make it fit.

The problem is that we cannot let it go at that level of defeatism,
because the questions being asked of the data bases are too important.
They are in many cases the broad policy questions that educational
researchers can hope to answer only from large-scale data sets.

Accordingly, we should welcome the quartet of studies presented here
(see chapters 2, 7, 8, and 13) because they probe the extent to which
we can borrow data elements from one set to substitute for missing
elements in another set or, in the ultimate case, merge data bases
completely to create what Tom Hilton refers to as a "standing data base,"
more or less abstracted from the population samples from which it was
created.

The chapters complement one another nicely. In chapter 2, Hilton set
the stage by sketching the large hope and the careful design behind this
NSF-supported effort. He pointed out that a real merger of data bases was
the ultimate goal to be achieved, approximated, or abandoned in the
overall feasibility study.

Susan Urahn (chapter 8) used data from the nationally representative
NAEP sample to predict the scores of a self-selected group of SAT takers.
Spencer Swinton (chapter 7) went the other way, using SAT scores for
a self-selected group to predict what the scores would be for a nationally
representative population. In each case, the authors tried to relate results
from two radically different samples.

Valerie Lee (chapter 13) bit the bullet of trying to really merge two
fairly similar data sets. She examined the possibility of merging two nationally representative data bases (NLS and HS&B), dismissed that
possibility for cause, and went on to draw from the two data sets as separate but related sources in predicting future enrollments in math, science,
and engineering.

I think these varied approaches succeed nicely in illuminating both the
promise and the problems of working across data bases or trying to combine them.

Swinton tackled a particularly tough but important problem: trying
to infer from the part to the whole or, more specifically, trying to predict
the scores of an unbiased sample of all high school seniors from the scores
of a biased sample of SAT takers. He derived the network of predictive
relationships between SAT and NLS scores by calculating correlations
across 24 subgroup means, where the subgroups are homogeneous by
sex, ethnic group, and geographic region. He found that the results show

utility in many respects but too much instability over time in the case of verbal scores: that is, the correlation of means across subgroups of the SAT and NLS verbal scores, even when adjusted for SES, was too low in 1980 to support using SAT scores to predict NLS scores.

The relatively low correlation of SAT-V and SES that shows up when he correlates group means is interesting and deserves further study. I suspect that it is likely to be artifactual. Accordingly, I think Swinton's suggestion of reanalyzing the correlational data on the individual level is a good idea. The greater stability in correlations based on individuals rather than subgroups might yield a more satisfactory basis for estimating nationally representative scores from SAT scores. The advantage would be substantial, because SAT data are generated annually. It would be very nice if they could be used to create approximations of data collected much less frequently in national studies.

The chapters by Urahn and Lee are fascinating for their substantive findings as well as for their contributions to methodology, especially because both presenters are courageous enough to hazard predictions about the future based on the strength of the associations they find between quite different data sets.

Urahn used NAEP data for 13-year-olds to predict the SAT scores that will be earned 5 years later by a self-selected subgroup from the same cohort, who by 1989 will be 18-year-olds. That is really quite a leap. The things that have changed include the nature of the sample, the test, the identities of the students, their ages at the two testing times, and the years (and hence the social and educational context) when the two tests were taken. The fact that Sue found a lot of consistency across the disparate conditions she studied is encouraging: We are certainly seeing the rejection of the null hypothesis, which would be that because of all the differences between the two data sets the comparisons would be unstable and prediction would fall around the chance level.

What Urahn predicts, of course, is subject to verification or disproof. She says that based on NAEP reading scores gathered in 1984 it looks as if SAT-V scores in 1989 will be higher in general than in 1985 and also as if Black students will continue to gain on Whites. Fascinating forecast! If it comes out right, whoever is President in 1989 will take credit for the change. Susan has advanced plausible hypotheses to account for the lack of perfect predictions in the past data between the data bases, in particular the differential changes in self-selection into the SAT population that have characterized different ethnic subgroups in recent years. I think it would be great if she would now throw caution completely out the window and predict specific subgroup scores on the SAT by sex and ethnicity, in 1989. I make the suggestion not to jeopardize her career but because comparing such quantified predictions with later actuals would be even more helpful in sharpening theory than comparing a predicted direction of change. As a gesture of scientific prudence, she might want to place confidence bands around the predicted scores.

Lee has taken what seems at first a more manageable problem, in that she is dealing with two data bases that were intended to be as similar as possible, even though they are separated by 10 years. The similarities, although substantial, were insufficient to justify the merger of even these two bases. It is useful to look at the kinds of differences that Valerie has cited. I suggest that they fall into two broad categories: (a) those that are theoretically controllable elements of study design, and (b) those that are not normally controllable.

Differences in controllable elements that Valerie found uncontrolled include differences in how the samples were drawn, how several crucial questions were asked, how answers were encoded, and how responses were combined. For two supposedly parallel studies, that is a discouraging list. Changes in uncontrollable elements that precluded merging the data sets were fundamentally different: substantive changes in students' interests over several years rather than methodological disparities. They appear to represent basic changes that came about in the value systems, interest patterns, and career plans of students over a decade. The existence of a trend toward an affinity with more education in general and more science in particular is part of the conclusion she was looking to confirm or deny. She found it reflected not only in the overall aggregate data but also in the subgroups stratified by ability, sex, and ethnicity. From the standpoint of the supply of trained scientists, that is a healthy trend. From the standpoint of data base comparability, it is an element of change or instability. Because those attitudes changed during the 10-year period, they can obviously change again, and we have to treat these data sets, gathered in sequential time slices, not as linkable through merger or consolidation but linkable only in the sense in which successive points on a trend line are linked.

The disparities in the controllable aspects of data sets are of course of methodological interest, especially such questions as: (a) How far can we go toward eliminating them, and (b) how much difference do they make anyway? These questions are especially important ones to answer, because Lee was working with the two national longitudinal studies, sponsored by the Center for Education Statistics, that Hilton identified as the best available framework for a unified data base.

Despite the absence of complete parallelism in the controllable aspects of even those two data sets, they were close enough in their design to allow Lee to predict that the supply of scientists will continue to rise throughout the decade and will include increasing proportions of women and minorities, although parity will not be reached in either case. Maybe

Lee could be persuaded to predict not just the direction of change but specific numbers, within confidence limits, that will constitute the yield of science students or graduates in some specific year. The more people who are willing to climb into the leaky boat of testing the predictive power of multiple data bases by putting up specific numerical forecasts, the better we will be able to judge how far we are from 20/20 foresight.

Hilton's chapter presents the overall strategy for investigating how we can capitalize on information resident in different data sets that, taken together, can illuminate issues in education. By pulling together the insights provided by these studies, and especially by noting the problems they encountered, we can perhaps develop a better taxonomy of the preconditions required for merging educational data bases.

Lee's chapter notes several such preconditions, including similarity of sampling rules; similarity of question forms, including the options provided; similarity of response coding and rules for aggregating response categories; and agreement on the treatment of missing cases. To these could be added similarity of target populations, simultaneity of data collections, and comparability of incentives or sanctions for responding candidly or slanting responses or omitting answers altogether. We need to inventory such requirements carefully. We also need to develop alternative procedures for testing and quantifying degrees of similarity and sensitivity-analysis techniques for deciding when it is or is not useful to merge the data bases for answering particular questions. The specific studies here presented help to fill out the strategy outlined by Hilton. Taken together, they move us several steps further towards the goal of an empirically grounded theory of how and when to draw upon multiple data bases in answering educational questions.

CHAPTER FIFTEEN

Summary and Conclusions

Thomas L. Hilton
Educational Testing Service

The strategy adopted in the author's investigation of the feasibility of constructing a unified data base of educational data was simply to try to merge several data bases on a small scale to see what problems would be encountered. If no unsolvable problems were encountered, we then would proceed with a pilot model of a unified base and run it on sample tasks as a way of estimating costs and evaluating the output obtained. The fact is that we never reached the pilot model stage, for reasons that are made evident shortly. To describe the problems encountered in constructing a unified data base and using national data bases in educational research, and simultaneously to convey our conclusions about the feasibility of the former, we review the strengths and weaknesses of each of the levels of unified data bases that we described earlier.

POOLED DATA

Pooling data from several sources with no effort to restructure the different files is the simplest type of unified data base. An example would be a pooling of SAT data for one sample and ACT data for a second sample without allowing for the possibility that the two samples might have members in common. The only advantages to such a file are the convenience of having the data all in one place physically and of having the data formatted in the same way with respect to labeling, density, and code convention.

264

We see no particular reason to create such a file in advance of a specific usage, because more data might be pooled than are actually needed, and the pooled data might inadvertently be formatted in a way that is not suitable for the data analysis software that is eventually used. On the other hand, pooled data can have definite advantages when the data are modified in any of several possible ways:

1. By Sampling Individuals. Confronted with data for a large number of individuals as, for example, in the case of the SAT population (approximately 1,000,000 students annually) or census data, the researcher may want to draw random samples from the population. In the case of SAT data, a sample of 1,000 cases is sufficient for many research purposes.

2. By Selecting Variables. Not all the measures available for each individual may be of interest.

3. By Standardizing Measures. To facilitate comparisons across samples of individuals, categories of individuals or measures of variables can be redefined. An example of the first type of modification would be racial-ethnic categories. One file might have only four categories: White, Black, Hispanic, and Other; although a second file might subdivide the Hispanic category into Mexican American, Puerto Rican, and Other Latin American. Collapsing the three Hispanic categories of the second file into one category would save programming steps if repeated comparisons are to be made between racial-ethnic categories in the two files. Yet, important distinctions among Hispanic subgroups would be lost, so the gains and losses would have to be weighed carefully.

An example of redefining measures of variables would be scales designed to reflect educational levels. One data file may discriminate between 2- and 4-year colleges, whereas a second file may have only one category for college attendance. Again, collapsing of categories may save programming steps, or—by drawing on other sources of information—the "college attendance" category of the second file might be split into 2- and 4-year college attendance.

4. By Aggregating Data. A possible way of greatly reducing the size of a data file is to include in the file only descriptive statistics of subgroups of the total sample for whom there are data. As discussed briefly in chapter 1, a possible set of subgroups might be those formed by cross-tabulating sex, race-ethnicity, socioeconomic status, and intended or actual college major (including a "no college" category). An example of a subgroup would be that comprised of all high-SES Black females who have intentions to major or actually did major in math, science, or engineering. If a second data base were aggregated in the same way and pooled with the first in the same file, then one would have a convenient way of generating tables comparing the characteristics of parallel subgroups in two or more data bases. One could, for example, readily compare—by means of the NLS and HS&B data files—the mean vocabulary scores of the high-SES Black females in 1972 with their scores in 1982. Or, by pooling aggregated data from the National Assessment files with aggregated data from the SAT files, one can compare the mean scores of corresponding subgroups in each file on roughly comparable measures. This is, in fact, what Urahn did, as described in chapter 8.

There are, however, problems with files of aggregated data:

1. As encountered by Urahn, the way in which subgroups are defined in separate data files may be so different as to make comparisons impossible. For example, there is no way of defining SES so as to achieve comparable categories in the NAEP and SAT data files. Similarly, educational aspirations could not be made comparable. This left Urahn with comparisons of males and females in each file and—for some years— Whites, Blacks, and Hispanics.

Similarly, in Hilton's study of visualization skills in 1960 and 1980 (chapter 6), it would have been desirable to report scores for racial–ethnic subgroups in 1960. However, the socio-cultural climate of the 1960s was such that the Project TALENT staff chose not to gather such data. Later, the data were obtained, but not for the full 1960 sample and not in time to be included in the volume that was the source of Hilton's data.

2. To what extent the data should be aggregated is difficult to anticipate. This suggests that more cells than may be needed be created by cross-tabulating many defining variables (e.g., sex, race, SES, educational aspirations, region of the country) and then, when confronted with a specific problem, that the desired cells be achieved by combining adjacent cells. Whether this is feasible depends on our ability to anticipate needs accurately. Creating too many cells defeats the purpose of aggregating, and not creating enough destroys the usefulness of the data base.

3. Aggregating data precludes the computation of product-moment correlations based on individual data (although rank-order correlations can be computed, and these, for some purposes, can be informative).

MATCHED MULTICOHORT DATA

In this second level of file creation, data from two or more surveys, test administrations, or other data collections are processed in such a way as to permit studies of trends over time or what Schaie (1965) would call time lag differences. An example would be the creation of a file covering the transition from high school to college by means of data from two or more cohorts of students. If a number of precautions are taken, such a file can provide valuable insights. Some of these precautions are as follows:

1. The sample members from each cohort should be comparable. Ordinarily, this means that both are from national probability samples, preferably drawn by exactly the same procedures in order to increase the probability of their being comparable. Or they may have been defined in the same way, for example, all Black students in New Jersey.

2. The data collection instruments should be as nearly the same as possible. Ideally, exactly the same instruments should have been administered, but this ideal is seldom achieved.

3. The data collection procedures should be the same, including:
   a. Invitations to sample members to participate (e.g., whether participation is voluntary or not).
   b. Explanations given for the data collection.
   c. Incentives provided to maximize participation.
   d. (When group data collection) make-up procedures for sample members who are absent.
   e. Whether group or individual administration of data collection instruments.
   f. Sex and ethnicity of survey or test administrators.
   g. Time allowed for completion of instruments.
   h. Rules for excusing certain sample members from participating (e.g., learning disabled students).

4. The data processing should be the same, including rules for handling:
   a. Double responses (i.e., two or more responses to a multiple choice item when the respondent is instructed to select one alternative).
   b. Inconsistencies.
   c. Nonsense responses and other deliberate efforts not to be cooperative.
   d. (In the case of performance tests) failure to respond to any items or only a small fraction of the items.

Many other processing problems could be cited, but these should suffice to illustrate the cautions that should be observed before concluding that two data files are sufficiently comparable to permit the study of time-lag differences.

In the Data Base study, two efforts were made to construct parallel segments. As described in detail in chapter 13, the first involved the 1972 NLS and the 1982 HS&B and, as described in chapter 6, the second involved the 1960 Project TALENT and the 1980 HS&B.

Comparison of 1972 and 1982 Cohorts

Numerous differences between the data files for the two national surveys had to be resolved before useful trend results could be derived from the data, including:

1. The Definition of the Category "Math, Science, and Engineering." In the base year survey of NLS, conducted in 1972, the sample members indicated their first choice of college major by circling one of 21 majors (Item 29 of the Student Questionnaire). Ten years later, in the base-year survey of HS&B, the respondents selected their choice from a somewhat longer list with slightly different descriptions of each major (Item 127 of the Senior Questionnaire). For example, "Predentistry" and "Premedicine" were removed from "Biological Sciences" and placed in a new category labelled "Preprofessional." "Prelaw" was removed from "Social sciences" and added to the same category. "Psychology" was removed from "Social sciences" and made a separate category. The modifications may have seriously affected the comparability of responses in regard to the social sciences. However, Hilton and Lee did not include the social sciences in the math, science, and engineering category and thus were spared the problem of estimating how seriously the change may have affected their results.

2. First College Attended. In the NLS, sample members were asked to report whether they were attending school during the "first week of October 1973" (Question 25); later in the questionnaire, the same question was asked for the "month of October 1972" (Question 29a). For each time period they were asked to write in the exact name of the school and, in processing the questionnaires, the Federal Interagency Committee on Education (FICE) Code of the school was coded. They also reported their actual or intended field of study at each time if they were attending school. In the study reported by Lee (chapter 13), a program was written to examine the relevant items in sequence to identify the first college with a valid FICE Code, if any, and what the student's actual or intended major in that school was.

In HS&B, however, the students were questioned about the first, second, and third school they attended and their actual or intended major "during the last month" they attended each school. We wrote a program to examine the schools sequentially until it reached a school with a valid FICE Code and a Postsecondary Educational Status code indicating the school that was attended in the 1982–1983 or 1983–1984 academic year. Then, the major "during the last month" was noted. Thus, this procedure—for which there was no alternative—required the assumption that the major "during the last month" would be comparable to the major reported by the respondents in NLS.

Other data processing steps that were taken to make the 1972 and 1982 maximally comparable could be described. We trust, however, that these two examples suffice to make the point that creating—from two or more sources—a file that has parallel segments can be time-consuming and expensive, even when the two data collections efforts (e.g., NLS and HS&B) were deliberately designed to be sufficiently similar to permit comparisons between the two age cohorts. A seemingly trivial change in a questionnaire item can make valid comparisons impossible, even though the change may improve the validity of the item itself.

Comparison of 1960 and 1980 Seniors

In chapter 6, a comparison of the visualization scores of high school seniors in 1960 with those of high school seniors in 1980 is described. Data from the Project TALENT files were not pooled with HS&B data because the published summary data from both surveys happened to include the mean scores and standard deviations required for the comparisons desired. (That this often is not the case is an argument in favor of preserving well-documented files of complete individual data.) Interpreting the results of the comparisons did, however, demonstrate why pooling data from two age cohorts 20 years apart may yield results that are deceptive. In 20 years, the social, political, cultural, and educational environment changed in significant ways. In 1960, 67% of the age cohort completed high school whereas, in 1980, 74% of the cohort completed high school. Thus, the 1960 sample was more restricted than the 1980 sample even though both were randomly selected.

Noncognitive variables influencing test performance change, including attitudes toward testing and authority, and beliefs about sex roles. Nevertheless, we view these observations as reasons to be cautious, not as reasons not to study important historical trends by pooling data from separate surveys.

The question remains, however, about the value of assembling a working file from separate longitudinal files. The answer, we now believe, is that it usually is not feasible to do so. Even when there is a specific question to be addressed, it is difficult to process the data so as to make the parts from different cohorts comparable. When there is no specific question at hand, it is inconceivable that any researcher or data manager could anticipate what use will be made of the data with sufficient accuracy to know what components, if any, should be transformed to enhance comparability.

LINKED COHORT DATA

This label was proposed for the situation where longitudinal data are simulated by pooling segments of data obtained at different times from the same age cohort. The study by Urahn described in chapter 8 was an effort to do this. Results from National Assessment were compared with results for the same cohorts from the SAT program and from HS&B. The question was whether early data for a cohort (e.g., mean NAEP Reading scores at age 13) forecast how the mean SAT scores for that cohort would compare with those of other cohorts. The answer was a cautious yes, but there were troublesome exceptions that defied explanation. Also, as we have found in other efforts to merge results from different test administrations, different definitions of key classificatory variables created problems. For example, in the 1971 NAEP assessment, the results for Whites were combined with the results for Hispanics. Separate results for Hispanic students were available for later assessments, but there was a question about how to define *Hispanic* for the SAT data where results were available for several Hispanic subpopulations. The final decision was to use the weighted mean of the Mexican American and Puerto Rican scores.

Our initial intention was to compare NAEP and SAT results at a much finer level of disaggregation, that is, by cross-tabulating sex, race-ethnicity, SES, educational aspirations, and possibly other variables. However, examination of the questionnaire items by means of which comparable cells would be created revealed so many important differences as to discourage us from proceeding. It may have been possible—by collapsing categories and by creating composite variables—to achieve sufficiently comparable cells, but the amount of data processing required was beyond the resources of the project. Our consistent experience, in this project and in others conducted recently at ETS, is that this kind of data preparation is demanding and time-consuming and, thereby, costly.

SIMULATED LONGITUDINAL DATA

The study described in chapter 13 was an effort to simulate longitudinal data by "merging" data from the 1972 NLS with data from the 1980 HS&B. Because the two files have no subjects in common, any merging would have had to have been at the level of subgroups. In other words, we would have acted as if subgroups created in one file by sorting on one or more variables could be assumed to be the same individuals as those in subgroups created for a second file by sorting on the same variables. For example, the high SES Black females in one file could be regarded as the same individuals as the high SES Black females in another file. Assuming that the subgroups could be regarded as individuals, we then could hypothesize that the "individuals" in the two cohorts would behave the same. For example, the same proportion would make the transition from high school to 4-year college. As described in chapter 12, however, this assumption is only approximately supported by the data. From 1972 to 1982, the transitional probabilities for subgroups of the sample are approximately the same. Whether they are sufficiently similar depends on the task at hand. For some purposes, predictions based on the assumption of no differences will be useful and better than any alternative, but for other purposes the error in such predictions will be unacceptable. Specifying precisely what these purposes are requires further study. We strongly recommend that this matter receive attention in the future.

MERGED INDIVIDUAL DATA

As described in chapter 1, the most defensible way of creating a unified data base is by merging data for the same individuals. An example is the addition of scores from the SAT and the Armed Services Vocational Aptitude Battery (ASVAB) to the data for the 1980 senior cohort of HS&B (see chapter 5). For those members of the cohort who indicated in the base-year questionnaire that they had taken the SAT, the College Board history files were searched for their scores. Simultaneously, the Department of Defense searched for ASVAB scores. The scores that were found were merged into the HS&B file, and copies of the merged file can to this day be purchased from the NCES.

Although the procedure was reasonably straightforward, implementing it was complicated and costly (approximately $40,000). Elaborate steps, involving scrambled identification numbers and multiple tapes, were necessary to protect the anonymity of the subjects. Equally elaborate programming was necessary to allow for the fact that students changed their last names (usually as a result of marriage) or used different first names (e.g., John and Jack, Charles E. and C. Everett) or misremembered their social security number or date of birth. (Frequently, year of birth was different in the two source documents.) As a final step in the SAT matching process, microfilms of the individual SAT records were located manually and examined for personal data that might resolve discrepancies between the two data sources.

Despite these steps and the carefully edited condition of both the HS&B and the SAT files, scores were retrieved for only 61.5% of the students who reported in the HS&B Senior Questionnaire that they took the SAT. Consequently, in an additional step, an analysis was conducted to ascertain whether the scores retrieved were for a representative sample of the SAT population. (The answer was yes.) Thus, merging data from two or more sources is not a step to be taken lightly; the time required and the cost may substantially exceed what one would casually estimate.

CONCLUSION

What then can be concluded about the feasibility of constructing a unified data base for the purposes of the National Science Foundation—or, for that matter, any other government agency or private organization? The answer depends on the cost and utility of precisely what is proposed. To this end, two possible products are described.

Unified File of Individual Data

The first possible product would be a longitudinal data file into which individual data from a variety of sources would be merged. Two obvious candidates for the longitudinal file are the 1980 senior cohort and the 1980 sophomore cohort of the HS&B. We recommend that the senior cohort receive priority of consideration, simply because that cohort will provide data on graduate school enrollments and completion rates 2 years before the younger cohort will. Also, focussing on the senior cohort first will provide the opportunity of repeating any analysis by means of the sophomore cohort. Such analyses would provide an added check on the validity of findings acquired from the senior cohort and also data on short-term (i.e., 2-year) change.

As mentioned before, SAT and ASVAB scores have already been retrieved for the senior cohort. Some other scores that might be retrieved and merged into the HS&B senior file are as follows:

1. American College Testing (ACT) admissions testing scores. These scores would usefully supplement SAT scores in studies of the quality of students in the United States who aspire to college.

2. Graduate Record Examinations (GRE) scores. The presence of these scores in a unified data base would permit studies of, for example, the

early origins of students scoring high on the GREs (and thus qualifying for graduate school). An estimated 3% of the HS&B senior cohort took the GRE as of the spring of 1986 (personal communication from NORC). An additional 2% or 3% may have taken the test subsequently.

There are scores available from other tests taken by a significant fraction of the HS&B senior cohort. Examples are the Graduate Management Admission Test (2%), the Law School Admissions Test (2%), and the Medical College Admission Test (1%).

In addition, because the schools attended by the sample members are known, as well as the occupations entered (by those who sought jobs), additional information about the schools and the occupations could be added to the HS&B file.

Lastly, there is the definite possibility of conducting supplementary surveys of all or of subgroups of the HS&B cohorts and then merging the results with the file data now available.

The question is, however, whether these efforts are justified in the absence of a definite need for the data. If funds were no object, it would be ideal to construct a unified data base by augmenting the HS&B files with all the data that might conceivably be useful in order that it be ready for analysis when the need arises. But, obviously, funds are an object, and the prudent course of action would seem to be to wait until a policy, planning, or evaluation question arises that requires the augmented file. At this time—with one exception—we can think of no supplementary individual data that are so likely to be useful and so inexpensive to obtain and merge that they should be obtained now, in anticipation of future use. The one exception is the GRE, including both test scores and responses to the personal history questionnaire completed by the examinees. The presence of these data in the files released by NCES would stimulate enough research on the early, concurrent, and subsequent correlates of the score to fully justify the expense of retrieving the scores (estimated to be $40,000).

Unified File of Group Data

The second possible product is a unified file of summary data for sub-groups of an age cohort. As described in earlier chapters, subgroups of the cohort would be treated as if they were individuals. Several efforts to pursue this possible data base design were undertaken in the present project, with mixed results. Urahn (chapter 8) examined the relationships between mean NAEP scores, mean SAT scores, and mean HS&B scores for students in the same age cohort. She found general correspondence among the means but methodological problems precluded a definitive investigation of the relationships. It was not possible, for example, to define SES in a way that would be common to all three data bases. Even the uniform definition of "Hispanic" posed a problem.

Also, Urahn encountered the problem posed by the fact that the SAT population is self-selected. Swinton investigated whether SAT data could be weighted so as to estimate what the mean scores would be if all college-bound students took the test. Initial results were promising, but in a cross-validation of his weights it appears that the stability of the relationships among the key variables was not sufficient to provide a method that we could recommend to NSF.

As mentioned earlier, Hilton and Lee investigated the possibility of merging data from the 1972 NLS with data from the 1980 HS&B so as to simulate a longitudinal data base covering the period from high school graduation through—for some—completion of graduate school. As previously discussed, whether the effort was successful or not depends on what test is applied. Application of the chi-square test indicates that nonchance changes in transitional probabilities took place (and thus, that the assumption was untenable). However, from a more pragmatic point of view, it could be argued that the method provides more accurate predictions than any known alternative method. Whether the method will be useful remains to be seen.

The foregoing uncertainty, combined with the data preparation problems described earlier in discussing matched multicohort data, raises questions about the likely usefulness of a unified file comprised of summary data for subgroups. Also, there is the question of cost. Our consistent experience has been that to reformulate a large data file, such as the National Assessment file, in such a way that the means of subgroups can be compared with the means of, say, parallel subgroups in the HS&B file, is costly, involving large amounts of programmer and machine time. For example, we can roughly estimate that creating a unified data file from National Assessment, HS&B, and SAT data could cost in excess of $1,000,000. This estimate indicates to us that more exploratory studies of the type conducted in this project are desirable before the construction of a unified data base is attempted.

Lest we leave the reader with the impression that there are so many problems inherent in trying to use data from two or more national data bases that the effort is not justified, let me review some of the unprecedented empirical studies that have been achieved by drawing data from two or more national surveys:

SAT Score Decline

Pooling tests and biographical data from Project TALENT (conducted in 1960) and the Base Year Survey of the National Longitudinal Study (conducted in 1972) provided one of the few, if not the only, rigorous explanation for a large share of the SAT score decline, namely, that share based on changes in the population of students taking the test. Without this pooling of Project TALENT and NLS data, this important finding simply would not have been possible.

National Test Score Changes from 1972 to 1980

Similarly, the pooling of data from NLS and HS&B permitted a definitive study of changes in verbal and quantitative ability from 1972 to 1980 (Rock et al., 1984), and when the original eight graders in NELS:88 are high school seniors in 1992, it will be possible to compare national performance in 1972 to that of 1992—provided, of course, that certain steps be taken to preserve comparability (these steps are referred to in several of the chapters of this volume). Integrating the findings from the SAT score decline study, the 1972–1980 study, and the study just mentioned will permit rigorous comparisons from 1960 to 1992, a feat without precedence in educational psychology in the United States.

Spatial Relations Study

The investigation of spatial relations (chapter 6) raises fundamental questions about the origins of such skills. Are there intractable differences between males and females or do the observed differences depend to a large extent on the cultural milieu? Research on these questions has been hampered in the past by the absence of samples large enough to permit any kind of conclusions about the culture or about changes over extended time periods. However, investigation of these questions is now possible for a range of human attributes, including values and attitudes, in addition to spatial relations skills.

The foregoing are only a sample of the studies that are now possible by virtue of the large national studies conducted in this country since 1960. The data resulting from these studies have hardly been tapped. It is the hope of the authors that this volume will facilitate the mining of this invaluable national resource.

References

Admissions Testing Program of the College Board. (1980). *National college-bound seniors.* New York: College Entrance Examination Board.

Admissions Testing Program of the College Board. (1986). *Profile of SAT and Achievement Test takers.* New York: College Entrance Examination Board.

Anastasi, A. (Ed.). (1965). *Individual differences.* New York: Wiley.

Anastasi, A. (1982). *Psychological testing* (5th ed.). New York: Macmillan.

Angoff, W. H. (1966). Can useful general purpose equivalency tables be prepared for different college admissions tests? In A. Anastasi (Ed.), *Testing problems in perspective* (pp. 251–264). Washington, DC: American Council on Education.

Angoff, W. H. (1971). Scales, norms, and equivalent scores. In R. L. Thorndike (Ed.), *Educational measurement* (2nd ed.) (pp. 508–600). Washington, DC: American Council on Education.

Angoff, W. H., & Schrader, W. B. (1984). Study of hypotheses basic to the use of rights and formula scores. *Journal of Educational Measurement, 21*(1), 1–17.

Arbeiter, S. (1986, May). Minority enrollment in higher education institutions: A chronological view. *Research and Development Update* (The College Board), pp. 1–9.

Beaton, A. E., Hilton, T. L., & Schrader, W. B. (1977). *Changes in the verbal abilities of high school seniors, college entrants, and SAT candidates between 1960 and 1972.* New York: College Entrance Examination Board.

Bianchini, J. C., & Loret, P. G. (1972). *Anchor test study: Final report.* Princeton, NJ: Educational Testing Service.

Borgatta, E. F., & Corsini, R. J. (1967). *Quick word test.* Itasca, IL: F. E. Research Publishers.

Broverman, D. M., Klaiber, E. L., Kabayashi, Y., & Vogel, W. (1968). Roles of activation and inhibition in sex differences in cognitive abilities. *Psychological Review, 75,* 23–50.

Center for Education Statistics. (1986, Nov.). Completion time for bachelor's degrees. *Bulletin OERI.* Washington, DC: Office of Educational Research and Improvement.

Coleman, J. S., Campbell, E. Q., Hobson, C. J., McPartland, J., Mood, A. M., Weinfeld, F. D., & York, R. L. (1966). *Equality of educational opportunity*. Washington, DC: U.S. Government Printing Office.

College Entrance Examination Board. (1982). *Profiles, college-bound seniors, 1981*. New York: Author.

College Entrance Examination Board. (1986). *Profiles, college-bound seniors, 1985*. New York: Author.

Collison, M. N. K. (1987, December 9). More young Black men choosing not to go to college. *The Chronicle of Higher Education,* pp. 1, A26, A27.

Cooperative Test Division, Educational Testing Service. (1957). *Cooperative sequential tests of educational progress: Technical report*. Princeton, NJ: Educational Testing Service.

Daniels, L. A. (1989, February 5). Ranks of Black men shrinking on U.S. campuses. *The New York Times,* pp. 1, 30.

Department of Defense. (1976). *ASVAB specimen set*. Washington, DC: U.S. Government Printing Office.

Donlon, T. F., Hilton, T. L., & Schrader, W. B. (1978). *Designing a test plan for the 1980 National Longitudinal Study "High School and Beyond"* (prepared for the National Center for Education Statistics, Contract No. 300-78-0084). Princeton, NJ: Educational Testing Service.

Earles, J. A., Giuliano, T., Ree, M. J., & Valentine, L. D. (1983). *The 1980 youth population: An investigation of speeded subtests*. Brooks Air Force Base, TX: Air Force Human Resources Laboratory.

Educational Testing Service. (1985). *The reading report card, progress toward excellence in our schools: Trends in reading over four national assessments, 1976–1984* (ETS Report No. 15-R-01). Princeton, NJ: Author.

Ekstrom, R. B., French, J. W., & Harman, H. H. (with Dermen, D.) (1976). *Manual for kit of factor-referenced cognitive tests, 1976*. Princeton, NJ: Educational Testing Service.

Fetters, W. B., Stowe, P. S., & Owings, J. A. (1984). *Quality of responses of high school students to questionnaire items. High school and beyond: A national longitudinal study for the 1980s* (NCES 84-216). Washington, DC: National Center for Education Statistics.

Fiske, E. B. (1989, September 13). Shortages predicted for 90's in professors of humanities. *The New York Times,* pp. 1, B10.

Flanagan, J. C., Dailey, J. T., Shaycoft, M. F., Gorham, W. A., Orr, D. B., & Goldberg, I. (1960). *Designing the study* (Tech. Rep. to the U.S. Office of Education, Cooperative Research Project No. 566). Pittsburgh, PA: University of Pittsburgh, Project TALENT Office. (ERIC No. 002198).

Flanagan, J. C., Dailey, J. T., Shaycoft, M. F., Gorham, W. A., Orr, D. B., & Goldberg, I. (1962). *Design for a study of American youth*. Boston, MA: Houghton Mifflin.

Flanagan, J. C., Davis, F. B., Dailey, J. T., Shaycoft, M. F., Orr, D. B., Goldberg, I., & Neyman, C. A., Jr. (1964). *The American high school student* (Final report to the U.S. Office of Education Cooperative Research Project No. 635). Pittsburgh, PA: University of Pittsburgh, Project TALENT Office.

Flanagan, J. C., & Jung, S. M. (1971). *Progress in education: A sample survey (1960–1970)*. Palo Alto, CA: American Institutes for Research.

Flaugher, R. L. (1971). *Project ACCESS research report number 3: Minority versus majority group performance on an aptitude test battery* (ETS RB-71-48). Princeton, NJ: Educational Testing Service.

Frankel, M. M., & Beamer, J. F. (1974). *Projections of educational statistics to 1982–83* (1973 ed.). Washington, DC: U.S. Government Printing Office.

French, J. W. (1964). *Experimental comparative prediction batteries: High school and college level.* Princeton, NJ: Educational Testing Service.

Haertel, E. H., & Wiley, D. E. (1978, December). *Rebalancing the test battery for "High School and Beyond": Analyses and recommendations.* Paper presented at the joint meeting of the National Planning Committee and the Test Advisory Panel for "High School & Beyond." Chicago: CEMREO, Inc. ML-Group for Policy Studies in Education.

Heyns, B., & Hilton, T. L. (1982). The cognitive tests for high school and beyond: An assessment. *Sociology of Education 1982, 55,* 89–102.

Hilton, T. L. (1967). *A study of intellectual growth and vocational development* (Interim Report, Project No. 6-1830, Office of Education, Bureau of Research). Princeton, NJ: Educational Testing Service.

Hilton, T. L. (1971). *A technical proposal for a national longitudinal study of the high school class of 1972.* Princeton, NJ: Educational Testing Service.

Hilton, T. L. (1982). *Persistence in higher education: An empirical study* (College Board Report No. 82-5, ETS RR No. 82-44). New York: The College Board.

Hilton, T. L. (1985, April). *Changes in student achievement.* Paper presented at the annual meeting of the American Educational Research Association, Chicago.

Hilton, T. L., & Lee, V. E. (1988). Student interest and persistence in science: Changes in the educational pipeline in the last decade. *Journal of Higher Education, 59*(5), 510–526.

Hilton, T. L., & Rhett, H. (1973). *The base-year survey of the national longitudinal study of the high school class of 1972* (Final Report to the U.S. Department of Health, Education, and Welfare, National Center for Educational Statistics, Contract No. OEC-0-72-0903). Princeton, NJ: Educational Testing Service.

Hilton, T. L., & Schrader, W. B. (1980a, April). *Alternative regression methods in data editing.* Paper presented at the annual meeting of the American Educational Research Association, Boston.

Hilton, T. L., & Schrader, W. B. (1980b). *Test analysis: High school and beyond field test.* Princeton, NJ: Educational Testing Service.

Hilton, T. L., & Schrader, W. B. (1985). *Students of the humanities in the 1970's and 1980's* (Final Report to the National Endowment for the Humanities, Grant No. OP-20092-83). Princeton, NJ: Educational Testing Service.

Hilton, T. L., & Schrader, W. B. (1987). *Pathways to graduate school: An empirical study based on national longitudinal data* (Final Report, GRE No. 82-21-R). Princeton, NJ: Educational Testing Service.

Hilton, T. L., Schrader, W. B., & Beaton, A. E. (1983). *Responses to questions on military service by 1980 high school seniors classified on ability and other variables* (Final Report submitted to the Army Recruiting Command, Prime Contract #300-78-0208), Princeton, NJ: Educational Testing Service.

Horvitz, D. G., Mason, K., Bayless, D., Jackson, D., Hunt, N., & Koch, G. (1972). *The design of a longitudinal survey of secondary school seniors* (2 Volumes). (Final Report, SU-160, prepared for the National Center for Educational Statistics, U.S. Office of Education, under Contract No. OEC-0-71-0752). Research Triangle Park, NC: Research Triangle Institute.

Howe, H. (1985). Let's have another SAT score decline. *Phi Delta Kappan, 66*(9), 599–607.

Jensen, A. R. (1968). Social class, race, and genetics: Implications for education. *American Educational Research Journal, 5,* 1–42.

Jones, C., Sebring, P., Crawford, I., Spencer, B., Spencer, B., & Butz, M. (1986). *High school and beyond: 1980 high school senior cohort second follow-up (1984).* Washington, DC: National Center for Statistics.

Joreskog, K. G., & Sorbom, D. (1983). *LISREL VI, estimation of linear structural equation systems by maximum likelihood methods: A program.* Chicago, IL: National Educational Resources.

Kish, L., & Frankel, M. R. (1970). Balanced repeated replication for standard errors. *Journal of the American Statistical Association, 65*(65), 1071–1094.

Kish, L., & Frankel, M. R. (1974). Inference from complex samples. *Journal of the Royal Statistical Society, Series B, 36,* 1–22.

Lesser, G. S., Fifer, G., & Clark, D. H. (1965). Mental abilities of children from different social-class and cultural groups. *Monographs for the Society for Research in Child Development, 30,* 4–73.

Lord, F. M. (1950). *Notes on comparable scales for test scores* (Research Bulletin 50-48). Princeton, NJ: Educational Testing Service.

Lord, F. M. (1980). *Applications of item response theory to practical testing problems.* Hillsdale, NJ: Lawrence Erlbaum Associates.

Lord, F. M., & Novick, M. R. (1968). *Statistical theories of mental test scores.* Reading, MA: Addison-Wesley.

Maccoby, E. E., & Jacklin, C. N. (1974). *The psychology of sex differences.* Stanford, CA: Stanford University Press.

McCarthy, P. J. (1969). Pseudo-replication: Half-samples. *Review of the International Statistical Institute, 37,* 239–264, 305–325.

Modu, C. C., & Stern, J. (1976). *The stability of the SAT-verbal score scale.* Unpublished report. Princeton, NJ: Educational Testing Service.

National Center for Education Statistics. (1970a). *Directory of nonpublic elementary and secondary day schools, 1968–69* (OE-20127, Vol. 5). Washington, DC: U.S. Government Printing Office.

National Center for Education Statistics. (1970b). *Directory of public elementary and secondary day schools, 1968–69* (OE-20126, Vols. 1–4). Washington, DC: U.S. Government Printing Office.

National Center for Education Statistics. (1985a). *The condition of education, 1985, statistical report* (NCES 85-402). Washington, DC: U.S. Government Printing Office.

National Center for Education Statistics. (1989). *Changes in educational attainment: A comparison among 1972, 1980, and 1982 high school seniors.* Washington, DC: U.S. Government Printing Office.

Parnes, H. S., Miljus, R. C., & Spitz, R. C. (1969). *Career thresholds: A longitudinal study of the educational and labor market experience of male youth 14–24 years of age* (Vol. 1). Columbus, OH: Ohio State University.

Pennock-Román, M., & Rivera, C. (1988). *Issues in ethnic identification in Part II: Effect of mean achievement means reported for Hispanics.* Unpublished manuscript.

Plackett, R. L., & Burman, J. P. (1943–1946). The design of optimum multifactorial experiments. *Biometrika, 33,* 305–325.

Project TALENT. (1972). *The project TALENT data bank: A handbook.* Palo Alto, CA: American Institutes for Research.

Raizen, S. A., & Jones, L. V. (Eds.). (1985). *Indicators of precollege education in science and mathematics: A preliminary review.* Washington, DC: National Academy Press.

Riccobono, J., Henderson, L. B., Burkheimer, G. J., Place, C., & Levinsohn, J. R. (1981). *National longitudinal study: Base year (1972) through fourth follow-up (1979), data file user's manual.* Washington, DC: National Center for Education Statistics.

Rock, D. A., Ekstrom, R. B., Goertz, M. E., Pollack, J., & Hilton, T. L. (1984). *Study of excellence in high school education, cross-sectional study, 1972–1980.* (Draft Technical Report: Background and descriptive analysis sections. Contract No. 300-83-0247, June 1984. Submitted to the U.S. Department of Education—National Center for Education Statistics.) Princeton, NJ: Educational Testing Service.

Rock, D. A., Hilton, T. L., Pollack, J., Ekstrom, R. B., & Goertz, M. E. (1985). *Psychometric analysis of the NLS and the High School and Beyond test batteries.* Washington, DC: National Center for Education Statistics.

Rohwer, W. D., Jr., Linch, S., Levin, J. R., & Suzuki, N. (1968). Grade level, school strata and learning efficiency. *Journal of Educational Psychology, 59*(1), Part 1, 26–31.

Schaie, K. W. (1965). A general model for the study of developmental problems. *Psychological Bulletin, 64,* 92–107.

Schrader, W. B., & Hilton, T. L. (1975). *Educational attainment of American high school seniors in 1960, 1965, and 1972: Feasibility study* (Project NIE-G-74-0050). Princeton, NJ: Educational Testing Service.

Sebring, P., Campbell, B., Glusberg, M., Spencer, B., & Singleton, M. (1987a). *High School and Beyond 1980 sophomore cohort third follow-up (1986), data file user's manual.* Washington, DC: National Center for Education Statistics.

Sebring, P., Campbell, B., Glusberg, M., Spencer, B., Singleton, M., & Turner, M. (1987b). *High School and Beyond 1980 senior cohort third follow-up (1986), data file user's manual.* Washington, DC: National Center for Education Statistics.

Semler, I. J., & Iscoe, I. (1963). Comparative and developmental study of learning abilities of Negro and White children under four conditions. *Journal of Educational Psychology, 54,* 38–44.

Shaycoft, M. F. (1967). *Project TALENT—The high school years: Growth in cognitive skills* (Interim Report 3 to the U.S. Office of Education, Cooperative Research Project No. 3051). Pittsburgh, PA: Project TALENT Office, American Institutes of Research.

Shaycoft, M. F., Dailey, J. T., Orr, D. B., Neymen, C. A., Jr., & Sherman, S. E. (1963). *Studies of a complete age group—age 15* (Technical Report to the U.S. Office of Education, Cooperative Research Project No. 226). Pittsburgh, PA: University of Pittsburgh.

Sherman, J. A. (1971). *On the psychology of women.* Springfield, IL: Charles C. Thomas.

Simon, K. A., & Frankel, M. M. (1973). *Projections of educational statistics to 1981–82* (1972 ed.). Washington, DC: U.S. Government Printing Office.

Stodolsky, S. S., & Lesser, G. S. (1967). Learning patterns in the disadvantaged. *Harvard Educational Review, 37,* 546–593.

Swinton, S. S. (1987, April). Estimating verbal and quantitative ability in the college-bound population. In R. Berry (Chair), *Drawing educational implications from multiple data bases.* Symposium conducted at the annual meeting of the American Educational Research Association, Washington, DC.

Tinto, V. (1982). Limits of theory and practice in student attrition. *Journal of Higher Education, 53,* 687–700.

United States Bureau of the Census. (1973). *Statistical abstract of the United States, 1973.* (94th ed.). Washington, DC: U.S. Government Printing Office.

Urahn, S. (1987, April). Do NAEP means predict later SAT means for the same cohort of students? In R. Berry (Chair), *Drawing educational implications from multiple data bases.* Symposium conducted at the annual meeting of the American Educational Research Association, Washington, DC.

WESTAT, Inc. (1972). *Sample design for the selection of a sample of schools with twelfth-graders for a longitudinal study.* Rockville, MD: Author.

Wiley, D. E., & Harnischfeger, A. (1974). Explosion of a myth: Quantity of schooling and exposure to instruction, major educational vehicles. *Educational Researcher, 3*(4), 7–11.

Wood, R. L., Wingersky, M. S., & Lord, F. M. (1976). *LOGIST: A computer program for estimating examining ability and item characteristic curve parameters* (Research Memo No. 76-6). Princeton, NJ: Educational Testing Service.

Description and Directions for Obtaining Copies of Selected National Data Bases (in order of listing in Table 2.1)

Research Triangle Institute National Survey of Science and Mathematics Education

This is a survey sponsored by the Directorate for Science and Engineering of NSF and conducted by Dr. Iris Weiss. Data are available on magnetic tape. There is one cohort per file or dataset (elementary principals, high school principals, elementary students, high school students, elementary science and math teachers, and high school science and math teachers). The file includes age, grade, sex, and ethnicity of subjects. Cost: No established rate.

Contact: Data Facility Administrator, Library
Rand Corporation
1700 Main Street
Santa Monica, CA 90470
(213) 393-4011 x. 7540 or x. 7351

National Assessment of Educational Progress (NAEP)

Federally funded, ongoing, periodic assessment of national samples of 9-, 13-, and 17-year-olds. Each year 75,000 to 100,000 persons are assessed in one or more learning areas taught in the schools. Public-use data tapes are available including the most recent full-scale assessments of citizenship/social studies, mathematics, and reading/literature. All original item response and background variable data fields are included and also documentation, including SAS, SPSS, and OSIRIS IV. The cost is $125.00 for each assessment age (e.g., 1977, 17, Basic Life Skills).

Contact: Norma Norris
            National Assessment of Educational Progress
            Educational Testing Service, 22-T
            Rosedale Road
            Princeton, NJ 08541-0001
            (609) 734-5898

Longitudinal Study of American Youth

Data are available for two national probability samples of middle and high school students who are being surveyed annually along with their parents and teachers. With support from the National Science Foundation, one cohort was first surveyed in 1986 as seventh graders, and a second cohort was surveyed as tenth graders. Public release files contain comprehensive test and questionnaire data. The data, including SPSS-X and SAS system files and codebooks, are available at no cost.

Contact: Jon D. Miller, Director
            Public Opinion Laboratory
            Northern Illinois University
            DeKalb, Illinois 60115-2854
            Fax (815) 753-2305
            Bitnet TIOPOL@NIU

National Longitudinal Surveys
of Labor Market Experience

Repeated interviews were conducted over a 20-year period with five groups, totalling 20,000, ranging in age from 14 to 59, including the children of one cohort. Data tapes, including CDs, and manuals are available at cost.

Contact: NLS Public User's Office
            Center for Human Resource Research
            The Ohio State University
            921 Chatham Lane
            Suite 200
            Columbus, Ohio 43221-2418

International Math Survey (US Component)

Data available on magnetic tape for two populations (eighth and twelfth graders). File contains age, grade, sex, ethnicity of subjects, achievement tests, and school, teacher, and student questionnaire. Data were obtained in 1981–1982. Cost: $50 (includes manual)

> Contact: Professor Ian Westbury
>   Department of Curriculum and Instruction
>   Education Building
>   University of Illinois at Urbana-Champaign
>   1310 South 6th Street
>   Champaign, IL 61820
>   (217) 333-6344

**National Education Longitudinal Study
of 1988 (NELS:88)**

Data are available from 24,599 eighth graders surveyed in 1988 and followed up in 1990 under the sponsorship of the National Center for Education Statistics. Biennial surveys will continue. Parent, teacher, and school data also available. Basic data set costs $175. Each tape also includes a SAS system file and SPSSX and SAS control cards. Data on CDs now available.

> Contact: Office of Educational Research and Improvement
>   Information Technology Branch
>   555 New Jersey Avenue NW
>   Washington, DC 20208-5725
>   (202) 219-1847 or (202) 219-1522 or (800) 424-1616

Project TALENT

Massive longitudinal study of 400,000 students begun in 1960. In base year, a large battery of cognitive tests and a background questionnaire were administered to the students, and long questionnaires were completed by their teachers and principals. In subsequent years, 1-, 5-, and 11-year follow-up questionnaires were administered. Data usually available on magnetic tape but can be made available on PC disk if requested. File includes age, grade, sex, and ethnicity of subjects. Cost: depends on the number of years being requested ($100–$200 each tape). A manual is included in the cost. Manual can also be purchased separately.

Contact: Project TALENT Data Bank
              American Institute of Research
              P.O. Box 1113
              Palo Alto, CA 94302
              (415) 493-3550

Metropolitan Achievement Tests

Psychological Corporation, (512) 299-1061
Data base not available for research purposes.

Iowa Tests of Education — Iowa Tests of Education Development

Riverside Publishing Company, (312) 693-0040 or (800) 323-9540
Data base not available for research purposes.

High School and Beyond (HS&B)

National longitudinal survey of approximately 60,000 high school sophomores and seniors first surveyed in 1980 and followed up in 1982, 1984, and 1986. Many supplementary files available. See entry for NELS: 88 for details about obtaining copies of tapes or CDs.

Armed Services Vocational Aptitude Battery (ASVAB)

This test battery is completed annually by nearly 1,000,000 high school students, predominantly juniors and seniors. Currently, planning is underway for future use of ASVAB data by educational researchers.

Contact: Personnel Testing Division
              Defense Manpower Data Center
              99 Pacific Street, Suite 155A
              Monterey, CA 93943-3231
              (408) 655-0400

American College Testing Service

ACT will make available their data bases to qualified researchers. Data include yearly test scores, age, grade, sex, ethnicity of subjects, and a manual or code book. Cost: Not standardized. Depends on what is requested.

Contact: Assistant Vice President
           Research Division
           American College Testing Service
           P.O. Box 168
           Iowa City, IA
           (319) 337-1000

National Longitudinal Study (NLS)
of the High School Class of 1972

National longitudinal survey of approximately 23,000 respondents begun in 1972 under the sponsorship of the National Center for Education Statistics. Follow-ups were conducted in 1973, 1974, 1976, 1979, and 1986.

Student test and questionnaire responses and also high school data, counselor data, and transcripts are available. Other files can be linked. Basic file cost is $275. See entry for NELS:88 for details about obtaining copies of files.

College Entrance Examination Board
Admissions Testing Program

Annually administers Scholastic Aptitude Test (SAT) and several other measures to over 1,500,000 students. Special arrangements can be made to obtain magnetic tapes containing student self-described information, including family income, years of study of academic courses in secondary school, ethnicity, college degree, and career aspirations, as well as SAT scores, scores of the Test of Standard Written English (TSWE), and achievement test scores in 13 subjects. Confidentiality of student and school data is maintained. Cost varies from $300 to $675, depending on size of sample.

Contact: Senior Customer Service Representative
           ATP Summary Reporting Services
           P.O. Box 6213
           Princeton, NJ 08541-6213
           (609) 734-7144

High School Equivalency Test — GED

The GED, sponsored by the American Council on Education (ACE) are directed to adults who need to show the equivalency of a high school education. About 800,000 tests are administered annually. Currently there is no standard data base available for research purposes, but data are made available according to the needs/specifications of the person making the request. ACE is in the process of developing two standardized data bases for graduating high school seniors and GED candidates. Data available on magnetic tape, but can be made available on PC disks.

File contains age, grade, sex, ethnicity of subjects, tests, and some questionnaires (occasional surveys). Cost: Currently depends on what is requested; a standard charge will be established once the standardized data base is completed.

> Contact: Assistant Director, GED Testing Service
> American Council on Education
> Assistant Director for Policy Research
> 1 Dupont Circle NW
> Washington, DC 20036
> (202) 939-9490

Cooperative Institutional Research Program (CIRP)

A large file of data on student attitudes and values is compiled annually from surveys of full-time college freshmen. Some follow-up data also are available.

> Contact: Dr. Alexander Astin
> Cooperative Institutional Research Program
> University of California
> Los Angeles, CA 90052
> (213) 825-1925

Integrated Postsecondary Education
Data System (IPEDS)

This is a new survey replacing the Higher Education General Information Survey (HEGIS). IPEDS provides comprehensive data on all postsecondary institutions in the United States. File includes enrollment data, financial statistics, and data on faculty salaries. See entry for NELS:88 for further details.

Current Population Surveys

Data are available from multistage probability sample of about 85,000 households from surveys conducted monthly since 1940. Microdata files available.

Contact: Customer Services Branch
           Data User Services Division
           U.S. Bureau of the Census
           Washington, D.C. 20233

Graduate Record Examinations (GRE)

The GRE data base contains information on persons taking the GRE during the four or five administrations conducted annually. The number of test takers in a given year is large (approximately 190,000). In addition to GRE scores, background information (e.g., parents' education, citizenship, and language) is collected.

Special ad hoc arrangements can be made to obtain GRE data at cost.

Contact: Jacqueline B. Briel
           Educational Testing Service, 26-U
           Rosedale Road
           Princeton, N.J. 08541-0001
           (609) 243-8286

National Teacher Examinations (NTE)

The NTE is the most widely administered teacher examination in the United States. Because the examinations currently are undergoing major revision, it is uncertain what the data files will contain, but it is expected that data will be available for research purposes.

Contact: Catherine Havrilesky
           Educational Testing Service, 20-U
           Rosedale Road
           Princeton, N.J. 08541-0001
           (609) 243-8205

Recent College Graduate Survey (RCG)

A national sample of approximately 18,000 BS and 2,000 MS degree recipients are surveyed 1 year after graduation. Conducted approximately every 2 years. Transcripts available for 1985–1986 sample. Basic cost: $175.00.

Contact: U.S. Department of Education
           OERI/IS/PID/Education Information Branch
           555 New Jersey Avenue, NW
           Washington, D.C. 20208-5641
           (800) 424-1616

Graduate Enrollment Survey (GES)

The GES is conducted annually by the Council of Graduate Schools and the Graduate Record Examinations Board and surveys universities that are members of the Council of Graduate Schools (e.g., in 1986, 385 graduate institutions were members, and 343 responded to the survey). It collects information on number of applications, full-/part-time enrollment by gender and race/ethnicity, and number receiving financial support.

Special arrangements may be made to obtain GES data. See entry for Graduate Record Examinations.

Survey of Graduate Science and Engineering Students and Post-Doctorates (SGSSP)

SGSSP is conducted by NSF on an annual basis and surveys colleges and universities that grant doctoral and master's degrees in the fields of science and engineering. In 1980, this included approximately 570 institutions. The survey collects enrollment data (by full-/part-time status, gender, race, source of financial support) at the department level.

Public-use data tapes are available at a cost of $100.00 for single years and $325.00 for multiyears.

        Contact: Ms. Esther Gist
                   National Science Foundation
                   Division of Science Resources Studies
                   Room L-602
                   1800 G Street, NW
                   Washington, D.C. 20550
                   (202) 634-4673

Survey of Earned Doctorates (SED)

The SED is conducted annually by the National Research Council of all persons who receive a doctoral degree from a university in the United States, which typically includes over 30,000 persons. The survey collects information on background characteristics, field of study, source of support, race/ethnicity, gender, and "postdoctoral" plans. The survey has been conducted since 1958, and a summary report has been published annually since 1967.

Raw data tapes are not made available, but customized data tabulations can be arranged.

Contact: Joanne Weinman
           Project Manager, Doctorate Records File
           National Research Council
           2101 Constitution Avenue, NW
           Washington, D.C. 20418
           (202) 334-3152

Survey of Doctorate Recipients (SDR)

Every other year the National Research Council surveys a 10% sample
of the subjects in the Survey of Earned Doctorates and then follows them
longitudinally every 2 years. An abridged data file (to preserve anonymity)
is available.

Contact: Data and Program Library Services
           University of Wisconsin—Madison
           3313 Social Science Building
           1180 Observatory Drive
           Madison, Wisconsin 53706
           (608) 262-7962

Author Index

Subject Index

A

Advanced Placement Program (APP), 2
Age, effects of
  and high school population, changes in, 89–90
  on SAT and National Assessment of Educational Progress (NAEP) scores, 143–148
  on spatial-visual ability, 114
  as a variable in equating, 76
American College Testing (ACT), 3, 10, 272, 284–285
Anchor Test Study, 67
Angoff's Design II
  and equating design of national survey, 66–67
Armed Forces Qualification Test (AFQT), 98
  and corresponding HS&B scores, 106
  defining composite weights, 107
  format of, 106–107
  relating scores to composite of HS&B scores, 105–112
  results of relating scores to composite of HS&B scores, 108–112
  tests to define scores of, 105–106

Armed Services Vocational Aptitude Battery (ASVAB), 98, 271, 272
  obtaining copy of, 284
  retrieving scores of, 103–105
    use of social security number in, 105
  scores of and merging with other data bases, 98–112
  types of abilities measured in, 105–106

B

Blacks, *See Ethnic background, effects of*

C

Civics education, test in, 154
Class rank, effects of
  in estimating ability in college-bound students, 126–127
Coleman study, *See Equality of Educational Opportunity Survey (EEOS)*
College
  changes in attendance patterns of, 250–253
  entrance, as a variable in equating, 75